MUSIC IN THE MARKETPLACE

Much recent economic work on the music industry has been focused on the impact of technology on demand, with predictions being made of digital copyright infringement leading to the demise of the industry. In fact, there have always been profound cyclical swings in music media sales owing to the fact that music always has been, and continues to be, a discretionary purchase.

This entertaining and accessible book offers an analysis of the production and consumption of music from a social economics approach. Locating music within the economic analysis of social behaviour, this books guides the reader through issues relating to production, supply, consumption and trends, wider considerations such as the international trade in music, and in particular through divisions of age, race and gender.

Providing an engaging overview of this fascinating topic, this book will be of interest and relevance to students and scholars of cultural economics, management, musicology, cultural studies and those with an interest in the music industry more generally.

Samuel Cameron is Professor of Economics at the University of Bradford, UK.

MUSIC IN THE MARKETPLACE

A social economics approach

Samuel Cameron

Routledge
Taylor & Francis Group

LONDON AND NEW YORK

First published 2015
by Routledge
2 Park Square, Milton Park, Abingdon, Oxon OX14 4RN

and by Routledge
711 Third Avenue, New York, NY 10017

Routledge is an imprint of the Taylor & Francis Group, an informa business

British Library Cataloguing in Publication Data
A catalogue record for this book is available from the British Library

Library of Congress Cataloging in Publication Data
A catalog record for this book has been requested

ISBN: 978-0-415-72327-5 (hbk)
ISBN: 978-0-415-72328-2 (pbk)
ISBN: 978-1-315-85777-0 (ebk)

Typeset in Bembo
by Wearset Ltd, Boldon, Tyne and Wear

MIX
Paper from
responsible sources
FSC
www.fsc.org   FSC® C013056

Printed and bound in Great Britain by
TJ International Ltd, Padstow, Cornwall

CONTENTS

FIGURES

TABLES

ABBREVIATIONS

ARIA   Australian Recording Industry Association
BBC   British Broadcasting Corporation
CD   compact disc
IFPI   International Federation of the Phonographic Industry
IP/IPR   Intellectual Property Right
MPC   Music Production Centre
NAMA   Native American Music Association
PRS   Performing Right Society
RIAA   Recording Industry Association of America
UNESCO   United Nations Educational, Scientific and Cultural Organization
VST   Virtual Sound Technology

1

INTRODUCTION

What is the opposite of music? Is it still music?

Let us start in a dialectical mode seldom found amongst the mainstream economists. It would be useful to define music before we discuss it. Academic studies of music tend to have very narrow terms of reference. Economists almost always discuss the demand for music even though other aspects of music would fall within the realm of conventional economics. Studies of music in cultural/media studies tend to focus on its social usage and circulation and its possible symbolic meaning. Hesmond-haulgh (2013) has lamented the tendency to overlook its important emotional role; but then everyone of a certain age knows the dictum of Noel Coward that it is strange how potent cheap music is.

It is not obvious that the study of emotional reactions to music is necessarily a study of music as such, as it may potentially be not significantly different in any way from emotional reactions to other cultural products like plays and books. If it is emotionally different from these this may, in some regards, be partly due to economic factors. Chiefly, it is the divisibility and separability of music that allows it to be consumed in fractions, and as background, to a greater degree than the above-mentioned categories. I shall return to this feature with some empirical data in the case study of Adele in the next chapter.

The ambient use of music has disturbed many in terms of moving music into thrall to the marketplace. This is very clearly stated in an interview with Stock-hausen (*Wire*, 1995). He says

> as soon as it becomes just a means for ambiance, as we say, environment, or for being used for certain purposes, then music becomes a whore, and one should not allow that really; one should not serve any existing demands or in particular not commercial values. That would be terrible: that is selling out the music.

It might seem that the definition of music is not very important for an economic approach as it might be considered to be whatever the producers and consumers say it is. Or, what government statisticians say it is. Once they give it a SIC (standard industrial classification) code and a formal name then that is the music industry. However a problem will tend to emerge when the welfare economics of so-called "market failure" is discussed for such things as television talent competitions. We then move into the sphere of old-world thinkers like Stockhausen and Adorno (2002) where "bad" or "not proper" music is driving out "good" music which needs special support to protect its fragile existence. Once we make such a move the "bad" music might be considered as ontologically not much different from "non-music" or "noise" in the sense in which it is used by the layperson. Chapter 3 deals with some works where non-economists are essentially using the "market failure" argument to rationalize the corruption of a form, which they venerate, into "non-" or "not proper" music.

A useful rhetorical strategy is to consider what might be the opposite of the thing to be defined. Is the opposite of music noise or is it silence? Or, is silence the opposite of both music and noise thereby making noise and music the same thing. Whichever of these it is, we should note there are likely to be some limitations in selling noise or silence widely in the marketplace.

Although we may note that in the increasingly noisy modern world, noise-cancelling headphones are literally selling people noise if they lead to an increase in costs.

Silence, like privacy, may be something which can be almost impossible to protect in the modern world. All music of course must contain some semblance of silence or it would be an incomprehensible blur with all the parts running together. The exception to this is the current vogue, on the internet, for creating "black midi" files using software to create musical performances with literally millions of notes being played. This is unlikely to appeal to the general listener and we should probably consider it a deviant case of anti-music made for frivolous purposes rather than any kind of polemic.

The ancient Japanese idea of *ma* says that music lives in constant dialogue with silence in the wider society. Thus the increased scarcity of silence in the general economy threatens the vitality of certain types of music. Some composers like Morton Feldman (and followers like English rock band Talk Talk) will argue that decisions about the placing and length of silence within a work are a crucial aspect of it. This would be a staple element also in discussion of jazz artists like Miles Davis. In more frenetic and populist music, like modern urban dance genres there will still be breaks where there appears to be no sound, even if it is only for a very small fraction of a second, but there is often still a very high level of sound/noise in terms of decibel measurements. In some cases, this will be due to the use of compression techniques to reduce the dynamic range of audio events to make them more palatable and possibly more exciting. This is the issue of the so-called "loudness wars" in modern music where the subtleties and finesse of music are being squashed out by sonic engineers and producers catering for mass markets. This is easier than ever as music is largely produced in the digital domain where little cost or effort is required to "squash" the mix of recorded music or even raise its level. These are arguments about music being noisy not that the music itself *is* noise. That is, that the music itself may still be "good" but is being ruined by a market-driven processing imperative similar to what happens to food ingredients as a few oligopolistic supermarkets take over the world. As with processed food, we find the argument that people become accustomed or even addicted to the overloud music. The market failure argument can also be applied to supposedly plain "bad" music as well as the ruination of good music.

One partial indication of the loss of value of silence in the modern world (because it is a "waste of time" in a harassed leisure universe) is the reduction in the length of gaps between tracks when older music, such as the Beatles, is repackaged.

Celebrated French thinker Jacques Attali's book, *Noise: The Political Economy of Music* is almost universally praised. This may be due to it not having been read by those who would be horrified by its contents. This is not a book that I have seen discussed by an economist although Attali himself is considered to be an economist. Indeed one who advises the French government. Its central thesis is one that attaches a level of importance to the social position of music that would surprise many. The term "political economy" is one that is a long-running and possibly even increasing source of confusion. Political economy is what the subject we now know as "Economics" was originally called before it became formalized and professionalized.

Currently it has a number of usages. Sometimes it is the term applied to discussion of economic matters by academics who are not themselves economists. Elsewhere it is symptomatic of attempts to spice up economics by making it more relevant or interdisciplinary. Just now there seems to be a vogue for calling works "cultural political economy". Confusingly, a lot of writings on political economy do not necessarily have anything to do with politics in the normal sense of the word.

The back cover of the 2011 printing of the Attali book contains this comment from *Ethnomusicology* (emphasis added):

> For Attali, music is not simply a reflection of culture, but a harbinger of change, an anticipatory abstraction of the shape of things to come. The book's title refers specifically to the reception of musics *that sonically rival normative orders.*

This quote follows Attali as the normative orders referred to are not canons of music creation but normative orders in the world. Thus like 1960s hippies, Sun Ra, early rap artists and British punks, Attali might be seen as thinking that music can change the world. It would seem that he and his aficionados, do not perhaps go that far as it is only a harbinger of change.

We might be inclined to say: so what? Why do we need a harbinger of social and political change? In terms of the marketplace for music, harbingers could be very useful as they may enable culturally minded entrepreneurs to make money by using the cutting edge of musical styles as a forecasting device for incoming shifts in consumer tastes not just for music but for whole lifestyles.

We ought to have a theory of why harbinger properties might be found in musical evolution. There are some obvious propositions that could be explored as follows:

- Creative musical people tend to be younger and more in touch with the zeitgeist.
- They may be more intuitive than others and thus pick up non-quantitative information.
- All musical work involves some degree of abstraction and removal from literary modes of thought and this may generate insights into incoming change.
- Creative musical people might be seen as living outside the conventional market world of mundane work existence and thus be able to see more clearly than those that are trapped within it.

These may also apply to film makers or other visual artists but music perhaps has the advantage of being a means whereby, historically, more people can be reached for less effort.

This might explain why (see Chapter 8) Pussy Riot are discussed under the heading of music despite the fact that their music itself is not discussed. Ubiquity of movement of music can account for some people, who are not necessarily that musically inclined, moving their art work into the musical sphere for either anarchistic or more focused political ends.

The itemized list above is premised mainly on some kind of "outsider" status and a degree of opposition to the marketplace. However, success brings the musician more into the discipline of the marketplace as Stockhausen laments. We may then envisage a long-run equilibrium where music simply becomes a product of the current normative order rather than a challenge to it or harbinger of change. Looking at 1960s protest "folk" music we can see this in such things as the promulgation of the early works of Sonny and Cher and Barry McGuire's "Eve of Destruction" as a sanitization of the works of Bob Dylan. Less musically stark (than Dylan) songwriting protesters The Third Rail unleashed an attack on consumerism in "Run Run Run" in 1967 and proceeded to end up writing advertising music. The ubiquitous co-opting of all sorts of music, into commercial advertising, represents an apex of market emasculation of the supposed outsider status. The noise has become the sound of the mainstream. The scene in the biopic of the Doors, based on Jim Morrison's anger at "Light my Fire" (seen as a counter-culture anthem) possibly being used in a Buick commercial now seems rather quaint. Nonetheless, an approach by another car firm, in 2003, led to a feud between the surviving Doors as one of them (Densmore) objected to ruthless economic exploitation of the band's name and songs as capital assets.

After the UK punk explosion we saw corporate encouragement of vague "Generation X" products like the hybridized sneer of Billy Idol. Attali generally would seem to be sympathetic to the idea that such marketization has removed the subversive power of music to be "noise" in his sense.

Attali's use of the term noise, however, is confusing and not really integrated into the "marketization leading to loss of essence" argument. In general, his use of the term noise is not in terms of acoustic theory, or even in terms of musicians who have sought to create theories and practices of "noise" music, although Attali confusingly provides brief historical accounts of both of these in his preamble. Rather, noise represents the derogation of revolutionary musical forms, by the established order, in the sense that they are not "proper" music. It might follow from the idea that noise is revolutionary that the opposite concept of silence might be equally revolutionary.

Silence as a form of music is obviously a somewhat limited career option for the consumer and equally restrictive for the listener. The only notable proponent of silence as a strategy of production is the American composer John Cage. In his case, this is done purely for polemical purposes (akin to visual artists presenting all one colour canvasses) and without any intent of being a viable long-term method. For consumption, the only notable proponent of a strategy of silent consumption is UK maverick anarchist Bill Drumond (formerly of the KLF).

This is discussed further in Chapter 3. Both Cage and Drummond are effectively concerned with the problem of satiation due to there being too much music and too little "real" listening as opposed to merely ambient and casual hearing. John Cage's "4 Minutes, 33 Seconds" is by now an easy source of rather tedious humour. His serious point was about the difference between simply hearing and actively listening to a subject on which there is (not surprisingly) much literature. There is also a belated ironic relevance to the issue of copyright to be found in the Mike Batt case. Supposedly Cage sued Batt for infringing his copyright of the silence. In 2010 Batt claimed on Twitter that this whole story had been a prefabricated scam done for amusement.

It seems darkly amusing that we could have a case of someone trying to copyright silence during an era of artist and corporate panic over the difficulties of copyrighting works of art and entertainment (or as we shall have to call them "intellectual property") which have got actual content.

In 2014, Michigan band Vulfpeck released a silent album *Sleepify* in order to extract money from Spotify. They made reportedly $20,000+, from over five million plays, before the entry was removed without explanation. There were ten tracks of 31 or 32 seconds which their hardcore fans left on streaming while they slept. This was an organized campaign to raise money to go on tour and some free shows were offered to fans as reward. Spotify only paid $0.0007 royalty per play meaning large numbers of plays are needed to generate much revenue. The length of tracks was chosen to be just enough to qualify for payment. Commentary on this has failed to point out that surely the silence element is irrelevant. The loyal fans could have slept and streamed short pieces of music with the volume turned down. Skoff (2014) sees the whole scam as indicative of the future scope for fan power to correct market failure which is penalizing the truly talented musicians due to a poor reward system.

The elements of music

So, if music is not in a state of crisis then it will be something that is not the opposite of noise or silence but what distinguishes it from other things? The obvious quality is sound. A painting by Picasso does not make a sound unless otherwise manipulated. It is thus "art" not music. But, galleries exhibit art installations which do have sonic content but are not deemed to be music and we find practitioners in "sound installation" which implies they are not musicians as such.

Music in the general sense may be conveniently divided into that which is performed and that which is recorded. Clearly this distinction is somewhat fluid. The majority of live performances now contain many recorded elements such as sampled parts and samples played in a musical style. In particular live percussion on traditional acoustic instruments has to be supplemented by additional triggered electronic (sampled or modelled) sounds or audiences will not be happy with the result. This is particularly the case where the live experience is required to reproduce the major elements of the recorded version.

In the rest of this section, I provide a distillation of the elements of music as catalogued over time in various musicological, psychological and other writings. I do not give chapter and verse for each aspect although one may refer to books on the psychology of the appreciation of music. Later, in Chapter 6, I discuss how these aspects can be more formally incorporated in mainstream economic analysis in terms of Lancaster goods characteristics model of utility. It is clear that some of these elements are also present in other cultural goods, the most relevant comparator being movies. Movies might be venerated or even successful because of an authenticity component, for example, such as in the current vogue for "real life stories" which have been fictionalized for impact. However, some of these elements are unique to music. We might talk about the rhythm of the narrative in a book or film but this is quite distinct from the type of impact to be found in ancient religious rituals with musical content or the pounding hedonism of night clubs. The discussion below is not about the musical analysis of the elements of music but is instead consumer reaction oriented. There is some relevance of the structure of musical consumption in Chapter 2 in so far as following rules of composition can lead to greater demand.

I will put the elements in alphabetical order by title just for convenience. Some of these are not aspects of music per se but of the social construction of its meaning but it will be less confusing if the list also includes these.

Authenticity

Most people exhibit some preference for that which is supposed to be "real" over that which is false. This could be tracked back to the problem of trust and lies in relation both to people and to commodities. Early fears of "unreal" food would be that it is dangerous. Insincere people would be likewise dangerous.

So far, we have talked about social construction of authenticity. However it is possible to verify empirically whether a musical experience is "real" in terms of its purported ingredients although this becomes a multi-layered task when we come to technology. In the case of tribute bands (see Chapter 5) we can easily verify that "Mick Dagger" is not actually Mick Jagger playing a prank. However, tribute bands receive more praise and economic success the closer they come to recreating an authentic experience of that which is tributed. So the degree of reality of the unreal becomes a motif of authenticity and a source of economic value.

Returning to the social construction of the overall experience, we have the authenticity of the artist with respect to the genre being exalted. Conspicuous examples of this are to be found in the UK where guitar band based musicians are often keen to flaunt their working class credentials of their street "edgy" nature which may be enhanced by flirtations with borderline criminality. The same kind of thing applies to black American hip hop and rap musicians many of whom came from comfortable middle class backgrounds.

The primary example of someone embodying their claims to authenticity in their actual work is of course multi-millionaire Jennifer Lopez who saw fit to inform us, in her 2002 hit single, that she was still "Jenny from the Block" with the clear message that tremendous wealth had not changed her and she was still true to her roots. In this case there is a dimension of ethnic identity to which I return in Chapter 9.

Relativity to genre is crucial. Thus we find that the idea of a white middle class English rapper is not easily accepted. The field of the higher social class white English rapper is then a comedy one such as the case of "Mr B the Gentleman Rhymer" (beloved of UK Conservative politician Michael Gove). Humour is the inevitable consequence of lack of socially validated authenticity as the producer can make a "joke" out of not having the identity they are supposed to have whilst working in the genre they have chosen.

Bodily stimulation

Popular forms of music have always been based heavily on being rhythmic which explains why more serious critics would find them wanting for being too repetitive. Stockhausen (*Wire*, 1995) exemplifies this in his response to listening to works by the Aphex Twin and others who were seen to typify new revolutionary movements in electronic music in the 1990s. He expresses contempt for the "permanent repetitive language. It is like someone who is stuttering all the time, and can't get words out of his mouth." One might even be tempted to detect an element of black origin racism in his remarks (even though the authors are white) as his disdain at one point is expressed in suggesting that the composer should stop his "post-African repetitions".

He goes on to specifically denigrate dancing as a low form of human activity. Speaking of Richie Hawtin he says: "I know that he wants to have a special effect in dancing bars, or wherever it is, on the public who like to dream away with such repetitions." Apart from not liking this, he actually offers an economic interpretation of why it is not a good idea in the first place. Specifically, that the artist in question will have a short shelf-life as before too long the process of competition will throw up a "new thing" which will depose the commercial status of the established work. This can be seen in the general field of electronic dance music (EDM) which shows the most dramatic tendency to proliferation of genre and sub-genre nomenclature ever seen in the history of arts and entertainment. Some of these are remarkable pieces of branding to wit, is the implication of IDM (intelligent dance music) that other works are stupid dance music?

Stockhausen also sees the dominance of rhythm as indicative of a harmful use of music as a drug which is effectively programming people's minds and thus opposing the evolution of their higher nature. He says "using music like a drug is stupid. One shouldn't do that: music is the product of the highest human intelligence, and of the best senses."

Much of Stockhausen's complaint is that there should be variability in rhythmic elements. But, too much variation will disrupt the psychosomatic benefits of rhythmic music. Much of this is related to dancing. It is not going to be easy to dance to complex patterns. One feature of simplistic rhythms is that they are democratic in terms of participation.

Types of dance have varied but the core principle stays the same. On occasions we have dance crazes, such as the waltz, the jitterbug and in the 1950s and 1960s we saw perhaps the more overt monetization of this in cynical attempts to engineer (now long forgotten) new dance crazes such as the Hully Gully. Long periods pass without there being a specific dance craze then we have intense peaks which inspire some surprisingly hostile social reactions. Typically a dance craze is for something which is not entirely new but has been smouldering or flickering for 20+ years without mass attention.

Although the last 30 years or so may not seem to have been a hotbed of dance crazes, we have had such flurries as the Macarena, in 1995–1997, and the breakouts of the Gangnam style by Psy (which is actually a K-Pop song – see Chapter 10). Twerking has become mainstream, entering the *Oxford English Dictionary* online in 2013 having been allegedly around for 20 years or so. Its substantial mainstreaming seems to be due to Miley Cyrus's video of her dancing to someone else's song.

The disco boom of the late 1970s is probably the largest ever economically exploited dance boom. This reached the point where the major music corporations would see the dance element as being almost mandatory in any popular music if it was going to sell. Thus stragglers and survivors of 1960s rock who had weathered the punk storm found themselves packed off to Florida with producers the Albert Brothers to lay the disco beat on top of their work. The fluke specimen of such thinking or, if we like, the exception which proved the rule, was Pink Floyd's "Another Brick in the Wall" in 1979 which gave the anti-singles band a massive hit (this was produced by Bob Ezrin who was keen to bring a "dance pocket" to work he was doing at the time).

We may note that dance and rhythm dovetails with authenticity issues. The Genesis hit "I Can't Dance" (1992), complete with supposedly amusing video, began as a parody of a song by the Clash ("Should I Stay or Should I Go") used in a jeans commercial. The joke we are asked to participate in is that Genesis are not young, sexy or glamorous. They are also from relatively upper class echelons of UK society (for the most part).

Such was the popularity of disco that a furious backlash emerged in the "Disco Sucks" movement crowned in the demolition of records and mass hysteria in Chicago in 1979 at a sports event. It is probably fair to say that there were homophobic and racist elements in this attack on this specific form of dance rooted music.

Catharsis/therapy

Hesmondhaugh's (2013) concern with the emotional impact of music is asserting something that is widely documented. To be of emotional impact, music could simply be evoking emotions like sadness, loss, regret without doing anything other than highlighting, underlying or recalling those experiences. More deeply music may serve cathartic or therapeutic purposes where it is essentially of health benefit to the consumer. This does tend to link back to authenticity in that people feel more strongly when they believe the author/renderer of the work has shared similar experiences to themselves. This can explain why people who are both singers and composers of their work may be hugely successful compared to singers of other people's work. Much of the huge appreciation of the work of Adele which is analysed in the next chapter, revolves around the catharsis element as her works to this point are essentially "break up" anthems.

Reverence/spirituality

Music in many countries and genres has its origins in essentially spiritual or religious uses. The obvious exception to this is the Amish faith in Pennsylvania. Music forms a core part of marriage and funeral services in many cultures being used in different ways. Increasingly secular music is used for these purposes the archetypal example being "Angels" by Robbie Williams. Outside such overt uses, there is ample documentation and evidence of people seeking reverential solace from music. Most music journalism analysing the success of U2 tends to lay emphasis on the pseudo-religious nature of involvement in the music. Even longer ago we can see certain musical instruments, chiefly the Hammond organ, as instant signifiers of reverence. The use of the Hammond organ in music of black origin tends to mirror gospel roots but this was later transmuted by white European ensembles into evocations of a more sedate white church music.

Relaxation and recreation

The music market is part of the leisure industry. People buy these products and services to engage in such things as rest, relaxation and even escapism. Part of the reasons for the depiction of the musical market as youth oriented comes from the emergence of spending power in these groups (derived from parents to some extent) and the easy identification of specific frustration alleviation and relaxation needs in these groups.

One person's relaxation may be another person's stress. So-called "easy listening" music (the key exemplar of which is the works of James Last) was overtly targeted at an adult audience seeking sedentary relaxation. For others, loud, frenetic and even aggressive music may be a form of relaxation. Particularly if it forms a vehicle to vent frustrations.

Besides the actual process of listening to music, surrounding aspects of the market may also provide leisure. These include making collections of recordings and equipment, maintaining and documenting these collections, shopping forays, reading about the subject and so on.

Tribal affiliation

Musical consumption may form part of an individual's identity but this may also have tendency to foster sociability. The facilitation of social interaction in normal discourse is one thing but it would not require that a strong social bond is formed which is specifically tied directly to the music. Popular music has tied together disparate individuals via basic "fan club" experiences. These became particularly emphasized in the 1960s and can currently be seen in the hysteria/mania of young girls following One Direction. With the emergence of performer websites and now myspace accounts etc., this reaches a new dimension where the consumer may even feel a tribal affiliation with the performer as well as fellow fans.

With the specific case of music aimed at young fans, there is an obvious economic production process at work where ensembles are constructed directly to appeal to the spread of fan mania in order to increase sales way beyond what is possible without this dimension. The first notable case of this was the creation of The Monkees as an attempt to deliberately replicate the seemingly spontaneous consumption mania inspired by the Beatles.

Conclusion

The elements of music listed above will be present in different combinations in different genres of music. Gregorian chants, and music of that ilk, are designed to bring reverence/spirituality. They must still, inevitably, have some rhythmic content but not to an extent that those seeking a hedonistic good time on a night out or a dance around to release their frustrations could base their activities on the genre. There may be synergy in the elements in that combining them in various ways may produce greater satisfaction. This is the essential job of popular music as a huge market force. The industry constitutes a laboratory where the various elements are endlessly combined in different forms in the pursuit of profit. Imitators of the work may have other aims in mind but eventually the market comes to play a significant part in the generation and use of their work. Even for more elitist forms of music, the marketplace is extremely important. Not just for the brutal fact of being a means of making money but also because most music is developed with an intention to communicate with an audience. In extreme cases, the musical performer or composer can find that there is a wilful blockage of such attempts due to critical disdain, rejection by commercial gatekeepers or hold-ups due to someone else holding their essential property rights.

In this chapter, we have discussed the nature of music as a general personal and social phenomenon and more specifically as a commodity which can be brought to market. These themes will be explored in more detail in the coming chapters. The next chapter is a case study of the huge success of one artist (Adele) chosen as a way of introducing the key elements, to be explored later, in a specific historical context.

The approach to be taken is a social economics one as I do not focus narrowly on costs and prices as the drivers of all outcomes. Social interactions are considered at all points and in many cases there is also an engagement with ethical issues.

2

ADELE-O-NOMICS

This chapter looks at Adele as an economic case study. It is intended only to be a platform to introduce themes that will be covered in other chapters by looking at a single artist. It is not intended to be taken as a critique or commentary on her music as such.

The Adele phenomenon

British singer Adele (full name Adele Laurie Blue Adkins) has experienced a phenomenal amount of success and, not surprisingly, become very rich in the process. The success has not been purely in terms of sales, her work has also been garlanded with critical praise and awards and social esteem (award of an MBE for example at a very young age for a person in the entertainment industry with a short career). According to Marcone (2013), Adele outsold the combined figures of the next two top selling albums in 2011 (in the USA), as "21" by Adele, shifted 5.8 million units; "Christmas" by Michael Buble, 2.5 million units; and "Born This Way" by Lady Gaga, 2.1 million units. These sales figures encapsulate a penetration of the US market which has not always been achievable by UK performers. Several powerful UK artists, such as Oasis, Status Quo and Cliff Richard, have failed to make a significant dent on the American market.

Her status was confirmed by being asked to contribute to the movie theme for *Skyfall* the resuscitated James Bond movie franchise. The extent of her successes is summarized in Table 2.1 with respect to the award of metal discs in some markets. Platinum awards dominate but she even achieves the rarity of a diamond disc in the USA. Other countries do not have a diamond disc, their silver, gold and platinum discs require figures that are correspondingly smaller in areas with smaller population. However, there is no formal proportionality; that is, a gold disc in country A is not the same as a gold disc in country B if we divide by some measure of potential

TABLE 2.1 Summary of the success of Adele

Disc awards	*Number/territory*	
Work/type of disc		
Singles	UK – 6×Platinum singles, 1×Gold	
From a population of 10 singles	USA – 22×Platinum singles, 1×Gold	Includes singles scoring 8×, 5× and 4×
	Australia – 10×Platinum, 3×Gold	Includes a 7× and a 3×
	Germany – 4×Platinum	
Albums		
"19"	UK – 7×Platinum	
	USA – 2×Platinum	
	Australia – 2×Platinum	
	Germany – 1×Platinum	
"21"	UK – 16×Platinum	
	Germany – 8×Platinum	
	Australia – 14×Platinum	
	USA – Diamond	Adele is:
		• the only artist or band in the last decade to earn an RIAA Diamond award for a 1 disc album in less than 2 years
		• the only British or European female solo act in history to earn an RIAA Diamond award
		• the sixth female solo artist in Gold and Platinum programme history to earn a Diamond award in less than 2 years
		• the only British or European artist or band in RIAA Gold and Platinum programme history to earn a Diamond award in less than 2 years
		• the artist who has had the most weeks of any album in US billboard top 40 (with "21")

Sources: data from RIAA.

sales such as population of a certain age. Also, there is no global metal disc awarding regularity body keeping an eye on consistency between countries.

I have not attempted to re-standardize by potential sales per country which would make the discs into fractions instead of whole numbers in most cases. I have aggregated multiples, e.g. a release which goes 4 × Platinum counts as four in the total. As metal discs are essentially industry rewards for sales performance, they provide some kind of benchmark of an artist with respect to the performance of others in the industry.

Perhaps not since the heyday of Michael Jackson's peak period has a single performer managed to satisfy simultaneously so many of the goals that an artist and their record company might aspire to. In a time of market fragmentation she is achieving huge sales and popularity in terms of *both* single songs and collections of these as albums. Indeed, it was said by James Donio, President of the National Association of Record Merchandisers, "An album like Adele's is a concept album, enjoyed when the songs are not disaggregated ... in cases like hers, the album is a work of art" (Pulley, 2011).

In terms of economics, we should also note that Adele's global success has come in a recording career that effectively begins in the midst of the worst recession ("the credit crunch") of modern times when one would expect that discretionary spending might be curtailed to focus on necessities. There is of course the counter-hypothesis that, in times of economic gloom, some forms of music will become more popular as palliatives. This is a relatively little explored topic.

A number of papers by Pettijohn and associates (Pettijohn and Sacco, 2009a, 2009b; Pettijohn *et al.*, 2012) in psychology journals have looked at the impact of economic conditions, in the USA, in terms of lyrics, tempo (bpm – beats per minute) and key of song.

Zullow (1991) analysed the optimism or pessimism of songs relative to economic conditions. However that paper tends to be on the reverse causation position, namely, that optimism or pessimism in songs can be used to predict economic conditions rather than be reflective of them. This has been taken further by Maymin (2011) in terms of the hypothesis that simpler mainstream popular music may presage market conditions because people contemplating complex future economic behaviour prefer simpler music, and vice versa. In contrast with other studies which use the bpm of a track, they use the annual average beat variance of the songs in the US Billboard Top 100 as the measure of complexity in a song. The data is from 1958–2007 using the standard deviation of returns of the Standard & Poor's 500 as the economic volatility measure. A significant negative correlation is observed between song volatility and stock market volatility. The study claims that the beat variance can predict future market volatility, producing 2.5 volatility points of profit per year on average.

It has to be pointed out that this is a case of inference from highly aggregate data and thus can be accused of the "ecological fallacy" a term from old school sociology and criminology. That is we have no conclusive demonstration of what any specific individual is doing so the correlation may be an illusion determined by data properties.

For the sake of completeness, I should enumerate another economic recession hypothesis. That is, at times of uncertainty and strife, it is possible that people may converge more readily on mass purchases of a smaller group of recordings and become less omnivorous in their tastes for music. They may also, within this restricted set, choose safer and more comforting music which need not have any messages per se within it about the specific times in which they live. As we shall see below, exegeses of Adele's musical appeal tend to lay stress on the dominant factor being a universal cathartic appeal rather than being comforting.

Adele's music does not divide into simply optimistic or pessimistic and it does not contain comments on political or economic conditions in the manner of 1930s depression era songs like "Buddy can You Spare a Dime", or even "Money's too Tight to Mention" the 1985 critique of Reaganomics from Simply Red (originally by the Valentines in 1982). Rather, Adele's work appears to synthesize a number of genres or idia. At the level of consumer appeal, its main thrust seems to be cathartic, in terms of surviving personal grief most commonly relationship breakups, in a way which straddles traditional soul anthems like "Young Hearts Run Free" or "I Will Survive" with the vague yearnings of U2 or Coldplay. This kind of blending of elements can be formulated in terms of economic theory as is shown in Chapter 6 using different examples.

It is not just the volume of Adele's sales that have been remarkable. It is also the spread of outlets into which her music has entered despite her record company being resistant to the prevalent tendency to pump out a proliferation of remixes. It has been said by Geronimo, director of electronic/dance programming for SiriusXM that "Adele has that once-in-a-generation sound that fits perfectly with nearly all genres of music" (Mason, 2013). Thus her music seems to have become such a perfect product for some people that it may be almost the only one they need in the genre like the Hoover, the Big Mac or the Panasonic Breadmaker. The same article attributes her ubiquity, in unexpected genres as a sampled element, to the warmth and authenticity of her voice which provides a contrast to synthetic processed textures in which it is placed in remixes in electronic dance genres. Vocalists in these genres have tended to be subject to heavy processing of their contributions regardless of whether or not they are technically "good" singers.

Adele's ubiquity has spread into "sync" markets (use of music in visual media such as films and television) which are seen as increasingly important in the modern marketplace. In such markets, original artist work which is intended for primary sale could be replaced by cheaper alternatives such as newly commissioned music or passages taken from library records. However, even cheap filler daytime television shows based around house purchases etc., seem to draw heavily on primary recorded artist repertoire for scene setting relying only on library music for transitions and themes.

I have compiled a crude comparative summary of Adele's performance in "sync" markets using the (incomplete) listings at the website Tune Find. There is a number of limitations in this data, in terms of estimating any type of proxy for use, which might for example signal revenues and/or cultural impact. However, my main interest is in artist and genre comparisons, not accurate level measurement and it is probably the case that the faults in the data work against Adele rather than for her in this imaginary competition.

The main problems with the data are that there is no specific attempt at completeness, so we do not find use in advertisements and coverage of British shows is limited to ones that are aired in the USA. We also have the frequency problem. A usage in a programme may be just a few bars or much longer and in some cases it may recur. The classic case of recurrence being the use of Fleetwood Mac's "The Chain" which is a constant in BBC Television's motoring programme *Top Gear* which is a massive worldwide success.

In the table, I have strategically chosen selected comparison artists. The data has not been standardized for the size of the artists' catalogue so Adele's performance versus the other heavy hitters is even stronger than it looks. The comparison artists contain heritage rock acts (Beatles, Who, Rolling Stones) and comparison contemporary acts including other female crossover artists. Adele significantly outperforms the Beatles even when solo work and solo work collaborations are added. The competitor female crossover artists can be assessed, to a degree, by looking at the "people who bought this also bought tag" at the bottom of Amazon pages. This brings up not just Norah Jones and Shania Twain but Coldplay.

We notice that some very successful and ostensibly similar (and also very high selling artists) have very weak sync ratings by comparison: the key case being Shania Twain. This brings us to the somewhat anomalous market position of what we broadly term "country" music. Shania Twain's music has country origins but its success is due to eradicating the more overt country nuances and her works have actually been distributed in different mixes to suit different territories. Other crossover country artists do not do anywhere near as well as Adele in volume terms. The Eagles, Dolly Parton and Lady Antebellum have relatively few entries despite being artists with very substantial record sales. They are also outdone by Adele "product line" precursor (to which theme we shall return to below) Amy Winehouse and another comparatively new white American female artist, Lana Del Rey. Lady Antebellum were explicitly ordered by their record company to tone down archetypal country elements (pedal steel guitars). Outside crossover artists like them, there are more mainstream country artists who sell masses of records and concert tickets but garner little mainstream attention.

It may be that country music is simply not suitable in its musical form and dynamic in terms of drop in edits to dramas and documentaries. Use of existing music is unlike the use of commissioned music where the composer can rework the piece to fit all circumstances. For example, in game shows to produce variations for big prize questions, going to an interval, back from an interval and so on. Given the degree of dislike in mainstream record industry circles of strong "pure" country elements, it may also be less used because of an unfortunate resonance of being too blatantly white and on occasions too working class. Country music with heavy metal would seem to be the most extremely "white" core music genres and both have a strong working class/blue collar constituency.

Biographical accounts of Adele indicate that country music was an influence on her work but this does not seem to loom large in accounts of why people appreciate it so much. The instrumentation and vocalizing are not notably country in tone. The degree to which her work is seen as country would be part of a more general feeling that it is "rootsy" which encapsulates a notion of authenticity. Her performance at the CMT Artist of the Year Awards in Nashville, in 2011, would seem to operate in

TABLE 2.2 Adele vs the rest: sync exposure

Artist	Number of plays
Adele	58
Lady Gaga	68
Coldplay	66
Stevie Wonder	55 + 4 collaborations
Phil Collins	13
Norah Jones	38 + 5 associated
Lana Del Rey	18 + 1 with different name variation
John Legend	19 + 7 associated
Amy Winehouse	24 + 1 associated
Macy Gray	15
Shania Twain	2
J-Lo	19
Katie Melua	1
Kate Bush	9
Madonna	37
Shania Twain	2
Eminem	20 + 3 associated
Pink Floyd	13
The Cure	44
Fleetwood Mac	30
+ Stevie Nicks	9 (and +2 associated)
Lady Antebellum	11
Dolly Parton	7 + 5 associated
Eagles	4
+ Don Henley	4 + 4 associated
+ Glenn Frey	1
Abba	15
Byrds	5
Beatles	14
+ George	4
+ Paul	9 (collabs not listed)
+ John	14 + 4 collabs
+ Ringo	0
Rolling Stones	107
Depeche Mode	30
Prince	6 + 1 by associates
The Who	43

Source: see text.

terms of making her work accessible to a country audience not the reverse scenario of putting more country in mainstream music.

The comparison with Coldplay may instance the fact that, subconsciously or otherwise, artists and composers are deliberately styling music into a formulaic structure which lends itself very well to gathering soundtrack usage. In economic terms supply is responding to changing characteristics of demand. Both artists have piano-based music, generally of a ballad nature, where there are shortish snatches of more overt piano which can be used to suggest or preface parts of the song itself in the context of a drama or documentary. Thus short pieces of the song can impinge powerfully on people who already know the whole piece but can still work for those with less familiarity.

Finally, we ought to consider the issue that sync "hits" may be even more skewed for an artist than sales, streamed or radio play charts with a lot of the success being due to one major song.

Adele's success is remarkable as it comes in the midst of endless woe and lamentation about the state of the music industry, outside any effects of global economic factors, with respect to both sales and quality. In the next chapter, we shall see that falling overall quality of popular music is one factor asserted as the cause of the "death of music". I will not be making any personal remarks about the "quality" of any Adele works, but simply observing on the evidence here that there is a remarkable lack of critical contempt for such successful recordings. I have elsewhere provided an economic analysis of the rationale for the negativity that full-time "serious" critics frequently exhibit towards popular work (Cameron, 1995, 2011).

Enormous musical success is not usually attributed to the power of product development and marketing alone. The idea of various types of "magic" and skill are commonly used to attempt to explain it. Skill is a conventional factor in economic production where it would be rendered as some form of "capital", e.g. songwriting capital, singing capital and so on. However "magic" is not a textbook economic factor of production. It can be surreptitiously adduced as an explanation in such things as entrepreneurship. We might confine this to the category of an explanation of "X inefficiency" in economic theory (see Leibenstein, 1966, 1978) whereby two identical operations, in terms of factor inputs, produce systematic large differences in output. This is pertinent to the "how to write a hit" thesis which we deal with below and return to, in a more nihilistic and provocative light, in the next chapter.

The ideas about magic and skill are enumerated below after a catalogue of the features that make the success so remarkable.

The dog that didn't bark in the night

Arthur Conan Doyle's Sherlock Holmes story *Silver Blaze* contains the famous remark to Doctor Watson about the important evidence of "the dog that did nothing in the night". This is often rendered as "didn't bark in the night" when it is mentioned in social science research. In this spirit of Sherlock, it might be useful to focus an economic inquiry about Adele by stating a number of things which she is *not*:

- dead;
- black;
- American;

- a prolific artist despite being in early career
  (she has released only two albums, "19" in 2008 and "21" in 2011 with rumours (May 2014) of the third continuing the "age at the time" theme to be called "25");
- a country and western artist;
- an ex member of a successful girl group or other ensemble;
- a purveyor of electronic beats oriented dance music;
- prone to have an aggressive male (*à la* Pitbull) vocalist appearing on her chart entries;
- a product of ruthless marketing by a major corporation
  (Adele remains signed to XL Records which is an independent record label focusing on more intense care of a small body of work (about six releases per year in total). *Music Week* (2011) describes the marketing campaign for the album "21" which is seen as clever rather than relentless);
- marketed on the basis of non-musical characteristics;
- a "brand" with a string of ancillary products such as perfume etc., despite being a single name artist (like Kylie and Madonna);
- from a family with a musical background;
- a product of cultivation by a ruthless musical entrepreneur;
- a winner or even competitor in a reality talent show;
- a heavy touring artist who can enhance sales by numerous and powerful live shows
  (one tour was cancelled at short notice on a whim and another tour was curtailed by throat surgery; some touring has taken place but television performances have been a more prominent driver of success).

Why is Adele's success of any economic significance? Does it not just represent the matching of demand to the supply of a popular product as occurs with cars, iPads or hamburgers? The vast success of Adele usefully highlights a number of currently debated themes which we shall discuss in future chapters. These can be broken down into:

1   The collapse of music sales.
2   The collapse of music sales on physical media within the sales that are left.
3   The position of female artists in the market.
4   The role of major record companies versus word of mouth.
5   The prevalence of talent competitions as a means of finding popular singers.
    (We should note that artists like Adele may have been indirectly assisted by the current revival of the TV talent show. These have helped revive the traditional emotional ballad as a popular form of musical output, at a time when it might be thought to be under threat from electronic modes of production.)
6   The mode of production of hit music – can it all be done in the bedroom or on the move on a laptop, tablet or even phone? Do ossified networks of intermediate producers prevent new entrants from emerging?

7   Music style – will "real", "organic", "proper" music always survive in the long-run equilibrium notwithstanding occasional threats from processed, artificial synthetic music?

Magic and feeling versus science

How do we explain large-scale musical success? There are a number of archetypal explanations which tend to cluster around different types of practitioners. One popular argument, in recent thinking, is to de-bunk the role of magic following Malcolm Gladwell's book (2009) *Outliers*, which claims that skilled activities require huge investments of time (10,000 hours) such as practising an instrument and writing bad songs until you finally come up with a good one. The concept of outliers is a basic one in statistics. Even in a randomly normally distributed population of events, some item somewhere must every so often turn out to be much larger than the rest. Many of the econometric studies of demand for music are preoccupied with the "long tail" feature of music sales where there is a small number of large hits and a large number of fails.

However, in the absence of proper scientific research on Gladwell's proposition, in the musical field, it is hard to establish causality. The fact that successful people may have spent long periods practising does not, by itself, prove that most of the hours were necessary or otherwise. Such huge labour inputs may instead be a proxy for drive and determination in self-marketing and formation of musical production units with other people.

Musicians and musicologists look for a formula of composition that will explain why a particular work resonates so much. The most detached view is to simply take a statistical view of sorting processes of the "if enough monkeys typed long enough on enough typewriters they would eventually produce the works of Shakespeare" type. This is the global uncoordinated "research and development" view of the music marketplace where an endless tide of songs/recordings is pushed out by corporations with only a few ever making a success of any note. It is not incompatible with Gladwell's 10,000 hours dictum as the time may just be a sorting process rather than an investment that is bringing productivity increases. Once a success has been achieved, there are economic incentives to attempt to produce more success with the same artist as there is brand recognition meaning less uncertainty for the consumer over a new product.

The complete opposite to these detached and scientific views is a view which is found in all works of art and entertainment but acquires some additional nuances in the case of music. At its apex, this is the idea of "genius" or, at least, greatness that goes beyond mere talent. These greats or geniuses have access to "magic" that the rest of us can never have. That is, they can produce works that exceed the mere sum of the parts that a "formula" of the type to be discussed can generate. There are attributions of genius to certain musicians, like Jimi Hendrix or Miles Davis or Eric Clapton, which imply that no one can ever produce their work even if they do exactly the same things. The genius is usually supposed to engage in some risk or suffering, outside the range of the normal person, such as the supposed selling of his soul to the devil by Robert Johnston.

The critical and commercial success of Adele's work has not been attributed to the presence of any genius musicians. In the case of Michael Jackson, there is more of a tendency for the attribution of genius to collaborators (specifically Quincy Jones). Given this we are left with the songs and the singing to focus on.

We live in times where there is an unprecedented plethora of technical instruction on how to be creative and succeed as instanced in the welter of creative writing courses.

It is therefore no surprise that we can locate guidance on how to write a hit like those of Adele given her enormous success. A feature in the *Wall Street Journal* (Doucleff, 2012) explicitly claims that "Science" has found the answer to why Adele is so successful.

It is more generally about why her work should (apparently) "make us all cry" as it says in the title but it does this by dwelling on the technical aspects of composition that go into a "hit". It should be pointed out that the scientific research, in this item, is general and did not actually include use of Adele's music in it.

The article seeks to link the impact back to classical music citing a passage from Mozart's Piano Concerto No. 23 (K. 488) where there is an octave jump in the violins. Emphasis is laid on frequent unexpected deviations in the melody or the harmony. It is claimed that music will only really be effective on an emotional level when it includes surprises in all of its core elements although the discussion conspicuously *does not* include the rhythmic part of the composition in this. This is not discussed in this article, or the next specimen piece discussed below.

We have to be careful not to conflate emotional impact with commercial success. Some might feel that audiences are becoming more sophisticated (in the mainstream if not in some genres) as regards melodic variation, if it is of such great impact on them. If not, we may wonder how some incredibly successful songwriters managed to have numerous hits, across long periods of time and working environments, with essentially the same melody repeated over and over again (not over songs but within a song that is the song is essentially more or less just one long chorus). The paradigmatic case here is British composers Roger Cook and Roger Greenaway with a classic example being their Coca-Cola song "I'd Like to Teach the World to Sing" (later the subject of a plagiarism case against Noel Gallagher of Oasis). The logic of the enumerated rules will be that no one finds that particular song moving. The success of it (and others like it) will be due to being memorable and thus lacking the emotional resonance that lifts on to a higher plane of socialized consumption.

The *Wall Street Journal* calls on Dr Guhn to analyse the specific structure of "Someone Like You". He notes that the song begins repetitively while Adele keeps the notes within a narrow frequency range. We then have the inference that an octave jump, in the vocal, in the chorus is significant especially when accompanied by an increase in volume. These are shadowed by concurrent increased complexity in lyrics and music providing a stimulus to the listener.

One scientific approach to the notion that there is high value added, for the consumer, by the features indicated is to link these as stimuli working on the consciousness. This kind of approach is becoming increasingly popular in economics, in the guise of neuroeconomics. It is claimed that an unexpected change in pattern in the music triggers a number of physiological responses arising from the processing of information by the brain. Such as increased pulse rates and sweating. These physical responses are reinterpreted, by the consciousness, as being states of happiness or sadness. This would be the scientific explanation for catharsis as an aspect of musical consumption.

Having dealt with the technical aspects of musical production, the neuroscientific discussion arrives at a conclusion that could harmoniously be linked to the Becker–Murphy rational addiction model in economics (Becker and Murphy, 1988).

In the rational addiction mode, the marginal utility of an Adele song would be intertemporally non-separable. Having listened in the past can make listening, in the future, more frequent with the specific rate depending on the discount rate of the consumer.

Doucleff (2012) cites the work of Robert Zatorre, at McGill University, as showing that emotionally intense music releases dopamine in the pleasure and reward centres of the brain, similar to the effects of food, sex and drugs. This induces us to want to repeat the behaviour. The exposure to music is correlated with the amount of dopamine released, even when the music was extremely "sad". So, music is a drug and more addictive drugs are more in demand, so the outliers at the pinnacle of musical success are the best drug dealers. This would be of no comfort to Stockhausen given his protestations discussed in the previous chapter.

The article concludes that "With 'Someone Like You,' Adele (and co-writer Wilson) not only crafted a perfect tear-jerker but also *stumbled upon a formula for commercial success*" (emphasis added). The formula seems to be to start predictably, introduce unexpected changes, use directly emotional words and ensure that changes from the expected are optimized to manipulate the listener's neural networks into a state of craving for more of the same song. Too many unexpected changes might confuse the message and thus weaken the directness of the product.

We should note that there is a lacuna here in terms of variety seeking behaviour, even if we were to apply the basic Becker–Murphy rational addiction model derived from standard neoclassical microeconomics. Why would the song/recording that embodies the above principles, necessarily induce a craving for more of the same song or same artist in such a high degree that it might ensure massive success for these songs or artists? The situation is not precisely analogous to the basic concept of diminishing marginal utility in static elementary economics or the more complex rational addiction model. With music, we have historically had a high degree of monopoly in the market supply but the listener has a wide range of choice in terms of how many individual songs or recordings are available. This choice is growing all the time. The consumer also has access to a wide range of substitute products that may have the same neural effects such as plays, films, books, etc.

So, why should reactions from endorphins, etc., lead to the addiction being focused on one song/artist rather than the category into which they fall? Falling in love with one person in an addictive way could be rationalized on sociobiological grounds but these do not apply to a song. For them to apply to an artist this would seem to require that they take the place of a "real" love object. We might think it is unlikely that masses of people could simultaneously be literally in love with the same performer so as to guarantee enormous sales. However, the teen market, from the Bay City Rollers and Osmonds to Take That and One Direction, may contradict this. This is not the market that is driving the huge success of Adele's work which would seem to focus more on the authenticity dimension that the author is "like them".

Thus the explanations from neurological responses, and compositional structure do not explain why a consumer should not become overwhelmed by Adele's "Someone Like You" and then run off and acquire cognate works by Ella Fitzgerald or Phil Collins or Coldplay to a level which prevents this specific song from becoming a massive success rather than just a big one.

The primary supplementary factors to deal with this objection are identification (or in the limit fanship), simple transactions costs arguments and herding or bandwagon effects. Some aspects of these will be taken up more fully in Chapter 6 but we can summarize these here as:

- Consumers' neurological reactions are heightened by the authenticity of authorship, they may reason that the singer/writer is "like them" and thus the experiences depicted are more real than those of some aloof or manufactured star.
- It is less effort and risk to seek out more of the same musical "drug" than to look for new but similar ones.
- Benefits of consumption may be greater if other people are engaging in the same consumption. This may involve a "pure" bandwagon effect where the pleasure is from the existence of other's consumption but also a network effect such as getting pleasure from conversations and interactions with like-minded consumers. Love of the same song essentially fosters a social network which may be implicit, episodic or, with the arrival of social media, fully embedded.

Some of these themes are embraced in our second foray into the "how to have a hit like Adele" field. This is given by Frederick (2013). He contradicts himself at one point. In the process of enumerating the formula for how to have a hit, he remarks that the writing of one song is "no mere formula writing". Leaving that aside here is his enumeration of the winning formula.

He gives analyses of three songs. As with the previous instance there is no mention of the rhythmic aspects. Indeed, the tempi of the works is not mentioned. In the statistical literature analysing the metric characteristics of hit records there are relatively few papers since the work by Crain and Tollison (1997).

Frederick begins with "Someone Like You" (which we may deem the paradigmatic Adele song) and goes on to "Set Fire to the Rain" and "Rolling in the

Deep". The presence of a production process is confirmed in the observation that all feature the same commercial song structure:

> Verse/Pre-chorus/Chorus
> Verse/Pre-chorus/Chorus
> Bridge/Chorus

A quantitative observation is made about the order of contents, namely, that the main chorus will arrive at the one-minute mark, which is claimed to be ideal for radio play. This is in spite of the claim by some (Kusek and Leonhard, 2005; see next chapter) that radio is "dead" as a commercial music distribution medium. No specific research is cited to buttress the "one minute" claim beyond the observation that this is the limit of listener patience for the emotional payoff to their neurological needs. We should note that quantitative aspects of "what is where" in a song seem to change significantly over time in ways that are not easy to explain in terms of psychological or socio-economic factors. For example, the hit singles of the Beatles almost always feature the rapid entry of the vocal part (as do many of the other records of the time such as Tamla Motown work) as do many contemporary "urban" recordings which is not always true of commercial singles music of the 1980s. One could justify some of these structure issues in terms of more time being available in later eras, due to technological changes, and changes in radio practice (such as the role of advertising). However, it does not follow that you must, or should, change the length of introduction or the time to the main chorus just because you can. A competitive economic market would be expected to drive suppliers to the type of decision, on these matters, that is most efficient in terms of overall success.

Frederick makes great play of titles, claiming that Adele's are often unique and intriguing with "Someone Like You" being a banal exception to this rule. For example "Set Fire to the Rain" seems paradoxical. He then offers a rather contradictory theory (given the stress that has been laid on the compositional structure and other aspects) that the mundane title "Someone Like You" does not matter because Adele was already an established star. The unusual titles are seen as helpful to the unestablished artist who is seeking entry into a crowded market. This is a clear "lay" economic theory – that you need a unique selling point or gimmick to get established but once you are established as a brand you do not need this anymore. There is little actual evidence to support or reject this thesis. Going back to Michael Jackson, his titles are generally of quite immense banality (as were those when he was with his siblings, for example "1–2–3"). However, the one word "Thriller" was rendered memorable by being underwritten by a very elaborate video to cement the title in the audience's brains. The unique selling point may be something else such as the flamboyance of the artist, as in the UK "Glam-Rock" era of the early 1970s, or the supposed outrage of Alice Cooper or Marilyn Manson. In some ways, the most logically economic user ever of song titles was Bo Diddley, as his own name was used in many of them. In terms of individual hits, the preponderant rule is that the title is the chorus, or very much in it, leaving aside exceptions like "Song 2" by Blur.

Bland and mundane titles have been perpetuated throughout their careers by many high selling artists, from the entry phase to the established phase. We can note for example Lionel Ritchie, along with Jackson and Coldplay as this is not exclusively music of black origin observation (although we might argue for Mr Frederick that the unusual step of making "Yellow" both the title and the catch line in the chorus of a song was unusual). Research on the disparity of titles of hit songs is very thin on the ground, for example the rate of return to using a person's name in the title has not been studied.

Or indeed the alphabetical position, and letter, of the first key word, which might historically have put the song higher up on lists sent out for promotion on radio.

Frederick lays considerable emphasis on the direct appeal of very emotional lyrics to the audience. He claims that they work better when some traditional ideas, bordering on the clichéd, are slightly refreshed by what we might term poetic innovation. The emotional appeal of words, that have been tweaked in some new way, is just a prerequisite and they require a supporting melody. It is rare that songs with little melodic content, however trite, will be highly successful products. We can always find exceptions to the rule like Laurie Anderson's "Oh Superman" but even in contemporary urban music, if we maintain that rap is "not" singing we often find that there is melodic content sampled from somewhere else as in the lifting of Dido's "Thank You" in Eminem's 1999 "Stan". "Stan" was nominated for numerous awards and features in list of all time great songs (note: not "recordings") for example it is number 296 in Rolling Stone's (2004) greatest songs of all time. His 2004 song "Like Toy Soldiers" repeats the same trick with Martika's "Toy Soldiers" (from 1998).

Frederick identifies the melodies of the three songs he has chosen as "paying respects" to a different style of music. He specifically identifies the chorus of "Set Fire to the Rain" as akin to great female pop hits of the 1960s, such as Dusty Springfield's "You Don't Have to Say You Love Me". "Rolling in the Deep" is said to rely on a Gospel–Blues feel. His discussion of the balance of familiarity in surprise in the evolution of the composition is similar to what was said above.

Now we come to the problem of needing magic as an input in the production process. Frederick observes that powerful, unique and appealing voices are naturally limited in supply but affirms that any singer-songwriter can overcome this basic economic scarcity problem by adjustment of the melody. In terms of an economic production function (see Chapter 5), this tends towards the argument that authenticity can be substituted for magic in the production process. Authenticity may even involve deliberately "faulty" production. He observes that, for a technically limited singer who cannot credibly achieve the highly valued upward octave jumps, it is more effective to break into (presumably a weak) falsetto and add more vulnerability "with honest emotion". This does seem to suppose that consumers will not be so impressed by "dishonest emotion" on a record and one could argue perversely that the consumer cannot tell, from technically correct singing, if the emotion is "honest". Thus an economist might think that consumers ought to reject technically correct singing in popular music as dishonest.

Frederick claims that "honest emotion" is much more important in the sync market than being a "powerhouse diva". Looking back at Table 2.2, given that the (not named by Frederick) Chris Martin of Coldplay would seem to exemplify the proposed strategy, there might be some empirical evidence to back this up. Off the back of Coldplay, we have also the surprise late commercial success of UK band Elbow featuring wobbly higher octave singing as a badge of emotion.

Frederick also comments on the sonic production of Adele's work mainly on the "less is more" aspects exemplified in the piano–vocal only presentation of "Someone Like You" which is extremely unusual in its sparsity for a hugely successful modern record. It is not clear that there can be formulae for production that transcend time and space. The huge Shania Twain global success partly depended on territory tailored production alterations. The popularity of some sparse productions may be a market forces phenomenon. The public may become tired of an over-supply of dense production. There may be a window for sparser and more acoustic music which can be seen as a return to authenticity. This has happened before. There have been singer-songwriter booms, such as the early 1970s, which would on occasions have more detailed production but "tastefully" situated so as not to disrupt the illusion of intimacy.

Authenticity and the sputtering production line

I have been sceptical of the magical musical formula argument. Not least because of the *post ergo propter hoc* aspect. I have also pointed out the relevance of there being black crossover elements in "white"-generated music in terms of reaching the range of modern markets beyond simple physical sales. The role of black elements in music (as we shall also find in the "death of genre" discussions in the next chapter) is intimately linked to the idea of music being "genuine" and "not just" a plastic manufactured product. Whether something is genuine or not is ultimately a value judgement. Someone somewhere is doubtless more emotionally moved by Kraftwerk than Aretha Franklin.

I now discuss the "blackness" in Adele's music before moving on to what is here termed "the sputtering production line" of white British female "soul" singers. The "blackness" of Adele's music has been analysed in an academic paper in a media studies journal. Edgar (2013) uses Adele's 2012 Grammy performance as a case study to examine the "racialized voice and the meaning of authenticity". The title draws attention to the presence of "disruptive authenticity". This study makes explicit reference to the actual physical appearance of the performer as white which can be deemed relevant as the case study is with respect to the Grammy performance, not the recording. Although we could still ask if this is a relevant or appropriate choice of inquiry.

Edgar sees Adele's performance as seemingly almost a radical event which challenges the racial bordering of singing performance into black or white (the article is *not* about the black/white content of the music itself). She constantly refers to Adele's performance as an "act of passing" in that she is aspiring to sound like a black singer.

The argument also rests on defining Adele as a "pop" artist with the follow-on that "pop" is dominated by white females. This threatens to mire us in tautology as it may be that female singers are shunted into "pop" by classifiers *because they are white* and shunted into soul and r'n'b *because they are black* independently of the actual nature of the performance.

It seems time to drag ourselves back a bit towards science. It is now possible to test people for their genetic racial composition. This has been done for a number of public figures in the UK (such as Mrs Thatcher's daughter) but so far as I am aware this has not been applied to singers with a view to awarding them certificates of how black or white they are. It is clear that there are many popular singers of mixed race and ethnicity.

We have popular female performers like Jennifer Lopez, who is Hispanic, and Rihanna, who is of direct Caribbean origin unlike the African-Americans typically thought of as "black" singers. Is she more "authentic" on this count or is she more inauthentic as she ought to be singing reggae to be authentic?

There seems to be little doubt that part of the reason for Adele's major success, as with Michael Jackson, is in terms of what is rather awkwardly termed racial transgression (given that cross-pollination of black and white musics is ubiquitous and long-standing). It seems slightly strange that anyone should specifically focus on this, in 2014, after years of Eric Burden, Joe Cocker, *The Commitments* movie and so on. These are all European instances of white men singing black. Black–white vocal crossover seems to be a sensitive issue in the USA. White American singers who might aspire to be in the soul genre seem to proffer a different product from European ones. The paradigmatic case may be Michael Bolton. He has performed with Ray Charles, BB King and Percy Sledge and managed to have a fairly large US hit (in 1988) covering Otis Redding's (last ever) song "Dock of the Bay". However, Bolton appears to carefully eschew black vocal mannerisms and his strive for emotional verity seems instead to incorporate elements of diluted opera singing.

The notion of black singing and music is also heavily coloured by the hegemony of American music. Recent UK urban artists, such as Dizee Rascal and Tinchy Stryder, use their indigenous black (London) diction and cultural references causing some confusion to American critics and audiences. Some recent UK female white-sounding white artists (Kate Nash, Lily Allen) likewise choose to sound London-English. The significant thing about Adele is that it is a globally assimilated voice that evokes many cultural nuances but does not blatantly signal any specific class or race or geography much like what is often desired in newsreaders.

The sputtering production line

Given Adele's huge success, we might expect that the struggling major corporations may seek to institute processes to generate similar artists, or attempt to buy
them from independent labels. They might look at our dog that didn't bark in the
night list and go hunting. However, Adele is not an out-of-left-field shock product
but the culmination of a specific product style.

Adele represents the greatest success of a long tradition of, black music imbued,
white female UK singers who are *English*. Their success in the American market
may not be specific to them being English so much as to them *not* being American
as white American soulsters are at more risk of implied racism.

Englishness may be important in terms of the supply of white female soul singers,
as being English has generally meant a good degree of access to the records of the
black role models amongst whom Aretha Franklin is the chief cited source. Other
black female American singers (for example Roberta Flack) have endured the criticism of their music and voice as being "too white". Speaking English as a first language would seem to be an advantage, though perhaps one day soon we will see a
Nordic or French equivalent to those being discussed.

One characteristic of this vein of English music is that the proponents of it have
not tended to be ruthless business people bent on their career furtherance to the
exclusion of other things. Nor does there seem to have been a charismatic svengali/
entrepreneur figure who sees the profits in this line of production and sets out to
snap up the talent.

This contrasts with Simon Cowell, the English boy band managers of recent
times and the Larry Parnes' "stable" of the 1950s and 1960s. The style begins essentially with the pop-rock explosion around the time of the Beatles' emergence.
Until this point, the UK female singer was essentially of a showbizzy cabaret style.
The 1960s saw Dusty Springfield as the pre-eminent English "blue eyed soul
singer" who achieved the status of "going native" by recording in the USA with
authentic soul musicians.

Apart from Dusty, there were less successful (at the time) northern English
black-oriented singers like Kiki Dee (Pauline Matthews from Bradford) and Elkie
Brooks (Elaine Bookbinder from Manchester) who were kicking against the trend
of cabaret and light entertainment female singing.

It would be a stretch to say there was a production line in the "blue eyed soul"
English female singer as it was uncoordinated and unsystematic. It seemed to sputter
out and come back to life in a series of performers leading up to Adele. These are
chiefly Amy Winehouse, Duffy and Joss Stone. The vexatious authenticity problem
comes up very specifically with Amy Winehouse, who was quite conspicuously
Jewish, leading the Jewish Museum in London to mount (in what has been accused
of being a spurious cash-in) an exhibition of her life in 2013. Would a young, white,
American Jewish woman be able to follow a career as ostensibly a "soul singer"?

Welsh born singer (Amie Ann) Duffy provides many templates for the Adele
success. Unlike her, she did have talent show experience (coming second on a local

television show) and also unlike her, and Amy Winehouse, she did not attend the BRIT school in Croydon. However she triggered a classic "market versus art/muse/authenticity" tirade from fellow singer (not of the same idiom) Alison Goldfrapp, in the *NME*, in an article entitled "Alison Goldfrapp thinks Duffy is an Amy Winehouse clone" on 12 June 2008,[1] which is derived from an interview at lipster.com. She claims that Amy Winehouse clones are being "manufactured" and that Duffy has actually been trained to work in the same idiom. She claims that Duffy's work is not her own idea but "a business plan". This accusation is predicated on the mistaken belief that she attended the same institution as Winehouse (and later Adele), rather than a music production course at Chester University. Interviews and material with Duffy seem to indicate that a vital part of her effective training in the idiom was education from her record label managers through the provision of suggested listening. We could say that she was, to some degree, benignly mentored as opposed to the product exploitation of some performers. Duffy has tended to drop out of sight after her huge record sales seemingly from her own lack of ambition.

Joss Stone became phenomenally rich and successful at an ever earlier age than Adele. She attributes her style to being exposed to Aretha–Dusty material at an early age via friends' music collections. She did not attend the BRIT school. She has shown a maverick resistance to the production line/business plan mentality. She fell out with her rapidly floundering record label EMI in 2010 over an album delay. It was reported that she offered to return almost £2 million from her advance (part of a £7.5 million four album deal) to free herself from her contract with the major label.[2] Although she had, by this time, sold 11 million copies of her debut album, she was reluctant to pass EMI the master tapes of her new record, "Colour Me Free". EMI however claimed that she had missed a December 2008 deadline for "Colour Me Free" and allegedly opened proceedings for the return of a £1.2 million advance. Elsewhere Stone complained that she had delivered the work but EMI was delaying its release without explanation.

It would seem these confusing disputes have a disagreement over the nature of the material produced at their heart. Stone supposedly completed the record quickly using a fairly basic production intending this to be the record that was released rather than something glossier or smoother. It may be an ironic reflection on the state EMI of the time was in (having been acquired by a venture capitalist firm) that the artist's opnions seem to point in the direction of the next upswing in the white female soul mode – that is Adele's rootsy "less is more" style.

So, being a white "English" female (leaving aside the issue of Duffy being Welsh and Amy Winehouse's Jewishness) seems to allow licence to supply authentic music, in a black idiom, that can be very successful because it ticks so many of the consumer's boxes.

One of the motifs of authenticity in the female singer mythology is to lead a tragic life (as did Dusty Springfield) with the epitome of this being an early death. Of the figures considered, only Winehouse has gone this far. Duffy and Stone have both had non-self-induced drama in their lives with the former having to be kept in a safe house in her youth and the latter the subject of a bizarre murder attempt.

However these facts have not been central to their appeal and in the latter case happened long after the success had arrived. Adele's life problems have been of a comparatively normal range. Her upbringing would be considered broadly working class. On which point we may note that the UK is currently generating quite a lot of successful female performers from (relatively) much more privileged backgrounds who *do not* attempt to place themselves in "rootsy/soul" genres.

What about prices?

Obviously we can have great singers with great songs and suitably "authentic" back stories and still not get massive success, or worse still, encounter abject failure. Music industry lore has historically been focused on marketing effort as the key to increasing sales especially in terms of translating large sales into truly astounding sales.

This seems to be inapplicable to Adele's success which has slipped through the typical routes currently advocated to achieve global market pre-eminence. She has worked in a fairly relaxed manner with an independent label, using people major labels would probably not have chosen and her label has not saturated the market with remixes, from the currently fashionable exponents of the genre.

Marketing exponents often downplay the role of price. Basic economic theory would suggest that one route to increased sales volume is to lower your price. If music is a "normal" good then price falls cause income and substitution effects that give rise to increasing demand. With entertainment media, a price fall some time after the initial launch can be used to re-situate the product in charts thereby getting it more attention.

More recently, early temporary offer low prices have been used to lure customers in, such as the one day only 99 cents deal on Lady Gaga's album "Born This Way" on Amazon USA, in 2011. This was a loss leader strategy carried out by Amazon *against* the wishes of record companies. However, repositioning over recent years has tended to focus on "expanding" the original product by issuing it with added content. In the last ten or so years the drive in the pricing of music is the supermarkets, with Wal-Mart being by far the key influence (see Hardy, 2012, p. 127), and to a lesser extent online stores. Aside from price, supermarkets have also served to create some of the massive successes by presenting a limited range of titles (as with books) to a very wide "passing trade" audience.

According to Pulley (2011), majors like EMI see lower pricing in general as a potent force in driving up sales of whole albums, with the key download price point (in the USA) being $9.99 per album in 2011 and around $11.99 in 2014. A lower price might also attract consumption from outside the immediate market sector. This is the logic of the corporate search for crossover artists who will bring in buyers who would "not normally" buy country music, classical music or whatever the flavour is.

Adele's sales of "21" are not to be explained by any low pricing relative to the rest of the market. Her figures far outstrip those of Lady Gaga for the same period, without the 99 cents for a day gimmick and with less aggressive promotion. Across the board persistent price cuts, for an artist, is simply not a strategy, that is used in the music sector. The cases are very rare. An offshoot of Alan McGee's Creation Records (Pop-tones), in 2000, released "Enjoy the Melodic Sunshine" by the Cosmic Rough Riders which went on to earn a UK silver disc. This was backed by a television advertising campaign drawing attention to the heavy discounting of the normal price (i.e. not a special offer). This album from an unknown band, on a new label, appeared to be a debut, but was actually compiled from their earlier two self-produced albums recorded in a community funded studio. Current discussion and listener reviews, on sales web-sites, of the album seem to draw little attention to the bargain origins of the work. Ironically, new copies of the CD now seem to be offered at quite high prices.

In the early 1970s, Richard Branson's emerging Virgin label released very cheap albums by Faust and others but this was severely *avant garde* music by popular stand-ards. In the mid-1960s to the 1970s, in the UK, sales of albums were to a large extent driven up by cheap labels like Saga, Music for Pleasure, Pickwick and K-Tel (Chapman, 1992) but these were mainly licensed compilations of existing work or non-current releases by hit acts. In the case of Saga, original new recordings were made but at extremely low costs. The outstanding case of price lowering has been the case of the Naxos label in the classical music field. However, this was tailored to concomitant cost reductions by using shorter production times, lower cost sites and musicians on lower wages outside the main unionized markets.

Unlike the economics textbook, the music market is not generally entered (in terms of final products) by using a lower price strategy. Musical outputs, such as CDs and digital downloads, are subject to lower price special offers from time to time but this is part of the normal sales strategy of the distribution outlets – what supermarkets refer to as EDLP (every day low prices). The market is generally entered by product differentiation which will be expounded in more detail in Chapter 6.

Conclusion

In this chapter, the success of Adele Adkins has been used as a case study to illumi-nate some of the key issues surrounding the position of music in the marketplace.

A key reason for this choice is the need to counterpoint a massive economic success, which also appears to inspire substantial emotional empathy from listeners, with the prevalence of negative and even nihilistic writings about music. Such views tend to come from the more intellectual end of the spectrum in which context they range from specific genre death theses to the all encompassing "death of all music" position. The next chapter looks at these views but also incorporates some analysis of the more prosaic death of music position, via falling sales, which has dominated popular discourse in the last ten years or so.

Notes

1 See www.nme.com/news/goldfrapp/37289#vpIMzw1ZzvEcpyxM.99 (accessed 23 May 2014).
2 See www.theguardian.com/music/2009/jun/01/joss-stone-emi (accessed 23 May 2014).

3

THE NEVER ENDING DEATH OF MUSIC

The death of music is still alive and with us

According to Mott the Hoople's 1974 UK number 16 hit single, "The Golden Age of Rock and Roll will Never Die". Thus we usher in the common linkage of the state of music with the concept of mortality. Being pedantic, we might note that the idea of a golden age never dying seems paradoxical as it implies we are always, and forever, living in a golden age. Reportedly, live performances of the aforesaid song were accompanied by ironic references to Don McLean's "American Pie" which alludes to the plane crash, in 1959, which killed Buddy Holly, Richie Valens and the Big Bopper as "the day the music died". From an economic point of view this is a very sentimental take as the death of three workers in an industry would rarely be seen as the death of production in the sector. Contrastingly, it can be argued that one emblem of the signs of a dead music sector is the living to be made out of canonizing dead artists. In the field of jazz, pianist Matthew Shipp (Nicholson, 2005, p. 144) has mocked it as the "death industry" where musicians can only be successfully marketed after death.

No doubt journalists will have written about the death of traditional fish and chips or thatched cottages, but nothing seems to attract commentary with the concept of death attached to it quite like music. For example, on 2 November 2013 the *Observer* newspaper ran the story "Is the album dead? Katy Perry, Miley Cyrus and Elton John hit by dramatic US sales slump". Such are the foibles of newspapers that this came quite soon after the piece, in another publication (discussed in the previous chapter) claiming that the album had sprung into new blossoming life – especially when the new concept of TEA (track equivalent albums) was used to agglomerate individual downloads that were not singles per se. The *Observer* piece quotes Radiohead's Thom Yorke's remark, concerning Spotify and streaming, that it is "the last desperate fart of a dying corpse". This appeared as Lou Reed's album sales had risen 607 per cent in the US in the last week following his death. They go on to point out the US music industry, the world's largest market, has experienced a drop in album sales from 800 million in 2002 to 316 million a decade later. In the week prior to the article, US album sales, as measured by Nielsen Soundscan, fell to a new low of 4.49 million units. They say Katy Perry's number one album "Prism" sold fewer than 300,000 copies, but that was still more than the next eight titles combined. The aggregate figures here are poor compared to the individual sales of Adele's work enumerated in the previous chapter.

The weak performance of heritage acts, such as Elton John and Paul McCartney, is dragged into the mix. A prime exhibit, offered to us, is that John's "The Diving Board" sold just 11,116 in its third week of release. They quote industry commentator Bob Lefsetz "The album is dying in front of our very eyes. Everybody's interested in the single, and no one's got time to sit and hear your hour-plus statement."

Spotify, YouTube and other cheap or free streaming services are identified as the murderers. Not only do they dent physical album sales but they also erode digital album sales by fostering the one-track-at-a-time "shuffle" culture. Clearly, there is a traditional statistical hypothesis here to be tested to which we come later. Even without detailed scientific analysis, the same source quotes Ed Christman, of the industry publication *Billboard*, as saying that there is no definitive data to show that streaming is cannibalizing traditional sales. Some additional "industry analyst" generated postulating is offered. Namely that album sales falls beyond the effect of streaming are due to:

- fragmenting of genres;
- the poor quality of music;
- shopping chains carrying a limited selection of discounted releases to bring in customers.

Let us look at these in turn. Fragmentation of genres is very much a feature which is created by digital distribution and low sales, rather than the other way round. In a difficult market, it is a logical entry strategy for new work as making up yet another genre identifies that the work may be "new" in some way and thus meriting investigation. From an economic theory point of view, any deleterious effect of excess genres on sales would be due to the problem of confusing the customers. Faced with too many options on which to decide, they may pass on.

In an emerging digital world, this is less of a problem and consequently may encourage digital consumption, as the use of online sampling of product may tip one into buying online. However it is not clear why this would be a specific factor leading to a fall in total consumption unless the fragmentation of genres reaches a very extreme level. Conversely, the Lancaster goods characteristics model of demand (see Chapter 6) implies that consumers may buy more due to the increase in choice.

Poor quality of music is hopelessly vague as an explanation. Leaving aside the vagaries of aesthetic judgement, it runs the risk of being a tautologous non-hypothesis if it is totally predicated on quality being a measure of median public taste. That is, if music sales are low then it must be because the quality is low, as if the quality was high then the sales would have been high! A more subtle explanation about declining quality, relating it to novelty and innovation, can be constructed in terms of exhaustion of production possibility frontiers. This is expounded later in this chapter.

The problem of shopping chains with a limited range of price discounted CDs in the early twenty-first century is well documented in Hardy (2012). It is not inevitable that this would contribute to the death of music or even just the death of the "album". It may have helped maintain sales by enforcing price cuts on lazy oligopolistic record companies who would otherwise have sought to maintain prices. Whether this increased sales revenue over what it would have been without supermarket (primarily Wal-Mart) intervention depends on the price elasticity of demand which is difficult to know given the limitations of existing empirical work.

The gist of the popular argumentation is that the album may have been the victim of evolutionary murder or even a form of unintended suicide. Only the Pink Floyd, in their celebrated victory of 2010, have achieved a measure of control over the dissection of the releases, in their oeuvre, into component parts. The band sued EMI over a contract clause to prevent unbundling of their work. The High Court in London found in their favour requiring sales of individual tracks on iTunes to cease. Not directly related to this, several of their complete works joined the Beatles in being absent from iTunes, as their overall arrangement with EMI was coming to an end. It might be cynically suggested that the Pink Floyd case was brought strategically to bring publicity (= free advertising) at a point where they hope to make large amounts of money from yet more reissuing of a static catalogue of work in ever more expensive editions by moving to a new contract. There is a lot of money in dead music.

Even with the unbundling judgement, control is limited as there is no way to prevent individual tracks being distributed as copies which are not sold legally. Indeed, regardless of format, it was never possible to enforce some Oliver Cromwell-type puritanical "unbundling embargo" by physically preventing owners of albums from listening to individual tracks out of sequence in freely chosen amounts. Or making mixtapes in the cassette era. Further, with the advent of sampling and cutting up of music, other artists are constantly unbundling the work of previous artists at a micro level beneath that of the individual track.

Digital technology was embraced by the recording industry with the intent to increase revenue, partly by inducing consumers to buy the same IPRs all over again in a new format. Part of the sales pitch or brand spin, for CDs, was the indestructibility of the new format which could supposedly survive being kicked around and having jam smeared on it. It was not, of course, this indestructible and skipping (and even decay due to bleeding in of print materials) was a feature of the emerging CD market. However its greater resistance to decay and abuse than prior formats enabled sales to grow through repackaged enhancements of pre-existing work. Thus we had the magic money-making formula of selling consumers something they already had repeatedly. The current wave of luxury high priced reissues of the work of premier heritage acts, such as the Pink Floyd, are tagged as "immersion releases".

Digital copying and the failure of copy protection and finally streaming take us to the question of whether the enterprise of making music can still be turned into a form of appropriable physical property or a viable analogue of it. But, first, let us get back to death in general.

The varieties of death

The above quoted newspaper article concerns the death of a *format* albeit without lamentation. In the rest of this chapter, I will look at a wider range of musical death tropes and relate them, as far as possible, to economic analysis. I move on to death of genres and then return to the more fundamentally economic issues of declining sales and revenue.

On a mundane level, it might be argued that the use of term "death" is simply journalistic and commentatorial hyperbole to "sex up" the more prosaic notion of a crisis. However, in the works of J.S. Mill, Attali and Bill Drummond there seems to be something more at work. Even in the mere "crisis state", the argument that death is coming rather than just a downsizing is worthy of analysis.

Music seems to have been dying ever since it was born. Jacques Attali's "Noise" monograph (discussed in Chapter 1) even seems to derive much of its momentum from a "death of music" thesis that is never explicitly stated in a clear form. Also, he sometimes seems to offer hopes of a rebirth. His position does not sit easily anywhere on the spectrum of views elaborated below. It seems also to be overlooked by some commentators on his work.

We start with the argument originating in J.S. Mill's autobiography. Music will not literally come to an end as people will still be playing, listening and (in modern times) recording. However it might be said to come to an end in terms of reaching a *satiation point* of some type. This is the approach we shall take to the idea of the death of music. Satiation may occur with the consumer who is no longer able to derive genuine pleasure, or with the impossibility of further additions in value by the musical producer. Although Mill's concerns are with consumer satiation, his argument runs in terms of technical limits to production and is thus chiefly about satiation in productivity. Polemicists, such as John Cage and Bill Drummond, focus on consumer satiation (a loss of value in music consumption or a loss of the sense of what it means).

John Stuart Mill and the exhaustion of the production possibility frontier

Liberal thinker John Stuart Mill wrote a candid autobiography about his life. From childhood, his life was dominated by his father's indoctrination of a dour version of utilitarianism – that only things that were practically useful, mattered. The archetypal form of this is founder Jeremy Bentham's remark that "push pin is as good as poetry" thereby denigrating the arts and culture in a way that had earlier been rejected by Adam Smith in the *Wealth of Nations*. Smith went into some detail in explaining that the work of an artistic labourer, such as a singer or dancer, was a genuine source of value if it provided utility to the consumer. The Benthamite utilitarianism foisted on Mill was allied to the economics of the time (mainly via Ricardo) but is out of step with the subjectivist trend in economic theory arising from "marginal utility" theorists of the 1890–1920 period.

Eventually, J.S. Mill recanted on his strict upbringings and produced a hefty, but ambiguous, work on economics which watered down Ricardian doctrines without going on to provide a clear direction for the future of the subject. His personal circumstances would appear to have triggered a nervous breakdown. His explanation for the inception of this is couched with reference to anxiety about the future death of music.

By modern standards, Mill treats his mental issues in a very circumspect and matter-of-fact way. Likewise his chief biographer, with respect to his economic ideas, Schwartz (1972) goes out of his way to downplay the significance of his apparent mental breakdown. Consequently Schwartz makes no attempt to link the event to any subsequent changes in Mill's intellectual ideas. The conventional treatment of Mill's breakdown is critiqued in Stewart (2005) as being in the realm of pointless speculation as we are, in effect, psychoanalysing a dead person. Hence, it is more informative about our own neuroses than those of the deceased.

In Mill's autobiography, the description of the basic circumstances is in a running header section entitled "A Crisis in My Mental History". Curiously, the discussion of the musical element is in the next section entitled "One Stage Forward" even though the mental crisis, at its darkest hour, is discussed there. There is no further discussion of music after this section.

Mill's mental crisis occurred at the beginning of his 20s in 1826/1827. His initial account of his mental crisis begins with the observation that he had been feeling a little bit jaded and had hoped "a good night's sleep" would cure it. It did not. He attributes the origin of his problems to a realization that he would not be happy if all his plans for instigating social reform came to pass. This came as a shock and not one to be linked to any possible criticism of the planned social reforms. Rather, he set off on inquiries about his own personal shortcomings and damage from his upbringing. He began to gravitate towards non-utilitarian ideas of thinkers (like Carlyle) who were seriously opposed to the doctrines his father had ingrained in him and thus were critics of contemporary political economy. This made them proto-humanist or social economists. Mill also questioned his lack of empathy on a personal basis. Boyle (2000, pp. 30–33) attributes Mill's torments to the tendency of a preoccupation with quantification of human activity to bring us unhappiness, of which Utilitarianism is an extreme case. Which is of course psychoanalysing the dead.

So, one of Mill's key reconstruction ideas was the "cultivation of feelings" (Mill, 1909, p. 82). Poetry became a crucial aspect of his search for well-being. The musical crisis is described thus:

it is very characteristic ... of my then state ... that I was seriously tormented by the thoughts of the exhaustibility of musical combinations. The octave consists only of five tones and two semi-tones which can be put together only in a limited number of ways, of which only a small portion are beautiful: most of these, it seem to me, must have already been discovered.

(p. 83)

He then goes on to claim that this must mean there cannot be a steady flow of composers of the quality of Mozart and Weber. Effectively, the gold mine of music is a fixed seam that will soon be worked out. He says that this is to be compared to the anxiety of philosophers, like Leibnitz, who fell into gloom on contemplation of the point when the sun would burn out. Thus by implication he is likening the decline of musical growth, to zero, to the cessation of all human life.

Mill's explanations, at this point, are somewhat out of sequence so this story comes after his description of the state his musical appreciation eventually tended to. His account of his recovery is that music did help but his enjoyment of it was not returned to his pre-depression levels. In terms of the major revolution in economics, that was to come after him, we may say he had problems of diminishing marginal utility. He says: "the pleasure of music ... fades with familiarity and requires either to be revived by intermittence, or fed by continual novelty" (p. 83).

It is obvious that this is the *complete opposite* to the addiction theory of mega-successful popular music we encountered in analysing discussions about the success of Adele. It is not contrary to Becker's theory of rational addiction. There is even a hint of permanent damage to Mill's music appreciation capital (as we would now call it; see Chapter 6 in this book) as he refers to Weber's *Oberon* as being of benefit to him in his recovery, more in terms of offering the idea of the level and kind of pleasure he once had than in actually delivering it. In terms of standard microeconomic theory, the last point he makes is essentially that of *option demand*. That is, some items may bring no utility in themselves to the consumer but they derive benefit from knowing they exist, in case the day ever comes when they do want them. This would form part of the argument for subsidizing comparatively unpopular forms of music.

I shall now interpret Mill's general musical problem in terms of mainstream microeconomics. I will proceed on the assumption that Mill's musical breakdown is not merely the product of transference of generalized anxiety on to the specific topic of music (e.g. why not develop the same phobia/obsession about the death of the literary novel?). Given this, we will explain his position in terms of the production possibility frontier or production function in economics. The production possibility frontier represents all the combination of outputs that can be produced if all the factor inputs are optimally used. That is, for example, that bankers are not paid too much relative to musicians with respect to their relative contributions to social output thereby leading to a "market failure" where there is too much banking and not enough music. For each type of output that can be produced, the production function is a mathematical relationship between the output and the inputs.

If we assume a very simple short-period situation where technology is fixed then the relationship is between inputs of labour effort and musical output. We are not here referring to the monetary value of musical output but to a hypothetical situation where it can be measured in the same manner as tons of steel or bushels of corn.

In such a situation, if we assume all of the stock of music could be aggregated into one composite output then we can write down a production of the form:

$$MQ = f(ML, u) \tag{3.1}$$

where MQ = musical output and ML = musical labour and u is a random disturbance term which represents all other influences. For ease of exposition let us disregard musical performance for the moment and assume that ML contains only work directed towards composition. This can be taken as the assumption that we are in an environment where performance skills are not relatively scarce but compositional skills are.

Mill's anxiety was that the limited production field of the chromatic Western scale means that "new" or worthwhile ideas cannot be found, i.e. that the production possibility frontier will become exhausted. This is of particular interest due to Mill being an economist who had a nervous breakdown due to this.

In terms of equation (3.1) exhaustion will come about when the marginal productivity of labour input declines to zero. This can be seen in Figure 3.1 where the graph of the production function plateaus at point DOM (death of music).

This is, of course, not death, in the literal normal sense of the term as the level of output at DOM will continue to exist in perpetuity. The existing stock of compositions will still be there but there is no further increase in the output. New compositions will be written and performed but they add nothing to existing value. At the time Mill was writing, access to different genres of music would have been very limited as recording and mass marketing had not yet been invented. His argument has then to be construed as being about the totality of music not any specific type even though his frame of reference was Western classical music.

Clearly, for some people the exhaustion of the production possibility frontier will have been pushed back by technological change. Technological change will mean the expansion of some non-labour limiting factor, which has held down the value of musical output. In Figure 3.1, this is shown in the second (higher) curve. Now the marginal productivity of musical labourers will rise. A competitive market would be expected to reward these increases in productivity. We have shown a one-off static exogenous upward shift in the production function. Obviously this just shifts the death of music farther back to the point DOM2. Unless there is an infinite expansion of production function shifting innovations then the death is somewhere in the future and this is what worried Mill. It might be considered a neurosis that he was fixated with the existence of such a point rather than the risk of its imminence.

If society followed rational economic principles in terms of its overall well-being, then we might expect that resources would flow out of "dead" music and

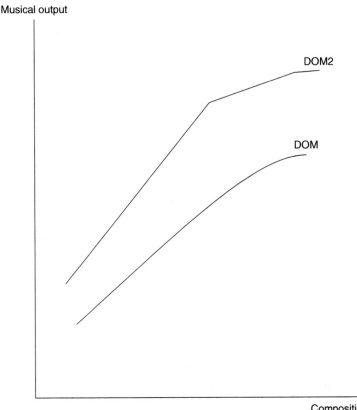

Musical output

DOM2

DOM

Compositional labour

FIGURE 3.1 Production function.

into other fields. For example, the potentially brilliant composer might move into another art form which is not yet exhausted. Logically this may occur before we get to the DOM points as the gains from further input, although not yet zero will be declining towards it and thus may be relatively less than in other fields. If the musical commentator or obsessive judges "death" of the field by a fall in the static increase rather than a complete plateauing then they may consider death to have arisen before the DOM point arrives.

Mill was writing when there were relatively few innovations. After his time these become available through simple changes in approach or technique and later through scientific innovations. As electronics have advanced especially since the arrival of digital methods, new sonic and rhythmic possibilities emerge with sound synthesis and sampling. These would not change music in the formal sense of its compositional methods but even in that area, after Mill we have expansions in the variety of scales that can be used. With digital sound generation this can be pushed to pseudo-infinite microtonality. For example, if we look just at the popular and relatively inexpensive composition software, Fl Studio, there are 19 scale files just to begin with.

Popular music instrument companies like Korg and Yamaha offered exotic scales for users to adopt even in very basic bread and butter sample-based electronic instruments from the late 1980s and continue to do so in performance oriented instruments (such as the Tenori-on and Kaossilator) that do not use traditional keyboards or analogues to guitar playing as input sources. One can easily download hundreds of scales in tuning file formats from the internet and it has long been possible to make any new scale you like by entering the appropriate maths.

It could be argued that the work of J.S. Bach was to a large degree inspired by trying to solve technical problems of the temperament of an acoustic piano. That digital synthesizers or virtual instruments, on computers, can relatively easily be set to produce not only endless scales but also auto-generated patterns would mean that music is now potentially limitless. It may not even need composers. With devices such as Guitar Hero and its spin-offs, Buddha machines or self perpetuating algorithmic composition software, the barrier between the producer and consumer may break down as the consumer can have access to music that they instigate themselves without having any musical skills or training. Although we must note the qualification in the quote from Mill above, that only "a small portion" of the possible combinations in traditional composition are beautiful. The same could be said of later innovations.

Notwithstanding these observations, we may still possibly find a modern "total death of music" advocate in the form of Bill Drummond's "No Music Day" that is absolutist in that it is not based on aesthetic judgements about the beauty of output. Bill Drummond previously had roles in the music market, most significantly of a subversive or insurrectionist nature. Although non-musical, we should note here the use of money from the sales of the KLF musical ensemble burned by its successor, the K foundation, as a piece of performance art. Films, books, exhibitions and documentaries have been derived from this and presented as works of art. The two main themes arising in commentary on this are:

i   doubt that the money really was burnt;
ii observation that this is not an original stance, as destruction of material wealth has previously been presented as art in many fields.

Surprisingly, Drummond and his partner Cauty, failed to give a clear explanation of what the meaning of the act was. Was it an indictment of the music industry as stinking and dead, and thus the completion of the nihilistic message of UK punk uncharacteristically (and belatedly in 1981) typified by Scottish group Altered Images' song "Dead Popstars" which refers to dead pop stars "rotting in the studio"? However irrational burning a million pounds might be, a thesis could be constructed from biohistorical information. The money derived from the KLF, which was clearly not an enterprise set up for the expression of sincere emotions, may have been burnt to exemplify the worthlessness of the music industry which has killed music. This is exemplified in their 1988 hit "Doctorin' the Tardis", a mish-mash of Gary Glitter's "Rock'n'Roll" and science fiction programme "Doctor Who" themes. "Doctorin' the Tardis" was a plank of the thesis in the book *The Manual (How to Have a Number One Hit the Easy Way)* published in 1988 which is a commercial "death of music" thesis as it claims anyone can have a number one if they follow a set of rules.

These are not the more glamorous rules of composition as discussed with respect to Adele's "Someone Like You", in my previous chapter, but more in the vein of a "Warholian" "famous for fifteen minutes" philosophy. However, the same fundamental problem of economic analysis of markets remains, as with pyramid schemes and get rich schemes of any type, that not everyone can succeed by following rules. The market is competitive, so if everyone follows the same rules, then the efforts must cancel out and so we end up with a ranking of winners and losers based on some other type of ability (whether musical or non-musical) or marketing effort that is not in "the rules". There is something of a puritanical streak beneath the mockery and cynicism. Burning the money from a "worthless" fortune can be seen as an attempt to redeem one's self other than by giving it to charity. At some points, Drummond reflects on how all artists are starving in the end. If the money had been given to (other and deserving starving musical artists) this would be nullified by a teleological belief that they too must become corrupt and "dead". Therefore why not cut out the middle of this process in a dramatic and nihilistic way and attempt to achieve a more transcendental status by presenting it as art? If the money had been given to non-musical charities it would simply represent compliance with the standard legitimization of the rich popular musician found in such events as Live Aid and its derivatives. Therefore nothing artistic would be achieved by giving the money away. Instead, the donors would be playing into the hands of the "dead" music world.

It is perhaps ironic that the book *The Manual: How to Have a Number One Hit the Easy Way* now (as of June 2014) appears to be rather scarce and quite expensive. The quoted current price of a new copy on Amazon UK is from £239.48 and a used one from £80.00. One might expect its price to have dwindled to near zero, given that it would seem to be a quaint irrelevance in the modern musical world of instant music creation and distribution at low transaction costs. However, price of such scarce items can be determined by the preferences of a few marginal buyers.

The puritan streak behind Drummond's "death of music" oeuvre is most manifest in the launch of "No Music Day" on 21 November 2005. This is a clear specimen of the "purity in danger" argument (see below), as the motivation was being "sickened" by the crass commercialization and degradation of music.

Similar complaints are often made about food but we see a clear distinction between food and this attempt to reconsecrate music. Attempts to subvert the commercial degradation of food and eating generally seek to promote "good" or "proper" food and eating situations not abstaining from food to bring back appreciation of it. The "food" approach does of course exist in other musical literature, and activism, which is not of this provocative or attention seeking nature. For example, Toop (2010), Voegelin (2010) and the work of Pauline Oliveros on "Deep Listening" (see Buzzarte and Bickley, 2012). These attempt to rescue us back from desecrated hearing and put us back on the road of proper hearing perhaps ultimately taking music back to the higher purposes sought by Stockhausen (see Chapter 1 of this book).

"No Music Day" was most active between 2005 and 2009.[1] Drummond's modus operandi is reminiscent of Cage. His claim is that he orchestrated it between 2005 and 2009 but from 2010 turns it over to other people to do their own "no music day" and send in documentation. The five-year plan period appears to have had little impact as few radio stations or arts/media bodies made any attempt to support it. Those that have can be found documented on the website. This also gives a contact form which basically asks the respondent to write a short statement explaining why they will or will not be observing "No Music Day".

Table 3.1 provides the raw statistics on the number of people moved to supply responses to the No Music Day website. It is clear from this that interest in the concept was dwindling progressively, during the five-year plan, after the initial bump of interest. If we normalized the 2005 data, by rescaling it to take account of the fact that it is year one and thus the data does not start on January, then the progressive decline is total. The 2005 data is only for about six weeks so if we made a crude *quid pro quo* scaling it would raise the 2005 equivalent messages to over 900.

I have not conducted any analysis of the annual changes in length or content of the messages although a superficial look suggests these do not change significantly. Perhaps one of the most pertinent comments is the following: "I am (or am not) observing No Music Day because: unless you lock yourself away in a padded cell or live on a desert island, it is virtually impossible" (Deppo 21 November 2007). Some people will not have the choice to participate in "no music" events by aborting consumption as they will have defective hearing to the point where they can not appreciate music to any significant degree as hearing sufficient of the elements is not possible. There is a charity "Music and the Deaf"[2] in the UK which helps the nine million people (figure on website June 2014) with a hearing loss to benefit from music. It was formed in 1988. It is not aimed merely at finding ameliorative

TABLE 3.1 "No music day" annual message numbers

Year	Statements deposited
2005	105*
2006	335
2007	219
2008	144
2009	58

Source: data from www.nomusicday.com.

Note

* Actual figure of responses without any adjustment for scheme only starting at end of year.

approaches to partial hearing loss but is actually aimed at totally deaf people also. Many of the key executive personnel have very profound or total deafness.

The primary focus is to raise the well-being of the target group by performing music. This seems strange in a world where people of full hearing agonize over the death of music.

Having discussed the ontological (as opposed to commercial) total death of music position we should now move on to the more common death of a genre of music claim.

Death of genres

Books and articles on the plight of supposedly "higher" culture threatened music genres have freely used the term "death". A work by Nicholson (2005) is entitled, *Is Jazz Dead? (Or Has It Moved to a New Address)*, and features a very rare incursion of (some) economic thinking into jazz literature. Commentator Nelson George (2008) in *The Death of Rhythm and Blues* does not employ any kind of social science theory. Both works dwell on the question of the "dead" form mutating into another form. George's book is essentially a quest to find out why the mutated form is of less worth than its predecessor.

Despite the title, George's book is a largely descriptive historical account which seems to veer into nostalgic veneration of older work in the genre. As he reaches the period when he sees the quality of the genre declining to the point of death there is inevitably an implicit analysis.

Underlying the whole problem is the search for profit. Intuitively, the standard welfare economics argument of market failure is presented. The claim is made that the desire to crossover to white markets causes a loss of value in black markets as black radio and black networks are used to "break" records before mainstreaming them in white markets. That is instead of those being used solely for the welfare of the black consumer. Undesirable endogeneity leads to the product being changed to fit this strategy leading to a "falling between two stools" problem. We get a product that satisfies neither artist nor any of the markets aimed at.

The commercial death of the genre is illustrated in analysis of the relative US Black Music vs Pop Charts positions of the top black records by Paul Grein (ibid., p. 157). He plots a fall in the conversion rate of number ones in the soul chart to their peak national pop chart position from before the disco era from nine before 1974, to 15 from 1974–1976, to 22 in 1978 at the peak of disco. The crossover represented by disco also eroded the scope for properly "black" artists to appear on "black" radio. George actually says on p. 157 that it became a breeding ground for "white negroes".

Inefficiency, specifically of the CBS label is identified in their failure to take seriously the recommendations of the "Harvard Report" which they commissioned (ibid., pp. 155–156). This in-depth study to the black music industry was conducted in 1971 by Harvard University Business School which identified that black stations were an entry point to getting mass general radio play as well as for black consumers. The study suggested that CBS should not use the "venture capital" approach to redressing its lack of soul/black music but it ignored this and sought simply to buy in existing successful black labels. The idea of growing a fully rounded indigenous network of black music under their corporate banner was ignored.

Ultimately George's position is about the death of a cultural identity which is indeed how his work starts. Underlying his death view is that music is supposed to mean something and embody a cultural identity of the group from which it emanates. If it just becomes a vapid hedonistic commodity, which is interchangeable with any other such item, then it is "dead".

This style of argument is not necessarily locked to matters of race and ethnicity.

The same kind of "corruption from within" thesis was to be found in peer generation critics and commentators of the supposed "revolution" largely spearheaded by the Sex Pistols in the United Kingdom. Here the purity and authenticity of "black" is replaced by "working class white youth" and the enemy is white middle class musically educated musicians of the prog rock genre playing interminable and complex solos.

Like George (2008), Nicholson (2005) proffers a death of genre argument, about music of black origin, that has elements of the standard welfare economics of market failure floating around in it. This is consolidated in the final chapter (9) entitled: "A Question of Survival: Market Place or Subsidy" which along with the preceding chapter, on Nordic countries, adds an "other man's grass is always greener" element of lamenting as to why the American government and audiences are not more like the Scandinavians. There is also a bit of local "grass is greener" argumentation as he argues at some points that the city of Chicago is not "dead", unlike the rest of the USA, in respect of this musical genre.

There is no explicit "death" theory offered in this book, not even by the copywriters of the dust jacket. However, the first sentence of the first page begins: "When Miles Davis died … jazz was plunged into a crisis of confidence as much as conscience" (ibid., p. 1). Having praised the work of Davis and documented his commercial achievements, we move swiftly on in almost Shakespearean fashion to the rise of the evil usurper of the dead "King" – Wynton Marsalis – who sows the seeds of the death of the genre of jazz music.

Of course this is not a wilful nihilist or anarchist intention like some early punk or "no wave" music. Marsalis is the snake of money in the garden of art. He provides the template for how a jazz artist is to be successful and thus creates a managerial syndrome amongst those marketing the genre. Nicholson implies that entrepreneurial sclerosis follows, with major companies unwilling to engage in meaningful attempts to cultivate audiences for the pure "genuine" work in the genre which, being more difficult, is an acquired taste. The power of such companies renders independent entrepreneurs, who may keep the genre alive, almost impotent.

Like many non-social scientist works analysing the state of the music market, much of the thinking in the book is derived from, or buttressed by, interviews with practitioners. At the end of the book these depict a "pure" artist, in the genre (as opposed to a corporate crossover vocalist) as doing pretty well by selling around 60,000 units of an album (in the USA presumably). This kind of figure dips perilously close to the sort of sales that would lead major labels, in the 1970s and 1980s to drop rock/pop artists from their roster. To further contextualize the numbers, we find that one of the target items in corporate discussions about the incoming challenges of the move to a digital and file sharing world, was how to handle artists below the 200,000 sales threshold.

Ultimately, Nicholson's position is another critique of "mainstreaming" musical genres via crossover acts. It is quite transparently a "purity in danger" (see further below) argument. That musical purity is a good thing so the existence of genres are not mere names to stick on folders where we can find the different "stuff" that we have stored away. This is very clearly evidenced in George (2008) where a fairly clear dislike of the work of Jimi Hendrix and Prince is to be found, originating in the complaint that they are "too white". There is even a hint of a market failure argument, rooted in human capital formation, in his observations that Prince mainly only heard white music when he was growing up.

All of the same kinds of thinking displayed by George and Nicholson are frequently found in journalistic, musicological and even academic economic writings on the fields of classical music and opera. The exception to this is the Austrian economics work of Cantor (2001) who puts forward the *completely opposite view on market failure* that government subsidy has ruined classical music by protecting it from the marketplace. Thus "weak" products buck the trend of Darwinian competition and the stronger work is driven out. One presumes its creators are driven into entirely different genres or out of the music market altogether.

In Nicholson's work, there is an unusual market failure argument in Chapter 5 which is directed at the education system. There is also a touch of the "other man's grass is always greener" position in this chapter as some European jazz courses are held up as superior to general US practice. This is presumably because of the superior arts culture, in Europe, where the market has not been allowed to totally degrade art. The point here is that, as the demand for the genre's music has declined, the supply of qualified practitioners expands rapidly due to the growth of the jazz education industry in universities and colleges. Thus, there is an imbalance in supply and demand that is not "corrected" by market forces as the excess supply is attributed to being an indulgence of rich people's children who fancy being a jazz musician. Familiar criticisms about the education system, in general, are aired (via primary sourced interview quotes) such as prevalent and serious grade inflation and the unwillingness to raise entry standards due to fear of choking off tuition fee revenue.

It is not claimed that the musicians from such courses are technically bad and incapable of playing. Indeed, the claim is the opposite that they are schooled in adequacy to the exclusion of any capacity for innovation and flair which means they are co-conspirators in ensuring the continued "death" of the genre.

In the field of classical music, the death metaphor shows no signs of abating. We find an article by Lee (2003b) which claims to be a "requiem" for classical music.

The revised version of Lebrecht (2008) *Who Killed Classical Music? Maestros, Managers and Classical Music?* quite clearly brings out the death imagery yet again. This work will be discussed in Chapter 5 rather than here. In a contrary vein, Botstein (2008) argues that classical music has been an "unsung success" in the same period.

At the less exalted level of quotidian discourse, the banal "generational death" theory that things are not what they used to be when the listener was in early young adulthood are trotted out relentlessly in YouTube comments pages for almost every type of popular music from almost every past period. Some have suspected that discussions by the likes of George (2008) are just a fancified version of such thoughts being passed off as something more than just a personal opinion.

Even within more mainstream spheres of music, we find death of genre claims. Britsh singer-songwriter-guitarist Richard Thompson, claimed in an interview on BBC Radio 5 Live Xtra (19 July 2014) that country music died, around 1962, when it became too overtly commercial.

There seems a degree of romanticism here as the product was a commercial product before but was different in its presentation. In the sphere of the generic rock band, the spectre of the death theory walks abroad following the demise of Oasis. Serge Pizzorno, leader of Kasabian, has recently lamented that "there aren't many rock bands left and that he hopes the experimentation on his group's new album '48:13' will help push new bands to look to the future". He also remarks that Kasabian are one of the few rock bands left. This is hardly true as there are still many musicians working within the genre. He would be busy if he started to count the number of workaday rock bands in the USA. His argument seems to be a fall from prominent market position. Rock has been replaced as the midpoint of music, and the default starting point for commercial efforts, by beats based urban black origin music. His reference to experimentation raises the same sort of problematic found in Nicholson's jazz lament and Stockhausen's (see Chapter 1) critique of modern electronic music. That is, if something has to evolve in order to maintain its credibility surely the paradox must be that it will eventually cease to be the thing it was in the first place. In other words, we are back to John Stuart Mill's exhaustion of the production possibility frontier problem.

What, in the end, are we to make of genre death arguments, if indeed there is anything in them other than "grumpy old man" syndrome? If we try to assemble some kind of analysis from them, the following themes seem to emerge.

- Money is the root of all evil.
- Gresham's Law (bad music drives out good which implies some weakness or imperfection in the body of consumers).
- The state is to blame.

Above all we have the "purity in danger" thesis.

Purity in danger

A clear theme of "purity in danger" runs through the death of music genre literature (not to be confused with anthropologist Mary Douglas' famous "Purity and Danger" thesis). Writers, and some musicians, are upset that some "pure" vision or style is being killed by entrants to the market who have no interest in "keeping the faith". Music, is not ultimately a religion or even the doctrine of a political party, so what is the faith that is being kept or the purity that is being protected from danger?

Inevitably much of the issue revolves around race. In crude terms, classical music is white and European, jazz and blues and gospel are black, country and western music is white and working class and parochial and rock music is white and global. These are not my own views but a blunt summation of what is implied in death of genre literature. Within the racial schism, there is also the "money is the root of all evil" thesis. That is, the corporate drive to chase the lure of global white rock music has seduced otherwise pure black musicians into life in a hellish crossover universe albeit a potentially well-paid hell. This is illustrated in the following comment in a history of black music in London: "it's when black music has opted to put itself in the hands of the regular music business that *progress* has fallen apart" (Bradley, 2013, p. 13).

We may also note the remark of Wynton Marsalis to the *Wire* magazine (in 1991), reported in Nicholson (2005), concerning the departure of his brother and another band member to play with Sting (ibid., p. 30) that "it was just another stab at the culture, the Afro-American culture". This pertains to Marsalis' previously expressed disdain about watered down "fake" jazz being served up in a palatable lightweight rock context.

Marsalis has also been prone to making aggressive remarks about white music critics which might be considered racist in their tone. One can extrapolate from this the notion that the music of his ethnic origin group "dies" when it becomes the victim of embourgeoisement and subject to evaluation in the terms derived from appreciation of elitist European music. We can see his cessation of classical performances and attempt to relocate jazz in blues origins as attempts to stop the music from dying by such decay into impurity.

Beyond the race issues, the other main types of purity in danger are some idealistic notion of artistic integrity and, perhaps, the most non-pragmatic notion of all, the idea of a whole genre of music having some kind of "meaning" that transcends mere dancing, dating, singing along and consumerism. We have here two fundamental conflicts with economic principles.

In the extreme, the "normal" consumer/worker has little choice about the work they are entitled to do. It is dictated solely by demand. The artist (and also in some cases scientist) is a romantic fantasy figure who not only has superior abilities but the strength of character to pursue a vision that is unique to them. They need money, and it is clearly nicer to have more of it, but money must not be allowed to override the drive to produce work that is good or, more ideally, a manifestation of genius. Music dies for some when this vision dies. This may become attached to an elevated role for some individuals or units but it can become attached to the idea that a genre must progress (as emphasized above) and will "die" if it does not progress.

Romanticism is not just foisted on the artistic integrity of the individual creator. It can also extend to whole genres as reservoirs of some social or political meaning. This can involve racial issues. That is that the genre carries the identity of the race which is being threatened by the shift to global consumerism comprising indiscriminate mixing of diverse influences. This is to some degree expecting the genre to be the embodiment of some deep "truth". For some consumers of all races, the truth expectation goes beyond a racial issue to unfocused wider aspirations. Assigning virtue to music creates an arena outside general market and political values to the extent that we might designate as a type of escapism indicative of a rite of passage of youth.

Death of consumption

The use of the term "death" in connection with falling demand attributed to digital innovation is surprisingly common in work by independent commentators (i.e. work that is not just industry-generated special pleading). A book published by Rogers (2013) is entitled *The Death and Life of the Music Industry in the Digital Age*. In a work by Kusek and Leonhard (2005) which is, on the whole, optimistic about the future of music as a whole, the back jacket features a line near the middle in much larger emboldened font: "**THE RECORD INDUSTRY IS TERMINALLY ILL**". Underneath are two columns. The one on the right is a list of bullet points. The one on the left is a text paragraph. The text paragraph tells us that the record industry as we know it is dying. It concludes by telling us that the book "punches gaping holes through the foundation of a record industry that refuses to adapt".

With consumption of production of music in all forms, we documented total death and genre (sub-market) death claims. In the recorded media field – radio, television, CDs, tapes, downloads – we likewise find total death and sub-market death arguments. The death of the vinyl LP (which has now been resurrected as journalist sources regale us with tales of its supposed massive popularity), the death of the cassette, the death of the minidisc and the death of the CD. None of these are actually, at the time of writing, dead. Indeed, we even find that wax cylinders are being produced again and some are even releasing music on the ultimate Cinderella format of eight-track cartridge. Minidiscs and cassette media can still be bought. Minidisc recording and playing devices are still being manufactured – the media announced death of this format was misleading as the termination date (of Sony's manufacture) was for the portable "walkman" style device not the professional or consumer standalone unit.

In 2013, the UK had its first national "cassette" day, admittedly a much smaller campaign than the global "Record Store Day", launched in 2007. The current "total death" argument about recorded music is exclusively about falling paid consumption. However in earlier times (the early 1970s), the lurking threat was environmental resource constraints especially petroleum in a market still primarily dependent on the vinyl LP and single.

Although it is not the case currently, pronouncements of death have stalked the live arena as prophecies have been made of the eclipsing of music by various threats – the various "new rock and roll arguments" – comedy, computer games etc. Around 2010 in the UK, there was frequent discussion of the regulatory threat, from decibel and public order legislation, which would have put small venues out of business. For example, an editorial in recording magazine *Sound on Sound* (White, 2010, p. 4), puts the claim that the mooted legislation is infringing basic human rights by attenuating the capacity to enjoy live music. This relates to small-scale events not the thriving arena and festival circuits. Day to day mundane live music, in the UK, faces the problem of the death of the public house as these are closing in large numbers in the wake of the credit crunch and the introduction of strict anti-smoking legislation.

For the purpose of looking at some long-run historical data let us confine ourselves to recorded music for which such data is available. I will concentrate on the period before downloading and streaming became prominent, to identify that recorded music consumption has spiralled down before and come up again. I will return to the more recent period in Chapter 10.

Table 3.1 in Grunow and Saunio (1998, p. 38) looks at the situation pretty much from the birth of recorded music as it covers 1921–1945. In dollar values, the USA had sales of 106 million in 1921 which dwindles to the all-time low of six million in 1935. On these figures, recorded music seems to have begun dying almost as soon as it was born. At this time, the feared killer of music was the growth of radio which would lead to such things as musicians unions pressurizing restrictions on broadcasting for a long time after. The impact of radio at this time is discussed in Liebowitz (2004). Radio may have been on the rise but the period in question was the time of the greatest economic depression in the history of the modern world with mass unemployment. As such it was likely to dent consumption severely. Even so, the decline in volume consumed was not as great as the decline in value. A footnote to the table suggests that physical sales 1921/1935 ratio was about 140/25 compared to a ratio of 106/9 on the value of sales figures.

Table 3.2 here, adapted from Table 7.1 in the same source, shows units sold in the four major recorded music territories of USA, UK, Germany and Japan over 1961–1980. These continue to be the major sales areas in the world to this day (see Chapter 10). Chapter 7 in Gronow and Saunio (ibid.) is actually entitled "The Period of Growth". In this period, the threat of radio as a substitute good was joined by that of home cassette taping. We should note that pre-recorded cassettes feature in the total unit sales.

Figures not shown (also in source Table 7.1), suggest that from the end of the Second World War to the rock and roll and pop eras (from the late 1950s) there had been a strong growth in sales. In Japan, there is a clear large trend of growth with only one reversal in 1977–1978. In the USA growth is strong and continuous until 1979/1980. Table 7.1 shows a slightly different pattern in the UK. Total unit

TABLE 3.2 Recorded music sales before the arrival of CDs

Year	USA*	UK	Germany	Japan
1961	640	76.4	–	–
1962	687	77.5	47.4	–
1963	698	85.5	42.3	45.9
1964	758	101.2	43	–
1965	862	93.8	49.2	72.7
1966	959	84.9	47.5	75.6
1967	1,173	90.2	57.5	80.7
1968	1,358	98.9	68.9	96.3
1969	1,586	106.4	76.6	105.4
1970	1,660	114	87	153.9
1971	1,744	126	86.9	171.3
1972	1,924	148.3	107.1	–
1973	2,016	177.9	109.1	159
1974	2,200	198.4	120.9	164.6
1975	2,391	202.1	127	162.9
1976	2,737	223.7	139.3	194.8
1977	3,500	231.6	161.1	218.7
1978	4,131	195.9	206.1	203.4
1979	3,676	187	202.4	208
1980	3,682	170.4	199.1	219.8

Source: adapted from Gronow and Saunio (1998).

Notes

Figures in millions of units sold.

* USA figures are in million dollars of sales *not* units sold so are not comparable in levels with the other figures.

sales actually fall in the UK at the time of the two main documented "revolutions". That is the "Beatles" explosion and the punk era. The perhaps surprising fall at the time of the Beatles boom has been noted elsewhere (Chapman, 1992). Unit sales fall each year from 1977 to 1980, and decline in 1965 and 1966 when the beat group boom supposedly took over from insipid balladeers and showbiz performers. Very strong growth is found from the late 1960s when the "death of the single" (45 rpm record) was being lamented as "progressive rock bands" such as Led Zeppelin and Pink Floyd tried to forbid even having singles issued and this genre of bands would sometimes deign not to perform their hit singles live in order to be taken seriously. The periods of dying UK unit sales find it behind Japan in terms of aggregate sales and also behind Germany in the latter phase. There are, of course, quite obvious population differences between the countries although this is immaterial to those seeking to profit from the sales.

Attempts to interpret such figures highlight the basic economics of supply and demand.

Revenues will be determined by the price times the quantity sold. The price in music markets is not determined exogenously to the firm. The number of firms has shrunk as global conglomerates have absorbed record labels. These have been the price setters. Entry pressure to the market has been through small labels supplying new music which has been overlooked not undercutting price. Adjustments in pricing will inevitably be sluggish and subject to inertia in such a scenario so it is hard to separate the effect of price from other movements in demand.

There will be other forms of inertia due to lazy and inefficient monopoly. The normal argument of the introductory economic textbook of "consumer sovereignty" does not apply here.

The firm is not the passive servant of the powerful consumer. There has been nothing in the music market to prevent firms from supplying a non-optimal bundle of products to the consumer.

This does not just relate to laziness or inertia but also the unpredictability of evolving changes in consumer preferences. If we take the specific cases mentioned. The "beat group" boom in the mid-1960s encouraged a frenzy of copycat signings by record companies but this petered out quite quickly leaving something of a void to be filled by ballad singers (see Chapter 7).

Firms have also had to determine whether the focus should be on songs/records or on artists. As the degree of monopoly increased, the focus tended to shift towards artists and away from songs as loyalty attachments to artists means that the quality of song/individual record supply may not need to be so high.

This takes us to a final argument about the death of pop music. Pop music was not initially meant to be a place for works of conscious art and lifetime careers. In such a vein, energies would be poured into a small set of works which embodied the vitality of youth.

The coming of album culture, serious embourgoisement into the world of music criticism and eventually college education to be a pop/rock musician erode this and leave us with another dead commodity.

Conclusion

This chapter has documented the frequent use of the idea that either all music, or a genre or an aspect of music is dying or has died. No doubt such claims are often entirely metaphorical or allegorical. Leaving this aside, I have looked analytically at the claims made in such accounts.

What we mainly see is that there is some tendency to misrepresent facts and to make ad hoc "lay" statistical inferences with insufficient foundations. Therefore we move, in the next chapter, to consider the very nature of knowledge in this marketplace. How do we know what we think we know and do we know anything?

Notes

1 See www.nomusicday.com the official website (accessed 23 May 2014).
2 See http://matd.org.uk/ (accessed 23 May 2014).

4

DOES ANYONE KNOW ANYTHING ABOUT ANYTHING?

Introduction

The trite and provocative title of this chapter has been chosen not just to avoid academic terms like hermeneutics, epistemology and empirical evidence. It refers to the types of comments made about Hollywood movies, that many economists have taken to investigating. This usually is that no one knows anything about what makes a hit a hit, yet they pretend to be able to forecast its likelihood based on various attributes – the most typical one being the presence of suitable stars. There is significant anecdotal evidence that the music industry too has over-banked on stars resulting in a loss of profits that was avoidable. However, there is no explicit testing of this proposition in the music industry.

In the case of music markets, quite a large number of people seem to think they know quite a lot. This can be seen in the extensive bibliography appended to this work.

Why do they think they know what they know? How did they come to know it? What penumbra of doubt should this knowledge be shrouded in?

To deal with these issues, we need to look at the nature of data and its construction and the processes whereby it can be made to "talk" to us and tell us what is going on. As data is assembled and tested by human beings, not artificial intelligence systems with neutral coding, we must be mindful of the psychological and social factors which impinge on the alleged evidence before us.

Why and wherefore?

Statistics may seem dry and impenetrable to many but they can be the cause of bitter animosity, the ruination of careers and even death in the case of medical trials and militaristic miscalculations. The normal ideas of "normal" science would be that "facts" can be interrogated following well-established rules that will enable us to decide who is right and who is wrong, subject to a margin of error surrounding any contested claim.

Inevitably things have never been quite that simple. Now, the haze of confusion is worse than ever, partly due to vested interests which are compounded by the impact of the spread of the internet. We now have the contradictory scenario of more information being available to more people than ever before but with seemingly less chance than ever of a clear or definitive conclusion on important matters. Already we have encountered in previous chapters claims, made within a short time frame, that the music album is dead and is bouncing back to vibrant life. A neutral observer might see a narrative in the successive DMRs (Digital Music Reports), provided by the IFPI of the last 15 years or so, of exaggerating the fall in musical markets when fear of piracy was rampant to exaggerating the rise of such markets in recent times as digital markets become regularized.

Ad hoc inference and insufficient awareness of data construction form the fertile ground in which statistical myths grow. Even well-educated people, who should know better, are apt to blithely repeat journalistic claims about such things as the extent of the fall in physical recording (in the form of CD) sales or the contradictory expansion of sales of vinyl recordings, without looking into the full basis of such assertions.

We should first pause to consider why we care about evidence at all. Evidence may seem only to be relevant, if it is possible that it will change the minds of people who believe the opposite of the evidence. If their mindset is so entrenched that this is impossible then we have ideas which have ascended into mythical status. Evidence may be used rhetorically, to attempt to persuade others into a change, whether or not the user believes in a mythic system of beliefs. There is also in social sciences, the possibility of a "glass bead game" of collective self-deception (*folie à deux*) where people think they are questioning their beliefs but the parameters are set in such a way that core beliefs cannot be overthrown. In some cases, this is because the core belief is central to the academic discipline to which a researcher belongs and will not be readily abandoned.

The key battleground where evidence "really" mattered for practical purposes, in music industry cases, was the merger wave coming somewhere between the maturing of the CD market and its shrinkage in revenue terms (see Hardy (2012) especially Chapter 4). The significance of approval for these mergers was more than a yes/no matter. Commission enquiries looked increasingly thoroughly into the impact of increased market concentration on consumer choice and issues about necessary costs of production. Examination of merger and takeover proposals dragged on for considerable periods and may have had serious repercussions in terms of providing information that would be instructive to venture capitalists seeking to enter the sector. Such was the level of detail sought.

This is a case where knowledge may in fact be power, but, as suggested above, more often statistical rhetoric is the driving force. The main recent area of statistical rhetoric is in the matter of declining sales due to unauthorized copying. The most glaring statistical fault in this context is that industry bodies, and pressure groups, have consistently presented estimates of monetary losses due to piracy which are obtained simply by multiplying the number of units illegally provided by the retail price of units which are sold.

The figure of foregone earnings has to be less than the price times quantity measures and could even, hypothetically, be zero if none of the unofficial units would have been bought without the copyright infringement. Fully accurate estimates would require a fully accurate estimate of the consumer demand curve to obtain the relevant areas underneath it. For example, in Figure 4.1, we assume price falls from retail price (P1) to (P2), stolen price from physical copies then to zero from unauthorized virtual distribution. We need to make the strong assumption that all other factors stay the same.

If all units sold at price P1 then the revenue would be ABCD. Normal economic thinking would suggest that it should fall to zero when the good is now

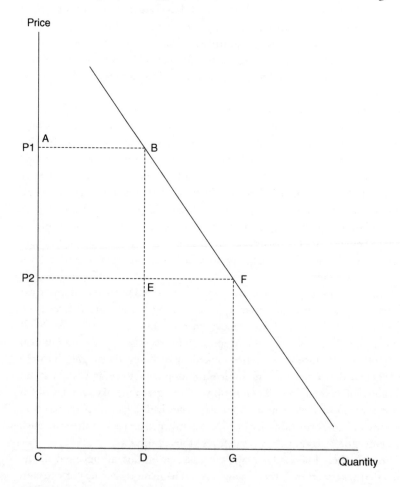

FIGURE 4.1 Demand with piracy.

available at price P2. However, some consumers will face barriers and thus will not buy at P2 because of guilt or not being able to obtain the good. If we assume that all the existing buyers are like this then the revenue from a fall to P2 which goes to the illegal copiers is EFDG but the original sellers will still get ABCD so the loss is zero. However, if a fraction of the original would-be buyers now switch to the P2 price then the area ABCD will shrink depending on how big this fraction is.

The principle is the same if the price falls to zero but in this case those involved will incur "hidden" costs such as unwanted advertising, trojan infections in their computers and so on which are the burden of "free" access. This could be represented by creating a notional copying price which includes such costs but this will have no bearing on the likelihood of such people buying the good at its original price.

To arrive at good estimates we need to model the share of people who switch suppliers in this scenario. This is extremely difficult and subject to severe problems of data quality and analysis which is one reason why it drives such heated debate.

If IPR infringement costs (as opposed to simple punitive damages) are sought, as in the Metallica–Napster case, there is a tendency to use the simple assumption that all shared (zero priced) music would have been bought by the end user if there was no P2P sharing. Regardless of accuracy, there is a strategic factor here. Any reduction in the claim amount below 100 per cent price replacement would probably weaken the impact of the lawsuit in the courtroom.

Mythical evidence which is impervious to the threat of real evidence is particularly problematic in the case of businesses who maintain ideas that are no longer supported. This is evidenced in the case of the major music industry firms who greeted the arrival of digital sales by welcoming an expert study (see Hardy, 2012) which assumed that legal digital sales would hold parity with the recent historical pattern of physical sales if digital download prices were exactly as per physical product prices. Firms would thus have been able to make massive profits as their production and distribution costs would have fallen substantially.

Expert evidence has figured prominently in music lawsuits. A classic case being in plagiarism disputes where a copyright holder claims royalties from unauthorized use.

The very idea of "expert" evidence is problematic giving rise to the kind of difficulty a car owner faces when paying for a repair. This is what is termed the problem of "asymmetric information" in the literature. If I hire an expert to tell me what is going on, how do I know the validity of what the expert tells me as it would seem obvious that they know more than I do? Do I hire another expert to check the expert and then another to check the checker and so on? Should I perhaps take three expert opinions as a rule of thumb (*à la* house repair estimates) and average them? This problem multiplies if the expertise is based on longevity and reputation rather than some kind of skill in applying a method. If a specific method is being applied, such as a complex statistical model, then the evidence can in some sense be evaluated by going through the steps of the method again and checking the impact of changes in key assumptions. In plagiarism cases, it would seem we do not really need a very high-level expert to tell us that work A contains the same sequence of notes or chords contained in work B. The real issue is the centrality of the "borrowing" to the final product. A typical case being the recent loss of royalties for the song "Down Under" by Australian band Men At Work long after its success, for using a small snippet of another work. If a work is successful, it is a difficult matter to establish that certain elements are *not* a vital contributor. In retrospect features of a work can seem as if they were central to the success as we are so accustomed to them being there. The more time passes the more they may seem to have been essential. We cannot go back in a time machine and take them out to test the hypothesis.

It is hard work trying to find plagiarism or authorship disputes being brought over commercially unrewarding works although one could construct an economic rationale for so doing, if they were by an artist who is becoming successful with other works. This is the pre-emptive strategy feared in other cultural industries – for example if you send a movie format to a film production firm in the anticipation that they will one day use something similar.

The presence of large sums of money, both in decisions and in the payment of experts, further clouds the picture in terms of obtaining unbiased decisions. Is the expert dealing with the analysis of real world history and business patterns like the neutral scientist in the lab pursuing nothing but the truth, or are they under some pressure to tell the hirer what they want to hear? In this context, we may note the fiasco of a frontier attempt to establish a popular music museum in the UK in Sheffield, South Yorkshire.

It only lasted from March 1999 to June 2000. This opened with a pricing structure determined by a report from the consultants (Arthur Andersen) and quickly ran into trouble due to poor attendances (well below half of the forecast) resulting in heavy subsidy by the local council. Closure came after a short time, despite a £2 million relaunch and the building has ended up as the Student's Union of Sheffield Hallam University. Despite this obvious economic failure, in which consultants colluded, this has been portrayed as a success in some terms by Kam (2004)!

On a psychological level, such situations give rise to the problem of pre-commitment. That is, if significant time and money has already been invested then there is an incentive to upgrade optimistic evidence and downgrade pessimistic evidence. This is the "oil well" problem. If one has poured vast sums into a barren oilfield, then it is foolish to pour more in hoping that the oil will eventually come. In terms of fledgling or medium ranking artists, record companies have tended not to display this specific cognitive bias. For major stars, and for record and audio equipment companies at the level of the market, and with some new technologies and other innovations, the optimistic cognitive bias is more prevalent.

We need to pause here to air a cognitive thesis that is difficult to test but nonetheless potent. To wit, the collective historical memory scar of the fact that the Beatles were turned down by Decca and were not seen by anyone (not even George Martin) as the colossal phenomenon which they proved to be. In themselves, rejection of a success and over committing to failures are banal phenomena found throughout the cultural economy. For example, the recent classic case being J.K. Rowling, the author of the Harry Potter novels. In statistical terms, these two opposite events are just Type I and Type II errors in forecasting. It would be most unlikely that significant failures do not occur and even with a standard normal distribution, of outcomes, some of them can be enormous as can the successes. That is, just because mistakes are very big that does not mean they are outliers and is not necessarily a reason to revise decision-making strategies.

In terms of decision-making under uncertainty theories, the traditional approach is that such outlying phenomena should not influence rational choice. For example, if Adele's huge success is just an outlier, it is not rational for record companies, and management teams, to go out scouting for someone with similar attributes to mould into a related product. Contributions, to decision-making theory, in recent decades have given more weight to behavioural features like "anchoring" and most pertinent to this case "Regret". Anchoring is a species of short-termism where expectations are linked to what has happened recently to the point of discarding other relevant information. The idea, of the major record companies, that digital downloads could be sold at equivalent prices to existing physical releases was perhaps anchored to past experience. In this case, the past experience was that all previous major technical innovations in the music market opened doors to enormous profits. For example moving from mono to stereo, the coming of clear quality reception FM radio and the arrival of the CD itself which allowed profits to be made from recycling the back catalogue of IPRs.

The Sony corporation may provide something of a classic case study of multiple cognitive bias business failures. This is manifest in their treatment of the technologies of DAT (digital audio tape) and minidisc and neglect of the possible potency of CD copying on home computer, and pirate commercial replication, equipment. The anchoring that went on here relates to the runaway success of the cassette tape walkman (see Hosakawa, 1984; Bull, 2002). The basic idea was that the market hegemony of this device could be maintained by simply updating it with the newest version of the equivalent technology. Thus we could have CD walkmans, laser disc walkmans, dat tape walkmans and whatever else came along. Little did they think that brand iconography would shift from the walkman term to the use of the term "mp3 player" even when the file is not an mp3. Or that a non-music-related computer firm and telephones would achieve significant hegemony in music delivery.

The small robust nature of the minidisc made it seem like the most inherently walkman-style media yet developed. The cassette tape was essentially a secondary market to the vinyl LP and, by analogy, the minidisc or DAT could be the improved cassette playing second fiddle to the improved vinyl replacement of the compact disc. Illegal copying was expected to be prevented by the use of proprietary encoding mechanisms. The success of the cassette walkman was not the result of a brilliant cunning corporate plan but, rather, was an accident arising from an internal request for a device to listen to music on flights. This is the issue of serendipity to which I return in Chapter 5 in the context of musical creation.

So, on top of cognitive bias in decision-making, we have the problem of hubris. If decision-makers, entrepreneurs and projects have been successful purely by accident, it will be difficult to prove that such success is not an accident, even if you were so inclined. Therefore, hubristic thinking will amplify the degree of such belief. There is a strong human need to believe in causation and the presence of meaningful patterns to explain events. In music, the apex of hubris is corporations believing that they should take credit for the success of artists over and above the quality of the artists' work.

The hubrism thesis is quite strongly evident in narratives of both the classical and commercial recorded music sectors (see Dannen, 1991; Lebrecht, 2008; Hardy, 2012). One has to be cautious about the colourful accounts in such books. It is not hard to find counter-claims by the participants about their behaviour and knowledge of the work of their artists. Institutional rituals, in industry, magnify the hubristic tendency – for example handing out achievement awards for selling lots of records to people who had relatively little involvement in making the actual records. However, it must be admitted that journalistic accounts also give a strong emphasis to the "sheer bloody minded decadence" hypothesis where senior executives, and medium to high ranking staff, lived a life of ease like medieval nobility not unlike the alleged behaviour of bankers in recent times.

It is clear from the above that many subtle psychological factors colour the interpretation of evidence. Let us return to the more tranquil matter of how evidence is supposed to be interpreted by a researcher who is not participating in business or policy decisions. An expert in the most rarefied sense of the term. In general, this involves the ideas of "classical" statistics as practised in economics and cognate disciplines, although the general ideas are the same in all fields of quantitative evaluation.

Evaluating evidence: the normal science part of social science

The dominant culture of evaluating evidence is the scientific paradigm. In social sciences, such as economics, the majority of work is carried out in the domain of "classical statistics" where one formulates a hypothesis and tests it using a model which does not incorporate any prior information from the researcher's beliefs. The opposite approach of Bayesian statistics is located in a thriving overall scientific community, but it has rarely reared its head in the analysis of music markets with a few exceptions such as Bradlow and Fader (2001) who model hot 100 Billboard songs and Lee (2003a) who models pre-launch sales forecasting of recorded music.

The classical statistics approach supposes that it should be possible to arrive at a conclusion which is not merely the product of, or severely contaminated by, personal opinion or vested interests. So-called "normal science" proceeds by formulating such hypotheses and collecting data to test them. The community of scholars should, in some way, check the validity of the results.

One of the most common slips in student work on statistical matters is the claim that something has been "proven". By its very nature, classical statistical testing can only deliver a conclusion qualified by a margin of error. This arises because we are using samples, from populations, that are generated by non-experimental means. Data relating to musical activity is rarely likely to be "controlled" in the manner of a laboratory experiment as there are numerous uncontrolled factors involved in the data generating pattern of any variable.

The remark "correlation does not imply causality" has frequently been repeated about statistical inferences. A statistical relationship does not necessarily demonstrate a "real" relationship when we are dealing with non-experimental data or data which has poor experimental controls. There has been a long debate on the notion of causality amongst philosophers. What we are talking about is the relationship between *cause* and *effect*. Our basic problem is deciding which is the cause and which is the effect, or do we have a situation where each is causing the other? The latter case is mutual causation. As the pattern of causes and effects are spread over time we face the difficulty of working out which is which from observed data.

The statistical method of causality testing attempts to determine which chain of cause and effect is at work. It does this by using a series of lags for each variable. Let us focus on a case of just two variables Y_1 and Y_2. We have here four possible outcomes:

Y_1 causes Y_2 and Y_2 causes Y_1

Y_1 causes Y_2 and Y_2 does not cause Y_1

Y_1 does not causes Y_2 and Y_2 does cause Y_1

Y_1 does not causes Y_2 and Y_2 does not cause Y_1

A musical example of this would be say the relationship between music sales and prices of musical items or the relationships between money spent on song "plugging" and chart position. The price may "cause" the amount of sales but the amount of sales may also "cause" the price via changes in the strategy of suppliers. We may say that a variable "Granger" causes another variable if appropriate results are obtained. The use of the term "Granger causality" involves exploring which of the four outcomes is correct by running an OLS (ordinary least squares) regression of a series on its own past values but also past values of the other variable. If an "F" test on the past values of the other variable are statistically significant then it is said to "Granger" cause the other variable.

Such a simple bivariate approach lacks the structural equations methodology which best typifies traditional economic models. At its simplest we would have an equation to explain supply and an independent equation to explain demand plus an adjustment mechanism to explain how these are reconciled.

This general positivist methodology, under which economics developed, was a distillation of the "logical positivism" of the philosopher Karl Popper in a famous essay by Milton Friedman in 1953. There are two main ideas – the "as if" postulate and the idea of *falsification*. The "as if" postulate justifies the use of models that are deliberately unrealistic. Friedman said, for example, we treat consumers and producers "as if" they were maximizing utility or profits. In the case of producers, we have to assume that there is perfect competition in the market if the relationship of a supply curve is to make any sense. This is patently not true in the case of recorded music or even in the case of musical production equipment.

The "as if" assumption brings in the use of untested assumptions. So, when we come to testing hypotheses we are testing the predictions of the models. We are *not* testing the assumptions on which those predictions are based. Hence it is always possible that the results, which seem to confirm or reject our hypothesis, arose for some other reason than the inherent accuracy of the hypothesis. It may be that some of the untested assumptions can never be tested, as it is impossible to formulate them in such a way that they can be tested. They may also be so fundamental to the core ideas of the discipline (in this case economics) that they are maintained in the face of all contradiction and thus there is no point in testing them.

We now turn to falsification. Popper argued that scientific research is not about proof or confirmation of one's hypotheses, rather it is about looking for evidence that rejects the hypotheses. His famous example is the proposition that "all swans are white".

If we go out to look for all the swans in the world, and find some more white ones then this does not mean we have proved the proposition. Instead, we should see the proposition as one that is not yet falsified. If we then find a black swan the proposition will be falsified and will have to be replaced with a reformulated proposition, that is more qualified than the one we started with. For example, do the black swans only live in the area where we found one or are there some in as yet uncharted regions?

Most recent economics of music literature is focused on the effects of downloading and streaming on total musical sales and/or physical music sales. If we go looking for such studies and let us say we find 25 that all support this proposition, the positivist methodology says we must not come to the conclusion that this proves that these digital innovations have "caused" a fall in sales. We must continue to look for some falsification. Let us suppose we now find three studies that do reject the proposition or, even more severely, support the opposite proposition, to wit that these digital innovations *have increased sales or at least had a null effect*. What conclusion do we come to? This matter is explored in an incisive forthcoming paper by Liebowitz (2016). He identifies that studies have not calculated the displacement, due to unpriced music procurement, in the same way or in consistent ways. He rebases all the studies to a common metric and also eliminates studies which were preliminary and incomplete and had been wrongly cited as authorities in support of the null or increase argument. He concludes that the rebased metrics show that almost all of the fall, in recorded music sales after 2000, was due to downloading.

He does not show confidence intervals but given that the underlying results used to compute the figures are significant at acceptable levels, any such interval would range around the 100 per cent central point fairly narrowly. It has to be borne in mind that such results are still derived from aggregate secondary data and acceptance of the chosen model specifications and estimation methods as appropriate.

I have had to make ad hoc judgements to deal with this balance problem in evaluating the hearing loss of musicians research discussed in Chapter 7. Literature reviews in this audiometric field have tended to give equal weight to all studies rather than giving more weight to those which seem to have a better quality of data and experimental control.

Contradictory studies may be seen as an anomaly if they are not compatible with the core theory. Revisions to theory may be made to attempt to deal with the anomaly. In some cases, anomalies are only apparent in that they are *not* automatically contradictory of the core theory but simply of some normative beliefs that researchers have collectively identified as part of the package of analysis. In the case of downloading and streaming, any apparent anomaly of an increase in sales attributed to them is explained by bringing in network effects. For example, with literal sharing people have to have something to swop with other people to obtain zero priced goods. Buyers may also have mixed motivations where they are omnivorous consumers who like a wide range of music and their free consumption simply liberates and stimulates more paid consumption.

The perennial social science problem is the use of non-experimental data that is not actually sampled in the literal meaning of the word of being drawn from the population in accordance with some specific criteria. In classical statistics, the margin of error which all findings are qualified by is the idea of statistical significance. The hypothesis has to be compared with the likelihood of some alternative happening under various assumptions including that of a normal distribution. Significance is the likelihood of a Type I error *assuming that the various assumptions made to construct the statistical tests are valid.* Thus we have the most popular choice of error level being 0.05 which is the 5 per cent significance level meaning there is a one in 20 chance the result occurs due to sampling accidents. The converse of a significance level is the confidence level which is in this case 95 per cent. The 95 per cent confidence interval will present a range of estimates within which 95 per cent of the actual values would be expected to lie. This can include both negative and positive results. The most common misinterpretation of research based on statistical models is that the findings do not lie in a confidence interval but produce a single definitive value for the conclusion. For example, 23 per cent of the fall in sales is due to downloading. This is an abuse of the "point" estimate – in this case 23 which is merely the most likely value.

Any subject relying on hypothesis testing requires its researchers to make decisions about what the significance level for a particular piece of work should be. It is unlikely that we would call "good science" the situation where an individual simply decides, for no apparent reason, to use a particular significance level. So there ought to be some criteria for picking a particular significance level. In strict decision-making theory this would be based on the costs of a mistake such as lives lost from wrong conclusions of disease testing methods. Like general academic work, empirical research on musical markets does not enter into any such cost quantification, instead simply using the convention of 1, 5, 10 per cent significance levels. These are the chances in 100 that a result came about by accident (assuming the assumptions used in estimation are correct in the first place), e.g. the popular 5 per cent level is a one in 20 chance.

One of the most commonly forgotten features of a brief statistical education is that statistical significance by itself is not sufficient grounds for a result to be of significance in the wider sense of the word. It may only show that we have very accurately estimated a very small impact. In some circumstances, a very small impact may be generally significant as well as statistically significant for example if we are talking about the saving of lives. However, in the musical case let us say it is found in a study that education level is statistically significantly related to musical spend-ing, this could be a very minimal impact, for example that a university degree adds 0.0000001 per cent to annual spending of a comparable individual. The tendency to overlook impact is more common when more complex equation estimation techniques are used to deal with categorical dependent variables (such as logit and probit models) as the evaluation of impacts is more difficult requiring specific assumptions about the values of all the variables.

If there is an agreed methodology, and all its users follow this, then we would expect there to be convergence to agreement on the evidence in the set of results. There are some obvious reasons why agreement is not guaranteed even within a narrow "pure" scientific paradigm which does not exhibit cognitive biases.

Reasons for disagreement

Quality of data problems

A considerable shadow of doubt can surround the reliability of any estimated equation. The most basic reason for this is that the raw material available to is itself never going to be perfect. This does mean that we will tend to have disagreements that come down to judgements about the validity of studies in terms of their underlying database.

Difficulty of operationalising variables

A common data problem is the extent of the difference between the data we have to use to measure a variable and the theoretical concept it is being used to represent. For example, any model in which risk is important faces the problem that there is no clearly defined way of measuring risk. For example, an individual-level study of "piracy"/copyright violation (Chiang and Assane, 2002, 2007) on US university campuses includes variables for risk, honesty and age in the estimated equations. The risk measures used are subjective ones related to knowledge of penalties and likelihood of being caught. The honesty measure is self-confessed cheating in exams. The latter would seem to be particularly problematic given issues about revelation of such activity.

In downloading/streaming impact studies there is often a problem of finding a proxy variable for non-purchase music use. Liebowitz (2016) cites some studies which use total internet usage rates in the country. The pattern of movement of this variable could diverge from the actual amount of streaming or piratical download-ing. Similarly, Parry *et al.* (2012) provide an extensive critique of the uncritical use of click stream data in studies which find zero or positive effects of P2P activity on legal music sales.

Data mining

Even if all the data, in all the studies conducted, was regarded as equally suitable we may still have problems. Say we find that studies overwhelmingly find in favour of the hypothesis, does this mean we can be contented and safely move our resources to other areas of research where there are unsettled or new questions to deal with? Unfortunately not, as all areas of science are open to the charge of data mining. I am leaving aside the problem of outright cheating in the form of "making up" data, which has certainly brought shame on some natural and social science researchers (e.g. Cyril Burt).

Data mining refers to the problem that the researcher may selectively engage in processes designed to produce a particular type of result. They may have a dataset of say 500 people and ten variables to predict the variable of interest such as per-centage of music streamed as opposed to owned. There is no canonical or definitive formulation of what the correct variables in the equation should be or how they are entered. Often the choice of variables is a convenience one as the sample used has already been collected by someone else. This may mean that some rather tenuous variables are included just because they are there. Different ways of entering vari-ables can be tried such as using a quadratic equation to allow non-monotonicity. Combinations of the ten variables in this case could be juggled until the researcher gets the kind of result they and/or their audience want. With so much leeway for obtaining different results we can meander towards the oft heard cynical claim that "a good econometrician can prove anything".

It is possible that the results presented, by a researcher, are totally atypical of the properties of the sample, and they have several hundred more contradictory results lurking in their undisclosed archive.

A methodology based on falsification is supposed to prevent this as we are meant to be looking for types of evidence that might reject our hypotheses, not going out of our way to confirm it. So we need to ask: why might the falsification principle break down in practice? This takes us into a "sociology of science" view of meth-odology. Producing publishable (and PhD worthy) research is an input into the long-run utility function of the academic researcher. It brings prestige, income and other benefits. Whether or not a piece of work is deemed to be fit to be awarded a thesis, or published in a journal, is decided by other academics who are then the "gatekeepers of science". In the case of academic journals and books, the gatekeep-ing function is performed by refereeing the work submitted for publication. This can be rejected outright or sent back to the author(s) for revision until it is in a suit-able form. Utility maximizing academics have an incentive to invest effort in increasing their chances of publication.

Whilst referees may be judging work on the basis of it contributing to the advance of the subject, they also seek to preserve the "hard core" propositions of the discipline against ridicule or loss of credibility. This may lead to some conservatism in terms of selecting in favour of work that is confirmatory in approach rather than falsificationist. In the extreme case, this will induce researchers to engage in "data mining" in the sense that they choose not to report contradictory findings and instead strive to get results which conform to those they are expected to find. This may come about due to changes in the variables used or the data or the techniques.

Unsystematic replication

The empirical literature on the economics of music has been surprisingly bereft of replication as the term is normally understood in scientific terms. Mittelstaedt and Zorn (1984) give a classification of types of replication. The most basic type is what we might call the "literal" replication where the study has to be exactly the same as the previous one. Taken to extremes this would mean exactly the same data using the same software on the same computer. This would be in the spirit of scientific replication where laboratory workers attempt to make sure that there are no variant factors that could account for differences in results between two laboratories.

The literal type of replication has to be systematic. The other types of replication should really be done systematically in the sense that we vary one element of the research design at a time in order to find out which factors lie behind discrepant results. The types of replication we can have then involve:

- changes in the specification of the model which, at the simplest level, means using different variables to "explain" the variable we are interested in;
- changes in the statistical techniques used;
- changes in the dataset used.

Replications are somewhat difficult in the field of the economic study of music as the data sources used tend not to be systematic across countries and time periods. We could use meta-analysis to bring some discipline into the process of reviewing the outcomes of this uncoordinated growth of research findings. The basic idea of this approach is that you treat the *findings of research as data to be subjected to further research*. Meta-analysis estimates an equation to try to explain the variations in some feature of the research. For example, if we were looking at the differences in the interest elasticity of the demand for money in developing countries, then a meta-analysis would include features of the studies – such as which kind of countries they were for, what time periods they covered, whether they were quarterly data or annual data, as factors that might "explain" the different findings.

Meta-analysis can be useful in condensing the kind of results found into a useful format. It may even provide useful "sociology of science" type information if the researchers see fit to look for it. I have yet to see any meta-analytical studies of the econometric research on musical subjects. I have seen studies in other fields such as minimum wages and cigarette smoking, which suggest that the magnitude of effects may vary systematically according to the type of journal published in.

Sources of evidence

Not all data is created equal, nor is it created for the same reasons. Data has to be collected. In order to collect it, decisions have to be made about the definition of the items in question and the degree of cost and effort that is going to be put into the gathering of information. For obvious reasons, total enumeration of the possible population is unlikely, hence we will be in the area of using samples to construct figures.

The body of classical statistical theory is premised on the assumption that we are not usually working with the total population but only a part of it. The technical term for a selection from the population (i.e. the total set of entities not the literal population of people) is a sample. A sample is used mainly because of cost barriers to obtaining data for the relevant population in any study. Often it is suggested that large random samples should be taken although this is not the strategy adopted by paid research companies.

For example, the RIAA data discussed in Chapters 7 and 8, is subject to changes in stratification in sampling, during the period, because of a belief that technological change was making the results more unrepresentative.

The desire for a large sample relates to the desire for representativeness when we cannot get the whole population. Interviewing only one household would be the extreme case of a small sample. Three would seem to be better than two and four better than three and so on. But why do we think this? The problem of using a sample of one is that it might come from an extreme of the distribution of values in the population. The concept of statistical inference is that we draw conclusions from an estimate made using a sample. We infer properties of the population from the sample. This means that we will often be making assumptions about the properties of the sample data. The beginner would be inclined to believe that the more observations we have the better, as more accurate estimates of the pattern of a variable and more reliable estimates of the parameters of a function will be obtained. Two observations need to be made about this:

i   Accuracy of estimates does not rise in direct proportion to the increase in the sample size.
ii Data is information. If it is to be used to test hypotheses, in the absence of scientifically controlled experiments, then the information has to vary enough for us to be able to observe the relationships between variables. There may not be enough "span" in the data, i.e. the relevant variables do not vary enough to enable us to observe the relationships between them. If we had genuine experimental data we can induce such variation (give the subject a bigger reward for completing a task for example).

Not all the research and information in the music industry is based on the principles of classical statistics as used in econometrics. Much of it is qualitative in the typical sense of involving a number of interviews with relevant people which are then quoted and moulded into a conclusion. When we approach this method we encounter the problem of rhetorical data use which is also present in classical statistics but in a different way.

A good example of this is the book by Rogers (2013) which interviews people in the music industry (such as artists, owners of small record labels, former executives in major labels) and commentators. These are thus deemed to be "experts". His sample is a little skewed in terms of over-representation of people in the Republic of Ireland. The sample is small and the validity of information is not checked in any way – for example working in an industry does not make one an expert on all aspects of it no matter what level one works at. This is typical of qualitative research. The justification would be that we are exploring information. This is fine but it does not seem logical that we can then draw meaningful inferences on the basis of it. To be fair to this work it also contains (pp. 35–41) a brief summary of some of the contradictory econometric evidence on the impact of file sharing on sales. This is however non-technical.

The rhetorical problem is that of the author finding numerous ways of repeating the same message in different guises so that it appears more likely to be true even if they have done nothing which helps establish the likelihood of its truth. In the field of musical interpretation, the unstructured interview is regularly used in a rhetorical way. One reason for this is that it is a comparatively cheap method (in terms of money but not time) of assembling a book. New interviews enable the publishers to say the book adds something new to the existing cognate works even if they are only "new" in the literal sense as they may add nothing to support any thesis that is being put forward. Books on musical subjects also sometimes face budget problems, of not being able to pay for the rights of reproducing some relevant materials, so the new interview can be a substitute for this.

A good example of all of this is the field of "Sydology" – writings on the life of original Pink Floyd front man Syd Barrett. There are at least five books and several documentaries on this man whose musical output was quite slight in volume and short in time span. His possessions fetched high auction prices when he died so he fulfils some of the ideas of neurotic celebrity worship. The dominant issue is the matter of his mental disturbances being due to early loss of father, taking LSD and so on. He satisfies a popular market archetype of the wounded individual who is a brilliant genius.

The most recent Sydological thesis by Chapman (2010) bucks the trend by arguing that his extant work was neither about madness nor a portrayal of it. This seems impossible to prove and falls right into the trap of psychoanalysing the dead mentioned in the previous chapter. The evidence given is largely a lot of new interviews with people who knew Syd Barrett which establish the literary antecedents of his work. It is difficult to see how these interviews, however interesting they may be, can establish any reduction in the margin of probability of rejection around counter-claims about this motivations and mindset. But, if one person after another who "really" knew him keeps saying the same things then they take on the spectre of verity.

Charts!

The use of more "hard" data, i.e. that which is actually in numerical format, is not without its problems. The most detailed type of "hard" data is on individuals. There are a number of ongoing surveys of this type and even some which are panel in nature, for example the NCDS (National Child Development Study) began in the UK, in 1958, and interviews the same people every seven years. Unfortunately these contain little specific information about music choices. There are some more specific cultural consumption surveys (such as those used in studies discussed in Chapter 7) but these only look at very broad categories of music consumption. They are also not panels so we have to conclude that there is no database which we could use to study the full life cycle of a music consumer. Likewise on the production side, there is no database of the entry and exit of musical performers, and their configurations such as in "bands", over time.

There have been a number of econometric studies of the determinants of sales volume before the problems of piracy/streaming/downloading began to dominate (e.g. Belinfante and Davis, 1978/1979; Burke, 1996; Cox et al., 1995). The focus of these was rather narrowly on the influence of price on sales. Such empirical work on sales has also highlighted the heavily seasonal nature of music sales. Specifically there are fourth quarter jumps caused by the celebration of Christmas. Music, like books and movie DVDs, are a convenient default choice of present for someone who may well get what they do not want. Economists would argue that vouchers should be used instead, and even more logically that we should not give presents at all as they are a constraint on choice which is inferior to the equivalent monetary sum.

Studies of specific artist performance, as opposed to market aggregates, have tended to focus on the data from the "charts". It would be nice if I could now cite a definitive rigorous analytical reference work on the history and use of charts around the world. Unfortunately such an item does not exist. There are many large books by Joel Whitburn on the various USA charts which usually form the source for econometric work on chart positions. However, these tend to be just reports of the data with pictures of artists. They also ignore the rest of the world. The nearest to a systematic analysis of charts is to be found in Llewellyn (2010) which is a broader work on crossover marketing of music.

The construction and regulation of charts has varied considerably. Within one country there have been rival charts using data collected by different bodies. In some cases, there have been different charts for different cities. In Belgium there are actually two different charts for the two major ethnic groups. This would seem obvious if the music was all indigenous but this covers all music, so Lady Gaga might perform very differently in the Walloon and Flemish charts. Given that the published data is ordinal (a ranking) it is not possible to aggregate the two in a meaningful way.

The problem of what is in the charts has reared its head again as downloads are now being incorporated and, as we move on, more other sources such as YouTube streams may be entered. It is not easy to see how we weight a physical sale relative to a stream. If we did it on revenues to the work, then the stream impact will be miniscule given the low royalty rates but then a substantial index of popularity is being shrunk. In the past, some charts included Jukebox plays, and in the Cashbox charts in the USA multiple versions of the same song were, at one time, aggregated.

Specialist charts encounter the problem of genre policing. The key problem is with crossover. Llewellyn (2010) discusses the case of artists being effectively banned from the classical charts because of their demeanour, or the inclusion of elements alien to the genre even when the artists are highly trained in the genre and perform-ing work within it.

Econometric work using chart data often claims to be looking for the "formula" for a hit with the conclusion that there is no formula (with respect to such things as key, tempo etc.). There is thus no real test of why something is a "hit" as per the discussion of expert advice on songwriting, in Chapter 2, as there is no analysis of failure data. The data is censored as it analyses degrees of being a hit and in so doing the statistical results may be severely biased due to the absence of data on total failures.

The various music "charts" and "hit parades" may be seen as the central scient-ific evidence site in analysing specific product performance. The chart has a number of dimensions, highest position reached, length of time at the top if reached, number of weeks on chart, position of entry to chart, chart re-entry after a period of exit. These dimensions could be aggregated, via weighting, into a conglomerate measure of success, but typically a single measure is used as the variable to be explained (such as weeks in the chart).

Charts can tell who is a great success, how their success varies across groups, e.g. are they a huge success in a sector, such as country music, with no crossover sales to the general charts. We can profile the trajectory of music releases in terms of their build up from release date, their length of plateau. We can isolate the case of so-called "one hit wonders" who failed to establish a lasting career. I use the term so-called advisedly as many journalistic profiles of one hit wonders that peddle "where are they now" type nostalgia are often dealing with people who had more than one (although not a lot more) substantial hits. There have been a number of econometric studies of chart performance (such as Stevans and Sessions, 2005; Strobl and Tucker, 2000; Anderson *et al.*, 1980; Cooper, 2010; Ceulemans, 2009; Hendricks and Sorensen, 2009; Bradlow and Fader, 2001; Gloor, 2011; Elliott and Simmons, 2011).

At the risk of pedantry, we must point out that the music charts are not a chart in the usual sense of the word, nor are they a parade. They are in fact tables of rank order with some other information appended (such as weeks on table, last week's rank and so on). A chart is typically understood to be a diagram, for example people who attempt to predict stock market prices from extrapolations of time series graphs are called "chartists". It is not a "parade" except perhaps in the case of specific broadcasts such as the UK's BBC chart shows which played all the entries in order.

The chart or hit parade does not, of course, actually show sales and is thus in some ways a purely relative measure of success. It is a weekly league table. Even within a short period of time, a more successful chart record may have less sales than a less successful one, e.g. due to the seasonal factors it may take more sales to get high up and stay in long at busy release times.

Even where charts are based totally on physical sales, before the advent of scan data, sampling of record shops had to be used. In the UK, for example, the same shops – chart return shops – would also be used. Clearly these charts are subject to sampling error and may contain more systematic biases which are discussed further below.

In statistical terms, charts are a rank ordering where the gaps in performance between successive items can vary from very small to very large. Some chart successes would have failed to enter in other epochs or vice versa. The use of metal disc awards can be used to some degree to overcome such temporal inconsistency.

There have also been variations in the relative buoyancy of singles versus albums charts. In the UK around the 1970s, singles charts were of low selling record volumes as product was being styled for the album market. Currently, there has been a renaissance in the significance of singles charts as the maturing of the legal download market continues. The waters are now being muddied by the increased usage of TEAs (track equivalent albums) formed by aggregating tracks, which were downloaded from an album as single tracks (but which are not "singles" per se), into notional album equivalents. This is potentially very confusing in conceptual terms. If an artist accumulates a large number of TEA units but these are mainly due to one or two tracks on the album does this not take us closer to those tracks being "de facto" singles?

It might seem that this is hair splitting irrelevancy as it does not alter the amount of records sold and hence does not alter the amount of money received. However charts clearly can themselves influence sales in the future. They function as free advertising and give consumers information signals about the status of products. Unlike conventional advertising, it is not supposed to be possible to buy chart positions. However there are a number of ways for suppliers to manipulate charts, in order to promote products:

Strategic organized buying by fans

This can concentrate the distribution of sales over time into a hump at one point which may even get a record that would not have charted into the record or push one which would have charted much higher. The classic case of this is for cult comedic performer John Otway, whose song "Bunsen Burner" reached number nine in the UK singles chart in 2002 despite a number of major retailers (Gibbons,

2002) refusing to stock the record or show its chart position in the shop. Otway's hit was manufactured as his requested birthday present from his fans. The process was scrutinized by the Electoral Reform Society. It also featured a very large number of his fans singing in the chorus on the B-side.

The reporting on this has not explored whether the "shop ban" was a reaction to the logrolling of the record into the charts. Llewellyn (2010) simply repeats Gibbons' claim that the record was omitted, in the shops in question, because they thought it would not interest their consumers. This does not explain why you should blank it out in the chart as per records banned for offensiveness in the past such as "Too Drunk to ★★★★" by the Dead Kennedys.

It has also been alleged that strategic voting of this type has sometimes propelled unexpected artists on to annual award lists.

Manipulation by suppliers

It is a very basic question as to what is the chart a chart of? For "single" tracks this is totally unambiguous for downloads and streams but physical music sales were for a long time two sided. Vinyl LPs, 45 rpm singles and pre-recorded cassettes had an "A" and a "B" side. For singles each had one track per side meaning that the chart could focus on the "A" side. The EP (extended player) or "maxi-single" would have typically 2×2 tracks. These tended to be treated as equivalent in singles charts. A significant feature of the emergence of CDs was that they were one-sided. They also had longer playing times which blurred the distinction between a CD single and a CD album as both were the same size and there was no distinction in the speed of play (33 rpm for album, 45 rpm for single) as all disks spun at the same speed. To the consumer, the CD single would seem to be simply a container for music which had been sold with a lot of empty space.

The CD single proved a hard sell and it may have been due to not finding a low enough price point. As manufacturing and distribution costs would not be lower for a CD single than album, the risk of selling it as a loss leader approaches if the general market price had fallen much. One compensating strategy for the supplier was to put more material and bonus material on the CD single which proved problematic. Time limits by official chart compilers blocked the first strategy. The bonus material trick was used to bump artists into the charts by relying on their fan base to buy the same single with different added content. The inevitable consequence of this was shorter times on the charts. The John Otway "Bunsen Burner" single also relied on the multi-version ploy as three versions were released.

Non-reporting of financial data

This would have the opposite effect, it would seem, of the other items reported here. It is claimed in Ribowsky (2009) that Berry Gordy purposefully forewent awards of gold and silver discs by some of his artists, on Tamla Motown, to avoid taxation.

Pay-o-la

The Pay-o-la problem has been a long tuning and notorious feature of the music industry leading to disgrace and decline for pioneering rock and roll DJ Alan Freed and a subsequent movie about this. The issue is one of corruption where radio station employees have taken bribes in the form of sex, money and drugs to give certain records priority over others. When the record industry consolidated into the hands of a few major corporations (Dannen, 1991) this settled into a more organized form of "song pluggers" who were paid agency fees for their skills in getting air time for records. The need to use pluggers constitutes an entry barrier for smaller firms and would make it harder for diverse music such as more ethnic work (cf. Chapter 9) to penetrate the marketplace. If the plugger did not use bribery then they were effectively just a salesperson.

Suppliers owning radio stations

Many liberal economies have been wary of cross-media ownership fearing that too much power, to influence the public, will end up in the hands of too few people. For music charts, the issue would be record companies owning radio stations. Pirate radio provided this option in terms of Radio Caroline (Chapman, 1992) but the impact was apparently minor.

False buying

If charts are based on sales then someone can buy multiple copies of a record to hype it into the charts. There are many documented cases of this the most noted being Brian Epstein's early support of the Beatles. The contemporary equivalent of false record store shopping is for artists to simply buy "likes" en masse for their Facebook pages thus trying to engineer a spurious bandwagon effect the logistics of which are discussed in Chapter 6. The case of the silent Vulpex tracks discussed in Chapter 1 substitutes false listening (in a low royalty rate context) in lieu for false buying.

These forms of interference with the charts are prone to moral objections. It would seem they are distorting the truth. But what is the value of this truth that they impeach? In terms of economic models, chart position should not influence utility to the consumer as the product itself is the same regardless of which number it attains or how many weeks it stays in. However, charts may help create bandwagon effects. They are the most salient form of achievement to the general public. So they are a signal as to what to buy. It does not follow that interference with the charts necessarily lowers the general welfare of consumers just because the truth has been hidden from them.

If the Beatles had not taken off at the end of 1962, due to Epstein's ploys, they may have split up for good and left the industry after slogging away for low returns for years. Not only might this have prevented their work ever appearing but it might also have removed a powerful influence from later work. The standard Mertonian multiple model of discoveries in science, if applied here, would suggest this would not be the case as the Beatles would just be one of many conduits for social and technological change.

Beyond this, we have the general problem that music is an information good with potentially high levels of uncertainty. Consumers use charts and the associated radio playlists to guide them. A more level playing field and a wider offering of product would not necessarily make them better off. If corruption is needed to improve the flow of information then this is one of many cases where markets may benefit from corruption (see Cameron, 2002).

Conclusion

Two things can be improved in terms of evidence. These are the quality of data and the capacity of individuals to interpret it. However, the reasons outlined in the early parts of this chapter suggest that ability to interpret evidence may be attenuated by inherent biases which are frequently documented in studies of decision-making. Biases occur not only at the individual level but can become an established norm within a group of practitioners. In the final part of this chapter, we also saw some endogenous biases where the economic agents (product suppliers) purposefully influence market data rather than being passive receivers of it. I now move on to the specific of music production and consumption.

5

THE PRODUCTION AND SUPPLY OF MUSIC

Introduction – problems of the market

Music has to be supplied to its consumers/end users or they will never hear it. The supply of music is both a vehicle of artistic creativity and a means of generating profits. Thus suppliers may also have other factors besides income, in their utility function, such as receiving acclaim for the high quality of their work or simply the prestige of fame.

Mainstream neoclassical economics would lead one to expect that the marketplace can potentially generate a harmonious outcome that is beneficial both to suppliers of creativity and to those specializing in its monetization. There are two main objections to this that we should lay out at this stage. First, it follows from the nature of the market relationship that there is a potential economic conflict between makers of music and those who assist its passage down the value chain. The eminence of this conflict would be emphasized in modern radical political economy or its traditional Marxist origins. Conflicts between creatives and capitalists became a dominant theme when mass youth culture and popular music emerged. The archetypal tale is of evil managers and corporations depriving the true generators of value of their just deserts and, in extreme cases, threatening to kill them such as Van Morrison and Neil Diamond (in the case of Bang records). The class conflict in music reaches another apex when the corporate owner of works prevents their creator from releasing them as has happened for example to Prince, George Michael and Roy Wood. This issue of exploitation of artists by corporations has not gone away. The monopolization and consolidation of the music industry led to conglomerates and venture capitalists being the oppressors of creatives, rather than shady managers. However, perhaps the artists now have more countervailing power. In a dispute between the Dixie Chicks and Sony over 30 alleged cases of fraudulent accounting depriving them of $4+ million (£2.7 million) they eventually settled privately.

Sony then gave them their own record label, better royalties and a better overall deal.

This is a case of an established artist and there was specific malfeasance by Sony. It may not adequately reflect the current configuration of markets. At present, the vogue in music industry discussions is to push towards the 360 degree deal following the example of Madonna. Under these, one firm, such as the record company, handles all of the musical unit's business transactions rather than there being separation of function by business manager, record company, tour agents etc. The drive for this is to capture the drift of revenue from recorded to live performance. In theory such deals might reasonably be prohibited on grounds of representing too high a degree of monopoly. They would seem to pose more of a threat in this regard than the mergers in the first decade of this century. For musicians below the elite with a massive catalogue of still flourishing IPRs, the 360 degree deal may signal the frontier of a new class war where corporate bodies find new ways to extract hefty shares of their income. They can of course opt out so it is useful that we, below, discuss attempts to run music-making businesses in contrast to the heavily profit driven imperative of major corporations.

The classic capitalist modality has been that the creative workers do not own the "means of production". Expensive recording studios and record pressing plants were in the hands of the capitalist. The creative producers could attempt to take over the managerial and distributive branches of their enterprise. This faces a classic problem of specialization and scarcity of resources. It is difficult to be both a business person and a creator, although we have exceptions such as Madonna, Handel and Andrew Lloyd Webber and also some smaller independent operators (such as the Projekt label run by the founder of the band Black Tape for a Blue Girl).

The need for a dedicated record company can partly be explained in terms of the transactions costs arguments espoused in the classic 1937 article by R.H. Coase where he asked: why should firms exist at all in the first place? The firm can achieve economies of scale, and scope, that the individual would not have access to if they executed each contract necessary to their operations themselves. According to IFPI (2012), record labels invest 16 per cent of their revenues in A+R and the costs of breaking an artist, in a major market, remain substantial at up to US$1.4 million per artist. The cost typically breaks down as payment of an advance (US$200,000), recording costs (US$200,000–300,000), video production costs (US$50,000–300,000), tour support (US$100,000) and marketing and promotional costs (US$200,000–500,000). A more anecdotal attempt to break down the cost of an individual hit song, by Rihanna, is given in Chace (2011) which is similar but identifies the high costs of buying in writers for team production in a short-run "factory".

From an economic theory point of view, many of these costs are not costs of production but expenditures to create monopolistic barriers to entry. A share of them may also be due to institutionalized bureaucratic waste. As music is an information good many of these costs are messaging or information costs. They are *not* costs of making music.

Market failures in supply are enumerated in "killing the goose that lays the golden eggs argument". The idea being that a malodorously arranged music industry may "kill off" creative work leaving us with less work in total and/or a decline in quality. One such putative killer is the TV talent show which lures hopefuls in, with the hope of amazing careers, but then spits them out in quick time with many winners losing their contracts soon afterwards. Perhaps surprisingly, some economists seriously attempt to apply standard supply arguments to the *Pop Idol/X Factor* genus of TV shows. Amegashie (2009) develops a highly mathematical model to deal with the criticism of *American Idol* (see also Zwan and Tom (2010) on the Dutch Idol competition) as not being a singing contest but more of a popularity contest. Awarding prizes which are not based on merit, but instead characteristics which are not related to output, might be thought to be economically inefficient. Amegashie concludes that popularity aspects may lead to a *more* efficient outcome as the supply of effort by the performers will be greater. Much of the conclusion rests on issues about uncertainty of information. It is of more importance that this is a purely theoretical paper which is also based on a partial equilibrium situation – only matters within the competition are considered. The wider issue of whether such competitions are detrimental to the global music market is not dealt with. Empirical work on this would be a very difficult and laborious enterprise given the matters elaborated in the previous chapter.

Similar issues, but with opposite conclusions, have been raised in work on classical music competitions. Glejser and Heyndels (2001) identify biases in the judges' rankings of piano and violin performance, using data from 1956–1999, for the Queen Elizabeth competition which is held in Belgium. In terms of statistically significant effects, candidates were higher ranked if they performed later in the week and later in the day. There is some evidence that women received lower rankings for piano but not for violin. Of concern to the authors was choice of piece. More recent compositions did better and more popular ones did worse. This suggests that the judges may be the source of a principal–agent problem in that they impose different preferences, on the outcome, than the public would. Thus the tournament that feeds into the final market may lead to a sub-optimal outcome for the consumers. This competition is different from the television style as those involve voting by the public and thus approximate to an external market of some type. We might conclude from these studies that experts should not be allowed to filter supply which should be left to the consuming public.

Musical production

From an economics viewpoint, music is produced and then it is distributed to the marketplace. From a musical point of view it is written, composed, created or whatever.

Like any industrial production process this has sequential layers in which value is added.

The word "production" in pure economic terms means adding value. So the person who writes and performs music is a producer. They have added value to the piece of wood that is a guitar, or to the collection of 0s, 1s and electrical current inside their laptop if using software. Economists' use of the word "producer" is in contrast to music industry usage of the term. There the producer is someone who shapes and develops a work germinated by the artists. The music producer is not an entrepreneur or manager but simply another co-worker in a small group enterprise but one on a short-term contract which may extend but does not have to. The producer, most importantly, cannot lay stake to the "name capital" of the musical unit. George Martin could not bring a claim that he was part of the Beatles. He was rather a co-worker with the collective entity.

Those designated as producers have held different positions within the overall production process. Beatles producer George Martin first encountered them merely in the capacity as a staff producer on fixed company (EMI) wages. At his time, named or superstar producers were comparatively rare. They were not allowed inside the major label system. For example, in the 1960s in the USA, CBS (Columbia) required musicians to use staff producers (those on permanent fixed contracts) and also use their own studios. They also required that a producer would be able to read and write music thus formally barring from entry many within the organization of a rock band. The outstanding British superstar producer of the early 1960s was the maverick autodidact lone individual, the unstable Joe Meek, who had a string of hits outside the corporate system produced in a flat above a shop in North London. In the USA, only Phil Spector carried individual name capital. As with Meek, he managed to crown his instability and dangerousness by shooting someone dead although Meek then killed himself.

From the 1970s onwards, more stable "name" record producers began to emerge such as Glyn Johns and Tony Visconti. Documentaries and literature on such figures typically gives them a "magic" aspect where they deserve credit as part of the production process rather than mere staffers fulfilling mundane functions. One of the mundane functions is simply to give an objective and unbiased assessment of work in progress. The more technical mundane tasks of audio mixing and processing would be performed by designated "engineers", meaning that the named producer is not literally producing the sound. The classic apprenticeship for a producer was early work in sound engineering with some starting as tea boys and general go-betweens.

As a member of the production team, the music producer delivers various nurse-maid services, which would require reliability and people skills commonly labelled "soft skills" in studies of labour markets. These include nurturing performers through self-doubt and negotiating conflict within the unit. Such skills might be devolved to a non-musical specialist, as is found in the documentary on the band Metallica entitled *Some Kind of Monster* (2004) where an expensive therapist was retained, for quite a long period. This has not been a common strategy.

Top producers tend to supply a "signature" sound (the most famous being Spector's "Wall of Sound") and may be important musically to the level of providing parts and arrangements. For example, Bob Rock filled in on bass for Metallica. Their later producer Rick Rubin advised them to change back to more conventional guitar tunings. Such activities are a potential source of conflict. An example of this was the falling out between Glyn Johns and the Eagles over his desire to impose his "signature" sound on them.

Meek and Spector supplied quite dramatic signature sounds whilst others, like George Martin, Norman Petty and Terry Melcher would more accurately be said to be supplying "good taste" and clarity in sound with some direction to those they shepherded. Demanding a producer for a signature sound has tended to be driven by popularity of a genre (such as Sly and Robbie for reggae), emergence of technology (such as Georgio Moroder and Trevor Horn) or perhaps a sheen to bland out the ageing artist (Daniel Lanois in the case of Bob Dylan) especially one who may have once been edgy or rule breaking but is now looking for a mature focus. In more dance-pop oriented genres, we see Madonna going through a whole series of producers changing them deliberately to attempt to keep up with the latest vogue in the genre. Her 2012 album "MDNA" employs a large number of different producers. At the point we have reached now, the "remixer" who appeared most prominently in the 1980s might be deemed to be a producer who arrives after all the component parts have been made. The boundary between producer and remixer is now fluid, i.e. the same person might regularly do both.

The producer may have a shamanic "rain dancing" type of role, where it is even possible that they have contributed nothing material to the process. There may be other such figures within a band. Bez from the Happy Mondays was a member of the band but appeared not to contribute an actual musical input. His stage role was largely confined to a non-professional form of dancing. Apparently he receives royalties despite doing nothing on records. Such persons may be of economic value through contributing some kind of ambience – for example their force of personality may raise the value of output generated by the ostensible creators. The shamanic designated producer may be best exemplified by the case of Brian Eno. His input style is formalized to some degree in the 1979 release of the "Oblique Strategies" deck of printed cards which is essentially a device to unlock creativity. It may not be immediately obvious to the listener what he has added to the mainstreamed-indie bands (U2, James, Coldplay) for whom he has worked. One can argue, from an economic theory point of view, that, in such cases, he adds to the utility of the musicians by convincing them that the work is in some way new and enterprising and not just "more of the same" which has established their position.

A clichéd trait of promotional interviews, by musicians, is that their new work is different from their old work thus making them "creative" rather than just peddlers of product. Often this is really about process rather than product – a producer who works in a different way was used, a different location was used such as the desert, or someone's garage or prescriptive equipment rules were used such as only using analogue tape or analogue synthesizers, or no computers, or no click tracks, or using one-take vocals instead of those which were "comped" together. As musical technology develops we can have a high level of observational equivalence, that is the same outcome can be arrived at in many different ways. Musicians and musical gear suppliers currently have an obsessive love affair with old school analogue equipment but it is not at all clear that this makes any difference to the ears of consumers.

Having discussed the nature of production, we need to delve into the despised nomenclature of "industry". The term tends to be applied to the owners of means of production and distribution. It is another cliché of performer interviews to despise being in the "music industry" allied with being uncomfortable about their work being "a job". An industry is a collection of firms making the same product. This is complicated by the presence of multi-product firms operating in a number of different areas. This has been common in the music industry where music has often been handled by firms working in a number of entertainment sectors. Growth of firms has often been typified by conglomerate mergers where the firm produces in widely diverse areas which would seem to have no connection at all. In such a context, there would be no reason why a music business concern could not be owned by a firm whose primary interest is in waste disposal or nuclear weapons. Further, modern literature on the theory of the firm in economics might suggest that this could be an efficient arrangement. The debacle of Guy Hands' takeover of EMI was essentially the intrusion of venture capitalism into music.

The SAD+ production function

We have briefly flirted with the idea of a production function in Chapter 3 whilst discussing John Stuart Mill's "death of music" problem. In the case of the art and entertainment sector, there is a capital dimension to the end user item, as a song, film etc., give long lived satisfaction. In the USA, this is now being incorporated in the national accounts on top of the consumption value (Soloveichik, 2010, 2011). There is an issue with drawing the line at recorded media and not valuing live performance (which will be reflected in national accounts in the earnings of live performance). However, Soloveichik, assumes that part of the asset value of original musical works is in its contribution to greater live earnings. For example, if the "hits" had not been written and recorded, then fewer people would want to see the artists and their ticket price would be lower. Incorporating estimates, that include these forms of value, she provides the following values for the USA, for periods around 2007–2009: $7.5 billion capital stock in original songs and recordings out of a total $51.6 billion (current) investment in all "artistic originals". These figures are from the 2011 paper. The music estimate in the music specific 2010 paper is slightly different.

In basic microeconomic theory we are introduced to the idea of a production function, such as

$$Q = f(K, L) \tag{5.1}$$

where Q is output and K is capital and L is labour. A given quantity of labour and a given quantity of capital will always deliver exactly the same output. We may have diminishing returns (falling marginal products) for musical labour and capital in a given state of knowledge and technology. For cultural work, we may even have negative returns to further labour input if there is insufficient discipline within the unit. For example someone may waste time trying to write a song which will never be any good.

Let us imagine a hypothetical caveperson long ago who is the first person to fully engage with the discovery of sound sculpted into musical forms. S/he has felt an emotion about the day's activities and begins to sing about them. This is pure labour production. The vocal style and skill may vary between singers. These divergences are, in terms of economics, neither capital nor labour. They are equivalent to "land" as they are a natural resource that has not been fashioned from other inputs. The best singers will get economic rent as they are natural monopolists.

They cannot earn a return in this non-money economy. However, the singer may acquire entitlements to relief from other labour. Time spent singing may have an opportunity cost such as being killed by an animal (which was meant to provide food) due to not paying attention. The group might support the singer/composer via transfers: a type of arrangement broadly found when we come to minstrels and jesters. In emerging market economies, the musical worker requires a patron from somewhere if musical markets are not yet organized. The system of a patron, as opposed to a general market, is a dominant factor in the supply volume of the canon of Western classical music (Baumol and Baumol, 1994; Tschmuck 2001a, 2001b, 2003). There have also been patrons in marketized popular music who fund ensembles with no expectation of a return such as in the early days of the group Supertramp. That case was a rich individual but earlier the Moody Blues derived their name from the initials (MB) of a brewery which sponsored them.

We also find implicit and explicit subsidies from other people such as parents and partners. Formal schemes, aimed at target group business enterprise, such as the Princes Trust in the UK, have also supported musicians. The most ubiquitous form of patronage, in marketized situations, is the unemployment benefit system.

Labour would be measured in "effort units" rather than hours put in. Most economics texts concentrate on cases where there is continuity and substitutability in the factor inputs. Capital and labour can be increased or decreased in infinitesimally small amounts as opposed to being "lumpy" where increases or decrease can only be made in large steps. Continuous substitution would allow musical creators to reduce the amount of effort needed to increase output by a given amount by replacing the effort with additional capital. In contemporary music, generated in DAWs (digital audio workstations) on computers, capital has replaced labour in many areas. These include use of samples, autogenerated patterns, quantization of elements that have been played manually and autotuning for pitch correction. Orchestral work has also been greatly reduced by these developments and time scarcity problems of demand (see Ekelund and Ritenour, 1999; Flanagan, 2008).

It is typically assumed that producers wish to maximize the output arising from a given amount of resources or, by "duality", minimize the costs of producing a specified amount of output. Gary S. Becker pioneered the concept of human capital, defined as any investment in the development of skills in order to gain higher returns in the future. A musical production unit will contain different individuals who have diverse initial endowments and acquired human capital. They may also have financial capital such as instruments or transport or rehearsal facilities.

Serendipity also plays a part. We may add this (S) and also authenticity (A) and drugs (D) to the production function. The SAD+ augmented production function becomes:

$$Q = f(K, L, S, A, D) \tag{5.2}$$

It is unlikely that a typical mathematical form such as the Cobb–Douglas (or more general multiplicative constant elasticity) model would adequately capture the relationships here due to threshold effects, synergy and lexicographic relations which may vary across different production units.

Serendipity is documented in many forms. For example, Brian Eno may be a supplier of serendipity if he is not a mere shamanic rain dancer. If titles of songs mattered for hits (which may be less true now) Lennon and McCartney were fortunate in their access to catchphrases.

"Paperback Writer" came from the utterances of a fellow Liverpudlian bohemian. "Eight Days a Week" and "Hard Day's Night" were Ringo-isms. Perhaps the classic form is making mistakes which turn out to be productive. Here we have such cases as Gary Numan's early hits arising from his inability to program a synthesizer properly and Ray Davies, of the Kinks, arriving at songs because he was unable to play those of others.

Serendipity is problematic in an organized market. Chefs in restaurants would presumably be sacked if they relied on it to make a dish excel. It is difficult to see how we can guarantee or induce its supply. So, the solutions are either to keep going and wait for it to happen or hire someone who is believed to be able to provide it. Relying on serendipity will inflate costs. We may find ourselves sitting waiting for it to come and having no idea when this will happen. Loss of serendipity is something about modern clinical production methods which worries commentators. Software studios tend to predetermine activity to a certain degree as creators are offered a substantial "buffet" of ready made options which limit the scope for beneficial accidents. This does not prevent any individual from behaving in an exploratory manner, on purpose to induce serendipity, but its overall tendency is to limit the typical person's choices to a narrow range.

Authenticity has been discussed in previous chapters. It is an interesting element in economic terms as it would, again, seem paradoxical to try to learn or manufacture it. We can buy it in by hiring someone who has it. For example, when artists seek to shift stylistically they often would go to the place where the "real" musicians are like Nashville or Jamaica. The idea that authenticity is best found outside the stuffy confines of formal linear musical training is frequent, from 1940s British jazz (see Godbolt, 2010), to the 1977 punk "rebellion" in the UK.

The idea that authenticity is enhanced by lack of formal skills is a useful form of rhetoric for those seeking to enter the market, as it means they cannot be barred on grounds of ineptitude. Generally speaking, where success is achieved there is often someone close to the heart of the enterprise who is more formally educated in music who may be operating as a translator of the ideas of the authentic "noble savage". Or such a person is eventually brought in. For example, the period of peak success for the Human League was characterized by bringing in a "proper" musician to the fold. Authentic urban musicians, such as Goldie or Public Enemy, were generally shepherded by someone with formal musical skills and the modern crop of such people is highly likely to have formally or informally acquired significant core musical skills or have associates who have.

Drugs constitute a serious issue for the economic analysis of the musical production unit as to what they actually are. Are they some kind of capital, which in conjunction with labour and recording equipment etc., generate the output? Or are they an unfortunate externality of the market which has become ritualized and institutionalized? Recent work by Clinton Heylin (2012) attempts to make the claim that drug use, and madness, were a significant factor in many of the recordings in the established canon of great works in popular music. That is they are *not* just random unfortunate and idiosyncratic by-products of greatness.

There is a constellation of dynamic issues with drugs to wit:

1   Are the suppliers of music using the same drug of choice as consumers of their genre format?
2   Are the members of the musical unit using the same drugs as each other?
3   Are there none (or light or even reformed) drug-users in the musical unit?
4   Are there differences in perception of use and amount of use between members, some of whom can't handle the drug? This applies to alcohol as well as lysergic substances. For example, some of the disenfranchisement of Lol Tollhurst from the Cure, documented in the court case he brought against them, is due to his incapacity to imbibe the same volumes of alcohol as other members during recording sessions. He had to go home whilst they worked on. So, his marginal productivity would fall below his internal market rate of return leading to dismissal as a logical outcome.

There are many documented instances where drugs have a bad effect on output. Leaving aside death and illness the most legendary case is the so-called "cocaine" albums where successful artists suddenly produce a very poor work because of their distorted perceptions. If they were less successful, we would expect the producer could exercise control over such poor outcomes, if necessary by bringing in outside musicians to complete the work.

It would be almost impossible to conduct any kind of meaningful classical statistical testing of the impact of drugs on musical output so we have to dissect shifts in historical epochs, which is, in essence, what Heylin does. One can also refer to the work by Derogatis (1996), which does not proffer any particularly relevant hypothesis but documents the rise of psychedelic music. Psychedelic and other forms of drug-heavy music may display features with respect to tempo changes, linearity of composition and sound textures that are not found in "normal" music.

These might be attributed to having taken drugs but the same sounds can be made by someone who has never taken any drugs. However this will be copying of an "original" idea so it may be that drugs were necessary to produce the idea of doing something in a certain way. There may be other ways of achieving the same effect, such as meditation or psychological self-abuse, but drugs became the ritualized and institutionalized method in the industry. Musicians, like the Beatles and the Byrds, in the mid-1960s claimed to be taking drugs, chiefly LSD, to promote creativity. Frequently the use of drugs in music would sometimes be simply to keep the weary worker going as per the original spread of cocaine for military use.

Purely hedonic consumption of drugs by musicians equates them to their fans. In some epochs, we could argue that certain drugs (like Ecstasy) simply perform the function of making both sides share the delusion that something is great when it is not. Delusion does not matter to standard economic theory. You might say it would wear off but social network sharing effects and later events like nostalgia (see Chapter 7) could perpetuate the delusion and even enhance it.

The most dramatic non-SAD change over time in musical production is in technology. There have been a number of distinct and dramatic shifts in music technology which are listed in Table 5.1. These are the invention of analogue synthesizers, hardware drum machines and samplers, the midi protocol, digital synthesis and sampling, the four-track cassette recorder the VST protocol and finally the emergence of low cost and stable music computing. Through all of this there has been the theme of deskilling the art of composing and performing so that almost anyone can do it. Or if not that, that the merely competent can replace the virtuoso.

The drum machine is seen by detractors as a particular evil of the 1990s eroding popular music via European dance genres, synth pop and hip hop. It is not uncommon to hear older people refer to it as something modern or new. On the other hand, it has arisen to the status of coffee-table book consumer fetishism (Mansfield, 2014) with lovers of specific models in reveries over them, willing to pay inflated prices for them and erecting quasi-museums to them in part of their houses. For the full obsessive consumption experience you may consult some YouTube videos of Moby's drum machine collection.

For musical performance and composition, electronic instruments initially, in many ways, marked a step *backwards* instead of forwards. Once tuned, a good violin, piano or guitar could be relied upon to stay in tune and if a particular method of generating a sound from it was obtained this could be reliably produced. Early analogue synthesizers had persistent issues of tuning and even picking up radio frequency communications (taxis, planes etc.) whilst on stage. There was also the problem of "patching" so that a sound had to be set up by multiple cabling operations and no recall method was available so that the user had either to take photographs or to use elaborate marked sheets.

There was also the persistent economic problem of establishing standards that dogs many innovations and is still an issue with computer OS given new life thanks to tablets and phones.

The use of Control Voltages, in analogue synthesizers, was not standard across different manufacturers and could lead to something being seriously out of tune if connected to a trigger using the other, voltage to pitch, standard. This lack of uniformity was effectively solved by the MIDI (Musical Instrument Digital Interface) protocol which used standard five-pin plugs to send the same information by pin across all manufacturers. The traffic between devices was organized by standard file formats. Midi also, in principle, provided efficient automatic tempo locking across different devices.

The humble four-track cassette machine was in some ways a genius invention as it repurposed humble existing technology to enhance its usefulness. The compact stereo cassette brought recording to the domestic consumer but given its track limitations was limited as a form of musical creation tool. Four-track recorders split the left and right of both sides of a tape into effectively four tracks on one side of a two-sided tape, enabling the kind of recording methods that were available to George Martin in the main Beatles recordings to be enacted in a small room by technically unskilled recordists. There was significant hiss, and copy degradation across such devices. However, the format gave the creator the opportunity to develop a sketch of the work for later more professional development. Many famous musicians (such as the Manic Street Preachers) developed their work in this context.

One result of the evolution of musical technology is that we move into a fully fledged "Sraffian musical economy" of production of commodities by the means of commodities. Artists in some genres would start their creative process by overtly seeking out samples from existing records (possibly "crate digging" in vinyl record shops). Even before cheap easy sampling, music was always made from other music (e.g. modifying someone else's song elements) but it did not directly lift the actual recorded product. Copyright protection has been strong in the sampling market to the point where some celebrated cases involved loss of all royalties to the user. We see the emergence of ancillary markets due to these issues. To avoid royalty claims, it is common to pay others to recreate the sample. There is also an agency market for crate diggers to find samples in order to benefit from bringing them to other users such as the unexpected show tune sample (Annie) in Jay-Z's "Hard Knock Life".

Co-operative efficiency within the musical unit and composition disputes

The simple efficiency conditions, of a basic microeconomics model (equality of marginal revenue products to factor prices) require perfect knowledge and also the ability to obtain separable marginal contributions which can be measured. In such a world it should not happen that the wrong person ends up in an unsuitable role or that there is conflict over task allocation.

How should any of the types of musical unit organize their production? We may call this a mode of production. A simple one in rock music is the dictatorial one

TABLE 5.1 Selected innovations in the history of music production technology

Innovation	Release/spread	Notes
Drum machine	1959 Wurlitzer Sideman (first commercial product). This and the first wave were sold as organ accompaniments. 1972 Eko rhythm composer – first programmable machine. Early 1980s Linn LM_1 costing around $5,000 introduced. First drum machine to use digital samples. Archetypal digital drum sample machine – Alesis SR16 released in 1990 is still in production.	Small digital drum machines highly portable widely used for practise, click tracks for writing and in rap and hip hop. In combination with portastudios and sequencers/samplers people could make viable tracks in their own houses without the need for "real" musicians. An Alesis Sr-16 would cost not much over $100 in present day prices but is limited compared with what is now available in dedicated software.
Moog synthesizer	Robert Moog's first prototype model was shown in 1964 being a control voltage analogue synth. Breakthrough came in late 1960s with Carlos' renderings of classical music. More portable usable models were developed (Minimoog). Company went bankrupt in 1986, relaunched in 2001.	Sparked a rash of cheaper alternatives. Russian clones are discussed in Chapter 10. Brand continues after Moog's death being a much more expensive brand than rival alternatives.
Portastudio	1979 Teac Portastudio One.	Benefit of small size and weight. Used domestic 2-track cassette tapes to allow 4-track recording when used as a 1-sided tape. Bruce Springsteen's "Nebraska" was recorded on a Teac 144. Used by many musicians for demos.
Midi protocol	1982	Later portastudios use DAT, hard discs, minidiscs and flash memory. Enabled instruments, effects and lighting to communicate reliability and efficiently overcoming compatibility problems with voltage based interfaces. Midi would allow accurate synchronization of cheap digital samplers, sequencers and drum machines. Discussed further in Chapter 10.
Yamaha DX7 (and variants)	1983 Price c. $2,000.	The digital use of 6 pure sine waves (operators) only as the tone generation method enabled low cost synthesis to be spread in cheaper 4-op and 2-op versions including computer sound cards and the Yamaha PSSS "toy" keyboards.

Roland TB303	1982 Price *c.* $400.	Benefit of small size and weight. Designed as accompaniment device for guitarists but creatively abused in "Acid" styles. Due to onboard sequencer and synth could be used to devise basis of tracks especially in conjunction with samplers and portastudios. Famous due to homage in Fatboy Slim single and is currently still the subject of many virtual, sample and physical instrument emulations.
VST protocol	1996 Steinberg releases specification. Many VST are now free and many are ported to mobile phone apps. Instruments which cost around $150–200 in early 2000s are now free.	Virtual Studio Technology enables computer software emulations of classic synthesizers and effects creation of new instruments and effects. Enables the DAW (digital audio workstation) to function with no physical instruments or effects at all.
Fairlight	1984 released by Australian company Fairlight, $25,000.	Had a profound influence on the sound of mainstream records. Very significant as chords could now be played using any sound at all once sampled. Sampling time was minimal. The core samples of the Fairlight can now be had virtually free in android/phone apps.
Samplers	1986 Akai S900 1987 EMU SP100	By the 1990s cheap digital samplers could provide "CD quality" sampling. Digital samplers effectively killed off much of the drum machine market, especially the Akai MPC series which are now becoming mainly software controllers. The original MPC models were developments from the Linn drum machine when Akai acquired the brand.
Digital downloading	1997 First digital download single (by Duran Duran) released 2001–2004. The heyday of Napster.	

Sources: various company websites, issues of *Sound on Sound*, music history websites such as www.vintagesynth.com, which do have some errors. e.g. the latter lists Akai SR-16 as ending production in 2003 when it is still being made.

Note

I have not listed guitar specific and effect processing innovations here in order to keep this to manageable proportions.

where one member is the composer and the others play. The problem of the appropriate model of production was considered for the Spandau Ballet legal cases in a paper by a practising barrister, Alan Coulthard (2000). He puts forward a typology of three modes of musical production. The three scenarios of Coulthard are:

Jamming: where a process of collaboration by the members of the collective composes the songs.
Group arrangement. One or more group members conceive the song prior to arrangement and the rest of the members develop an arrangement in rehearsals.
Cover versions. If the song has previously been recorded, then the new version may seek to add value via a different arrangement.

It is difficult to identify separable marginal products for the inputs even *ex post* to the production of a song/performance. Long after a unit of production has failed to be artistically and/or commercially successful people still debate which ingredients were the key to the achievements in the successful period. There is also a question as to whether revenues are actually accruing to the song per se but rather a style of performance (trademark) of which the song is an embodiment.

Given these issues, musicians are now generally advised to register a formal partnership with their band mates. Before they first broke up, Spandau Ballet had an interesting arrangement of this type (see Cameron, 2005). The group traded through a company called Marbelow Limited which received recording and performance income. Marbelow divided this income six ways with one-sixth going to each group member and one-sixth going to their manager. Publishing income was paid directly to Gary Kemp. Kemp instructed his publishing company to pay approximately half of the royalty profits to Marbelow to be divided equally as per the recording income. Thus he was making a side payment to his colleagues for their difficult to measure contributions.

Sometime after the band broke up the arrangement ceased and a series of disputes over the name, trademark and composition royalties ensued.

The volume of song writing authorship disputes have grown in the music industry as the role of recorded music has increased. According to Keyes (2004) there were around twice as many such cases in the USA in the second half of the twentieth century as there were in the first half of the century. New claims come forward all the time, such as recent claims that Led Zeppelin's "Stairway to Heaven" was derivative of an instrumental by Spirit. In a more high profile example, Katy Perry has been accused of plagiarizing recent religious music.

The key issues are: the burden of proof, the definition of the relevant work to be owned, the passage of time until a claim and the impact on supply of works. The notorious cases around Procol Harum's "A Whiter Shade of Pale" illustrate all of these points. The first legal contest took place in 2006, 39 years after the song was written and was found in favour of the plaintiff (Fisher). He was deemed to merit 40 per cent of the musical composition rights but only from the date of his application onwards. In both the original case and the appeal, a distinction was maintained between "the song" deemed to have been written by Brooker and Reid and copy-righted before Fisher had any involvement and "the work" which is the well-known Procol Harum recording of the song. Fisher's award was for *ownership in the work not ownership in the song*.

Precedents for overruling the delay issue featured prominently. Previously substantial royalties were awarded to singer Clare Torry for her contribution of word-less vocals to one track on the "Dark Side of the Moon" album by Pink Floyd. This was 31 years after the release (2004).

Delay by itself does not render a legal case invalid. Judge Blackburne (2006, p. 17) stated of Fisher's case:

> his admitted failure between then *(1967)* and 2004 even so much as to hint to Mr Brooker that he should be acknowledged as a joint author of the Work is quite extraordinary. In itself, however, Mr Fisher's silence over so long a period is irrelevant to whether he can assert a share in the ownership of the musical copyright in the Work resulting from his contribution to its composition.

The delay issue comes under the doctrine of *laches*. This is not judged on the basis of the literal amount of time. The onus is on the defendant to prove that the delay was unreasonable and prejudicial to the defendant and would have been to their detriment. That is, the defendant may have taken actions which weaken their position such as spending the money that had accrued to them in the intervening period when the right had not been notified or they may have put more effort into promoting the disputed copyright than they would have done if they had known there was a dispute.

Torry's claim is that she was told to improvise something at points in the track, likewise Ray Clements says the same about his contribution to Rod Stewart's "Maggie Mae" (for which no case was brought). Matthew Fisher's claim was that he added to an arrangement and thus he becomes a composer of "the work" as the judge saw it if not "of the song".

However these *are* issues about contract. Why could the parties not have produced an optimal contract at the time instead of leaving the aggrieved parties on fixed wages? The key aspect is risk sharing. Those on royalties will engage in effort which has a wide variance in its predicted rate of return. Those on fixed rates cannot obtain the high levels that can occur but they are guaranteed not to suffer the low returns those on royalties may get per effort unit. Making explicit connections between rewards and activities may lead to excessive concentration on measurable aspects of the job (Holmstrom and Milgrom, 1991). Those with a comparative advantage in playing, rather than composing, may spend too much time in composing and even engage in wasteful rent-seeking to attempt to get their compositions on the recorded outputs (cf. Cameron and Collins, 1997).

Such employment contracts can create an "incentive to rely" (Craswell, 2001), which alters the decisions of those receiving the offer as regards their search efforts in seeking alternate employment or partnerships (cp. Mortensen, 1982; Diamond and Maskin, 1979, 1981). This is similar to the marriage problem where a partner has specialized in activities to the benefit of the union without formal payment above the implicit level.

The record company as a firm

In the Marshallian model of perfect completion, we have the seeming paradox that the efficient size of a firm is infinitely small. It operates at its minimum average cost per unit but the concept of average cost includes "normal profits" which, assuming away various problems, achieves private efficiency (what is best for the firm) and social efficiency (what is best for all of us) will both be met at this point. A fundamental break from this is where firms become large through monopoly power and seek to control the market. The firm may be privately inefficient in the sense that the owners (shareholders) are unable to control managerial extraction from the profit stream. Similar tales of managerial and corporate waste and inefficiency are found in histories of both the classical music (Lebrecht, 2008) and popular music industries (Hardy, 2012). The external shareholders can be dispersed so that no individual shareholder can exercise voting influence or there may be majority or significantly large shareholdings. The logic of external ownership is that more finance can be raised to spur future growth and investment. However, the firm may expand through benign or predatory takeovers and mergers.

A key factor in efficiency is the design of the operation of the organization. The extreme case is to have a supermarket mode of production and simply to buy in product from somewhere else. This has been prominent at some times in the music industry where record labels simply license product from other firms (such as labels in another country).

One view of the process of production is as a "factory" with connotations of dour, methodical and potentially soul-destroying and oppressive effort. In the history of popular music it has been common to talk of certain units (typically record companies) as "hit factories". The primary example of a hit factory was the original incarnation of Tamla Motown. Many of its factory style attributes are documented in Ribowsky (2009). One of these was the maintenance of a set core of fixed wage workers who were the session musicians. Classic Tamla Motown processes could be seen as an attempt to routinize serendipity.

In the heyday of Tamla Motown, Gordy was ruthlessly determined to pursue hits – he did not simply release what he thought was good and hope for the best. He engaged in creative allocation of his team resources by reassigning people across writing, performing, singing and arranging according to their skill set. He also created songwriting teams by experimenting with the combination of different writers. He held internal monitoring committees to assess the hit potential of the planned singles. As success increased, he set up the infamous "charm school" where the lead artists were groomed in how to present themselves in the media for best effect.

One key economic characteristic of the Tamla Motown factory, was that individual product lines (artists) were treated as long-term investments. He did not drop artists automatically just because they had failed to bring success quickly. This tended to the reverse investment profile of the television talent show where the "factory owner" signs up an already successful artist whose revenue stream frequently then declines rapidly.

Although less labyrinthine and grandiose in its organization, Pete Waterman's PWL setup was to a large degree modelled on Tamla Motown and was a self-styled "hit factory". Both invite the factory metaphor further on grounds of being headed by individuals who emerge from areas characterized by declining heavy (motor vehicle) industry. We may also find the term applied or implied to certain recording studios because a consistent stream of successful works emanated from them. However those cases really represent serendipity and brand reputation not a factory mode of production.

The central economic idea of the factory is the notion of division of labour and the pivotal organizational motif tends to the highly autocratic owner who, in the novels of Charles Dickens, grinds the face of the poor. The Gradgrind figure may well also have the hard work ethic of a self-made man who started out as a mere worker and rose without the assistance of family wealth or connections. Gordy's Napoleonic dictatorial tendencies have been highlighted by a portrait he commissioned and some rather risible passages in his memoirs. But this should not blind us to the fact that he might well be considered an economic genius of his day. Although factory like in its modus operandi, his operation was at the same time both more militaristic and more flexible in a liberal, creative way.

The hit factory metaphor has the central feature of the notion of there being some form of highly profit oriented central direction. In terms of sheer economic logic, there is a well-defined range of alternatives to the factory mode. The suitability and feasibility of these will change as technology changes. The most glaringly obvious factor here is the arrival of digital media as a force. Going back to hardware analogue times, the reason we do not seem to have factories of any type until fairly late is the use of a literary/thespian type model in music. The performer, composer or performer/composers bring their works or performances to agents of distribution who have access to the means of production of reproducible media. Some of these will fail and some will succeed but if there is an elastic supply of them then there seems to be no particular need to cultivate or hone the artists collectively. Some people will do this because they want to, but it is not an imperative of the market.

In some cases, a simple rule of thumb can be followed such as looking on one's doorstep or looking in the same place as where the success came from. If we take the case of Brian Epstein, he did groom the Beatles to eradicate their rougher Hamburg image and initiated some manipulative practices to get their first record into the charts but he did not have a factory of artists. His roster of artists were all lesser talents from the same town of Liverpool. He did not seek to create a recording and distribution network around his artists. This was left to the Beatles themselves with the fairly disastrous Apple. This represents the idealistic alternative of a record label that exists for the primary reason of promoting artists and good work rather than the pursuit of profit. There have been numerous other artist founded labels which have generally failed to sustain in promoting the careers of artists other than the founders.

The traditional key method in popular music, as with old time sports, was scouting. Someone with expert knowledge (an A + R person) would seek out people with potential. In economic terms, a high quality scout can make great contributions by finding someone in advance of rival buyers. This advantage dissipates if the quarry does not sign up on advantageous terms before rivals can begin to bid. This type of method is still common. The major record labels put people on development contracts (New Zealand singer Lorde being so placed at 13 is in a similar position to Kate Bush in the 1970s), which may involve placing them with experienced mentors until they are ready to be taken to the market as a product.

There are a number of obvious explanations for lack of sustainability of hit factories. The most obvious ones are rigidity, burnout and the Marshallian "lazy river" argument. In the Tamla Motown case, the relocation to the West Coast, would be seen by some as one of the factors in its decline. Successful industrial production of the traditional type was able to transfer its operations to other locations. If Tamla Motown had been an electronics manufacturing firm it could have duplicated its operations perfectly well with lower wage labourers in India and Korea.

The factory mode may have mutated. It would seem (Chace, 2011) that short-run factory style arrangements are used to produce hits for the established frontline superstars rather than manufacture new stars who are often short lived. She documents the case of a Rihanna writing camp session where large numbers of hired writers on retainers are brought to bear in work going on in a large number of expensive traditional studios over a short period of time.

Those who are attracted to the music industry, in managerial and entrepreneurial capacities, may prefer not to operate the factory mode. Works such as Dannan (1991) suggest that they are often seduced into the idea of a glamorous lifestyle and trying to live more like the artists. Some people will be living vicariously through the artists they direct.

In pure logic, the antithesis of a hit factory is to have no hits and no factory. In practice, we find a range of more nuanced antitheses. The idea of a factory has been shunned and demeaned by some, along with the ideas of industry and business as being contradictory to the notions of art. The unifying factors are a degree of "consumer-fan turned producer" and quixotic artistic romanticism where profitability, stability and obtaining a career are sacrificed for such things as leaving behind something of "true" value, providing people with memories and having adventures.

We can distinguish various models. First, the *hippy mode* as typified by the Grateful Dead. The Grateful Dead's business practices have become enshrined academically. At the University of California, Santa Cruz, a Grateful Dead archive has been established:[1] exhibitions of selections from this archive have been held in museums. Through their Rex foundation, they enabled the public dissemination of obscure

English classical music composer (Havergal Brian). The Rex foundation was not established solely for cultural subsidy. It provided support for whatever aim the governing body saw fit. It is difficult to think of any other rock/pop ensemble who have gone to the lengths of establishing such a significant charitable foundation. Philanthropy in the mainstream music fields generally consists of performing in benefits although there are occasional one-off donations by some artists to good causes and we should give an honourable mention to Dolly Parton's book promotion charity.

The "Dead" pursued a reciprocal relationship with their fans which made them trailblazing pioneers and maintainers of counter-cultural production which bypasses the mainstream capitalist market model. The most noted feature was their radical treatment of "unofficial" recordings or as they would commonly be known "bootlegs" which were encouraged. They began on a major label (Warner Brothers) and made compromises in their music in order to be bailed out by major labels on a number of occasions.

We can identify other hippyish ventures which simply perished such as John Peel's Dandelion label (1969–1973). The original Virgin record label of Branson eventually morphed into a conventional capitalist firm with some slightly alternative trappings which would be sold off for a handsome profit. Both these cases involved human capital transfer. Branson had a record shop and Peel was a prominent alternative/underground DJ. It would seem that these base positions, and the information sources they represent, would provide a launch pad for record label success. Branson might, at the inception, be termed a proto-bobo (bohemian business entrepreneur).

The second mode to be considered is more energetic and anarchic. The word punk is probably best avoided here given its appropriation by mainstream corporate media. The same goes for "indie". The LOFI/DIY ethic is essentially anti-capitalist in saying we do not need to have expensive equipment and training to produce music.[2] In its own way it is a rebellion against the prostitution of music deplored by Stockhausen in Chapter 1. There are well-known and much documented UK enterprises in this modality but these generally tended to drift quickly towards being "proper" businesses if the originators displayed sufficient entrepreneurial acumen. The authentic DIY ethic experience tends to be found in the disdained geopolitical backwaters such as Scotland (Postcard record label), Northern Ireland (Good Vibrations record label) and in the exemplary case study of New Zealand's Flying Nun record label which was active from 1980 and began its journey into absorption into more mainstream businesses via takeover and merger from 1990 onwards. New Zealand was not only a long way from the thoughts of major executives, it was considerably harder and more expensive to relocate to music industry centres than for people in Scotland or Northern Ireland or Canada. Its social and economic backwardness, low and spread population made the active support of youth culture very difficult back in the 1970s. Prejudice against New Zealand musicians has not dissipated as some of the humour in the successful music parody act "Flight of the Conchords" (1998–) derives from mockery of the low status of New Zealanders in the music industry. Flying Nun pursued a policy of simply putting out work that the owner (filtered via a key technical person) liked without any proper business planning, leading eventually to the situation that they could not get records into the shops at the crucial time of potential breakthrough of their most promising act.

Let us continue and conclude with the paradox of disdaining the imperative of making profits being potentially good for profits with the alleged situationism of Anthony Wilson's, ironically named, organization "Factory Records" located in Manchester whose primary success was with the band New Order. As with Flying Nun, formal contracts were formally eschewed leading to inevitable problems later on. Still, there is a net economic gain here (widely construed) if the ethos and modus operandi led to output that would otherwise not have been forthcoming by producers who otherwise might not have been there. Factory achieved dizzy heights of anti-capitalist modality with the 12-inch single of "Blue Monday" in 1983 which lost the company money the more it sold, as the cost of production exceeded the price of the item. Factory records eventually collapsed because of the heavy dependence on New Order.

Factory also launched one of the numerous failed attempts to reposition classical music with a younger audience with its dedicated classical label.

Besides these alternative modalities of running a record label, there continued to be independent labels that comply with quite a simple economic model (such as Mute, New Hormones and the independent labels that have handled twenty-first century UK artists like Adele, the Arctic Monkeys and Kasabian). That is, they aim to make a satisficing level of profits but they are willing to trade-off profits for the well-being of the artist and for "quality" of output. They may even use the profits from some artists to cross-subsidize others for longer than might be justified in terms of long-term investment plans.

The decline in vinyl and move to CDs made it somewhat easier for such labels. Such labels, even with truly independent manufacturing and distribution, remain prey to the risk that their artists will be poached by mega-corporations. Retention requires that the artist retains sufficient non-pecuniary orientation. The shift to digital distribution, whilst it lowers costs, making independent labels easy to establish, due to low costs may increase the risk of poaching as more expenditure is needed to hype one's work in a crowded marketplace.

Financing

The origins of property rights in the industry have been largely determined by record companies who are large multinational firms who, since the age of concentration in the industry (see Gronow and Saunio, 1998, ch. 7), are corporations who have primarily crossed over from the film or consumer electronics industries, often buying up a roster of artists from small specialist music labels. Their relationship with musicians is one of employees on contracts, generally exclusive ones that can lead to forestalling of output and prevention of collaboration (which has on occasions been overcome by use of pseudonyms for guest appearances).

Such contracts have been heavily asymmetric. The artist cannot leave before the contract end but the firm can drop them early. This formal structure has been replicated within partnerships, when disputes between musicians themselves rather than record companies, have come to court. This process has been assisted by the chief income earners from a group (as in the Smiths case) resorting to formal registration of themselves as a company making their fellow band members into employees. There are other cases where "original" members have left and new ones have arrived and the new members have explicitly been on wages with no entitlements to the group name revenue (such as Bananarama and Jethro Tull).

Large companies have access to more finance than individuals and are thus able to underwrite their ventures. In the case of recorded music, a settled pattern (akin to the agricultural production cycle) arose in the 1970s. The creators would retreat to an environment where they attempted to "grow" the new product, which was intended to be both respected and financially successful. There would be a formal contract to deliver the product but, at times of poor company financial performance difficulty, major artists would sometimes be offered additional premia to bring completion forward (Dannen, 1991) with a consequent risk to output quality.

It is normally expected that creativity is difficult whilst engaged in other pursuits like marketing, travelling, performing etc. This is an issue of time, motivation and also inspiration.

Thus we have specialized creative phases. Whilst the creative phase is in process, no new income is being generated and potentially high costs are being incurred. So, the artists need income to cover themselves if they do not have past income to live off. They also need "front" money to pay for the production costs. These costs will be even greater with a new artist who has to be nurtured before they are ready to be launched fully on the market.

How high the costs are going to be also contains a risk element due to the speculative nature of the enterprise as exemplified in the SAD+ production function. Depending on the technology, costs may already be high for an individual to self-finance due to the quality of equipment required. Even now, digitization of recording processes cannot totally erode the specialist functions of rooms with special acoustic properties. Attempts have been made to do this with the mathematical process of convolution but this is now not seen as being as good a substitute as it was initially. The case of microphones presents a difficult frontier to move. The price of very expensive microphones and analogue equipment to accompany it, have come down due to competition and low-wage manufacturing but still remain prohibitive to entry level musicians. Especially if they want to acoustically record "real drums" etc., as many different types of microphone will be needed and the skill to use them properly. Such knowledge and capital is still impacted in traditional studios – for example, Abbey Road.

It has now become commonplace for artists to use the "pledge" system on the internet to overcome these fundamental problems of market capitalism as a delivery mechanism. There had been uses of this before the saturation of social media reached us (for example the Marillion album "Anoraknophobia" in 2001) but these were isolated with no dedicated vehicle to deliver and manage this process. Many still see pledging as a "new" thing. Moderately successful Liverpool 1980s group China Crisis announced their 2013 pledge campaign as a "new way" of making recordings. They had last released new material in 1994, to poor results, having come back after a falling out with Virgin in the late 1980s. This campaign typifies the moderate campaigns we see. A specified time was set to achieve the required sum. Amounts raised above the sum are remitted at a fixed rate to a designated charity. Members can offer set higher pledges to receive unique offers (such as, in this case, accompaniment to a football match in Liverpool with a band member). Others have even offered genetic material (phials of blood). Some concrete examples from the kickstarter.com campaign of virtuoso jazz-rock ensemble Led Bib in 2013 are shown in Table 5.2. This raised £10,221 from 151 backers, with an average of just below £7 per backer. Information on their backers is necessarily incomplete but where it is given, it seems most people backed *only* this campaign. The exception being a gentleman who backed 64 campaigns in total, of which only one was musical.

Apart from being "nice", what is the economic significance of this? One view is that it exemplifies the ideas of French economic sociologist Pierre Bourdieu about the fluidity of the boundary between the producer and the consumer. Pledge creates an incentive for the marginal tergiversating giver to come in with the added "bonus" of loosening up their unexpressed altruism as per the current vogue for Nudge economics. What is the required sum for? In most cases it is to go into a studio rather than simply make the work in members' houses using computer based equipment.

TABLE 5.2 Distribution of pledge rewards for Led Bib fourth album

£ amount (= shown and above)	Number of takers	Details
1	2	Good karma and thanks
5	5	Twitter thanks
9	3	Postcard from Mark
10	12	Thanks in CD booklet
12	0	Request played and name checked in concert
15	11	Digital album and thanks listed
20	32	CD album with thanks listed
30	13	As last + T-shirt
30	7	As 20 pledge + score sheet of a band piece
35	5	As 20 pledge + specific pot of hummus loved by band
45	1	Copy of the new Led Bib live vinyl, a pot of the hummus and a special request at the next local Led Bib gig + a credit in the liner notes
45	14	A CD copy of the new Led Bib album and a vinyl edition (with download code) of the new live LP + a thanks on the CD liner notes

continued

£ amount (= shown and above)	Number of takers	Details
55	3	A CD copy of the new Led Bib album, a copy of the limited edition live vinyl and a pot of the hummus + a credit on the CD liner notes.
60	4 (from limit of 5)	A signed test pressing of the new Led Bib live vinyl release
60	2	The new CD, the limited edition live LP, and 2 tickets to the closest show to your area during the 2014 tour and a credit in the liner notes
70	5	Instrumental lesson with any member of Led Bib in London, or travel must be paid, or for Mark, they will take place in Vienna, or London when he is available … + a copy of the new Led Bib CD and a thanks in the liner notes
75	0	A copy of all 5 Led Bib CDs plus the new Led Bib CD and a thanks in the liner notes
95	2	A copy of all 5 Led Bib CDs plus the new Led Bib CD and a copy of the new limited edition LP and a thanks in the liner notes
95	0	As 70 pledge + copy of limited edition LP with download code
115	3	Trip to White Hart Lane with Chris Williams to a Tottenham Hotspur league or cup match + a copy of the new Led Bib CD and a thanks in the liner notes Includes food + drink
120	1	A guided tour around Vienna with Mark! Also comes with the new CD signed by all the members of Led Bib and a credit on the liner notes
125	0	Liran and Mark (trading as aBoBp) will write you a personalized song in their inimitable style *or* produce you a remix of a Led Bib track of your choice and present it to you on CD Also a copy of the CD and a thanks in the liner notes
130	1 (out of a limit to 5)	Appear in the next Led Bib video! Just send along a picture and we will get you into the video! Also includes a copy of the CD + a copy of the limited edition LP both signed by all the members of Led Bib and a thanks in the liner notes.
150	1	As 125 pledge + a copy of the limited edition LP (and a download code) signed by all the members of Led Bib and a thanks in the liner notes
200	2 (was limited to 10)	A trip to the studio with Led Bib in London + A copy of the CD + A copy of the limited edition LP both signed by all the members of Led Bib and a thanks in the liner notes
250	0	At next local Led Bib gig, will play a version of any song of your choice, from Kraftwerk to Billy Idol + a copy of the new Led Bib signed by all the members of the band and a thanks in the liner notes
650	1	A special concert from 3/5 of Led Bib, has to be in London or have travel covered + a copy of the CD and the live vinyl signed by all the members of Led Bib and a credit in the liner notes
1,000	0	Private Led Bib concert be at your house or your party in London or somewhere we are available on a tour Plus all the CDs and the vinyl signed by the members of Led Bib and a credit in the album!

Source: compiled from text on https://www.kickstarter.com/projects/ledbib/led-bib-new-studio-album-and-live-vinyl-release (accessed 2 September 2014).

Notes
Median is £30, mode is £20.

This Led Bib campaign highlights the possible inefficiency and inconsistencies of the popularization of the method. The band bring out the archetypal explanation that it was a "cool way" to fund the album and it is really putting them in touch with their fans. Yet, the call is actually in conjunction with a record label and many of the pledges are actually just advance purchases of standard goods. In this case the more personal and unique type items did not get taken up to much degree. This crops up also in the econometric work on the band, Third Eye Blind, that is reported in the next chapter. It is probable that resurfacing 1980s pop bands may do better in this regard.

There also seems to be a terribly over complex "buffet" of options here. Given the outcomes, one might suggest that it might be more efficient to simply use a range of special T-shirts for sale with a few other items. It is perhaps slightly specious to claim that these smallish sums of money are actually needed to fund recording of the work identified. They seem much more to be part of a continuous product placement campaign.

More specious use of the idea of crowdfunding is to be found in the case of how Macklemore's "Thrift Shop" got to number one in the Billboard charts in 2013 (see Chace, 2013).

The artists used social media to boost about the roots nature of their success growing from their social network support when they were supported by distribution from one of the remaining major record labels.

Jumping from the middle ground of normal range pledging it is instructive to look at the case of Amanda Palmer. Palmer would be best described, prior to this, as a "cult" artist emerging from the Dresden Dolls. Her work may be considered quirky such as having a song about (unsuccessful) UK soccer team Leeds United. She has some wider name brand capital due to being married to comic book novelist Neil Gaiman and also being a provocative controversialist who takes full advantage of conflicts with more reactionary mainstream media.

Palmer's call was massively oversubscribed leading to an expression of anger from people outwith the call. On 20 April 2012, the Kickstarter project was supported by 24,883 backers for a grand total of $1,192,793 – at the time, the most funds ever raised for a musical project on Kickstarter. To put this in context, non-musical projects are funded for more. As of 14 August 2014, the highest funded project was over $10 million for an iPhone watch and a movie had also been funded for over $5.7 million. These cases are different to a degree in that the funders hope to obtain shares of future profits.

Palmer had already caused controversy in 2012 by trying to employ local musicians without wages ("beer, merchandise and hugs" being given in lieu). She eventually backed down on this after outrage from musicians, the president of the American Federation of Musicians and prominent producer Steve Albini. Before backing down she had claimed she could not afford to pay the local musicians. She also invoked a revealed preference argument that many a free market apologist economist might be proud of – that the volunteer musicians were incredibly happy and enthusiastic to be there so everything was alright.

One conclusion that might be drawn from the Palmer cases is that pledging has mutated away from its original purpose as a supplementary market to overcome the barriers of an ossified capitalism. Bluntly it can now function as a form of advertising which will lose this specific potency if it becomes too widespread. It also faces competition for funds from the now pervasive use of crowdfunding to support a wide range of things including consumer goods.

It might seem that the internet pledge could fulfil the most cherished dreams of hippy, situationist and lackadaisical entrepreneurs in the record industry by usurping traditional misguided capitalist firms and putting the musicians right in touch with their fans.

However, it would seem on balance that it will remain a supplementary market that is used to lever entry into a relationship with the major oligopolistic firms in the music industry.

Or simply to augment the Indian Summers of the seasoned performer which are discussed in Chapter 7. These are increasingly 360 degree deals with the live performance business being integrated with the recorded music deal.

Whats in a name? Tribute brands

Popular music outstrips even horse racing, in the leisure sector, in terms of the colourfulness of names (see for example Dolgins, 1993). This extends beyond pop and rock bands to the monikers of rappers and other urban music operatives who are very unlikely to ever use their birth names as their market title. These names constitute brands and trademarks and thus, by themselves, can embody economic value which has enthusiastically been extended into ancillary good merchandising amongst urban musicians.

Traditional brand names and trademarks are freely tradeable in the marketplace to the presumed benefit of all. It does not matter whether a particular jam or sauce is still being made in the same place by the same people as when it was first launched. The musical situation is different due to an attempt to enforce authenticity requirements. These are not recognized in law hence litigation has to sail under the brands and trademarks flags of convenience. In the Byrds case, in the late 1980s, the judge favoured giving ownership of the name to the former drummer, who had only one-third of one song authorship in the whole catalogue of the band. It was argued that the name was a commercial asset which the former members were not only not exploiting but also chief original name owner Roger McGuinn had frequently expressed strong distaste about ever trading under the name again. Thus, the judge was treating a band as no different from a guitar pedal. No one bats an eyelid that modern Vox or Danelectro products have no credible link to the revered originals.

In the Meat Loaf case (Tomlinson, 2002), Jim Steinman refused to let Meatloaf use the term "Bat Out of Hell" in a record title on the grounds that he had effectively copyrighted this franchise. Meat Loaf sought to claim that he had contributed to the franchise many years earlier via various key ideas. Additional Spandau Ballet disputes arose in the late 1990s when three ex-members (Hadley, Norman and

Keeble) sought to revive their careers by reviving the dormant band name. The decision was that Hadley *et al.* had wrongfully registered the name of the band and were violating use of the trademark. A temporary injunction against using the rider "ex Spandau Ballet" in advertising was granted. In summer 2003 a third case, on the use of the term "ex Spandau Ballet" was settled out of court.

The key argument for upholding trademark ownership is that (cf. De Alessi and Staaf, 1994) trademark capital not only guarantees quality but it also assures specific performance thus affording customers some protection from breach. In the popular musical field, the validity of trademarks has constantly been strained by the continued use of band names when key personnel (and even in some cases all key personnel) have left. This raises the question of the economic role of tribute acts. These could have emerged as a franchise operation from the trademark holder but that was not the case. Their emergence is spontaneous but it may have had the beneficial effect of polarizing markets in such a way as to eliminate "bogus" bands.

The phenomenon of tribute acts is now extremely widespread and generates considerable income. Relatively little academic work exists on this topic and what there is tends to be in music/musicology outlets (Gregory, 2012; Homan, 2006; Frith, 2006) or in law journals concerned with the copyright infringement issue (Geary, 2004–2005; Newman, 2012). There have been many journalistic and blog pieces on the tribute act industry which seem to be the primary source of data quoted in academic papers. Even though there is no officially documented consistent time series of the volume and value of tribute acts, there would seem to be no one in the world who doubts the massive growth of this sector since the late 1980s.

There seems to be little interest amongst economists or marketing researchers. This may be surprising as the tribute act is clearly a phenomenon full of economic and monetary issues.

How can we define the term "tribute act"? A tribute act will perform *only* the work of a specified performer. They will not perform any work of their own and they will seek to reproduce some well-known idioms of the target performer. That is they may represent only a specific era of the Beatles, Pink Floyd etc., rather than the whole repertoire. This will require capital goods of dress (clothes, wigs etc.) and staging (lightshows etc.). A tribute act to a musical group will typically have a soundalike name which is often humorous as in Nearly Dan (Steely Dan), Bootleg Beatles, By Jovi (Bon Jovi). Less commonly we may find portmanteau tribute bands who combine more than one performer's works, e.g. from a style in an epoch. This will require fewer capital investments to accurately reproduce, as exactitude in copying a specific visual style is not so important,

Tribute bands have been embedded in tourism and music festivals which in the current century have been buoyant features of the cultural economy. Examples of these are the Beatles week in Liverpool, Trieste at Driffield (East Yorkshire, UK), Glastonbudget, three days in a farm in Leicestershire (not in Glastonbury), Big Tribute Festival, Fakestock, the Bootleg Festival and others.

In legal terms, the tribute act would seem to be violating trademarks with the consequent risk of being prosecuted for infringement. Although rare, this has cropped up. Widow of Frank Zappa, Gail Zappa, has sought redress that some tribute performers are not sufficiently competent to render his work as per the original. For more mainstream popular music, tribute acts have been accepted, and even in some cases encouraged by the original trademark holders.

The tribute act would normally be thought to be an example of a textbook economics case of an imperfect substitute. Thus if it costs the same as the original good it would simply have no reason to exist. The most blatant reason for existence is the death of the target performers such as Michael Jackson and Frank Sinatra. If the target is not dead they may have reduced their output to few, difficult to access performances thus depriving audiences of many opportunities to see them. There may be further scarcity factors in that the target may have evolved (such as losing key members) and may have decided to abstain from parts of their repertoire.

If the target is still alive and not comparatively scarce then textbook economics would suggest that the price must be lowered proportionately to the degree of imperfection in the substitute. Tribute acts have experienced both an increase in supply and in demand for their services. Given that musical events are experience goods, there is a degree of synergy. That is, you might not know how much you want something until you get a proper demonstration of its existence and uses. There are some non-standard sources of utility to the consumer such as the "parrot factor" of being excited at how close someone can come to imitating something.

This is very prominent in comedy impressionists. The popularity of the television programme *Stars in their Eyes* helped promote the parrot factor. Karaoke and "karaoke" musicals based on such artists as Queen, Rod Stewart and Madness have helped promote tribute act consumption.

The tribute band provides a way for struggling musicians to make a living as other sources of income have dried up. This may be supplementary to preferred work or be full time.

Tribute acts can potentially earn much better money than lesser "name" artists. The Abba tribute, Bjorn Again, have made huge sums of money partly due to being officially blessed by Abba at the time of major reissues and times of revival of interest.

Some idea of potential earnings can be gleaned from Table 5.3 which is taken from agency data for UK performers. These fees would be considerably more than the musicians involved can obtain when trying to promote their own new work in other combos.

It is notable that the fees for bands are often twice as much as those for solo artist tributes. This would not logically be due to the number of people involved as the solo artist should need a backing band. However, as we see in the table a cut price Amy Winehouse without band can be had whilst she is very expensive with band. I have not compiled a set of ticket prices for tribute bands but many of these regularly perform on the regional theatre circuit at similar prices to established (but not superstar) performers including musicians and comedians. We should note that the costs of being a tribute band can be quite high due to the need to accurately emulate the source works. A Pink Floyd tribute band performing a specific big album tribute show will need extensive use of lighting and effects. Tribute band

TABLE 5.3 Tribute band fees

Act	Price (£)	Comment
Bootleg Beatles	11,363	Beatles
Classic Beatles	3,099	Beatles
Paperback Writers	1,054	Beatles
We Will Rock You	1,983	Queen
Queen Rocks	831	Queen
Fabba	2,603	Abba (there are also much cheaper Abbas)
Beach Boys Gold	1,983	Beach Boys
Not Fade Away	22,293	Rolling Stones
Purple Patch	1,240	Deep Purple
One Step Beyond	1,859	Madness
By Jovi	1,395	Bon Jovi
Reflex	1,364	Duran Duran
OK Sis	1,240	Oasis
Tribute to Fleetwood Mac	1,488	Fleetwood Mac
Vintage Van	1,240	Van Morrison
Kasabian LSF	1,364	Kasabian
Led Zeppelin Experience	1,265	Led Zeppelin
Absolutely Amy Winehouse	651	Amy Winehouse
Absolute Adele	620	Adele
Whitney	496	Whitney Houston
Confide in Kylie	682	Kylie Minogue
Robbie Williams Robbie to the Max	620	Robbie Williams
Michael Jackson UK	992	Michael Jackson
Michael Jackson Tribute Band	1,550	Michael Jackson
Totally Elton	620	Elton John

Source: data from www.alivenetwork.com/bandsearch.asp?style=Tribute%20bands (accessed 1 May 2014).

Notes

Since I compiled this table, the figures have changed slightly. In general the lower bound of a range is now given, e.g. for Not Fade Away is listed as £1,800+, Absolutely Amy Winehouse is now listed as £630 solo or + band for £2,820. Similar figures apply to other Amy Whitehouse tributes.

It may be of interest that the Alive Network classifies sub £1,000 as a "cheap" act.

musicians may need to carry a wide range of guitars etc., which might not be the case if they were performing their own compositions in their own bands.

Conclusion

This chapter has looked at music production in terms of standard microeconomic theory with some appropriate augmentation. Unusual features specific to the industry have been considered. It is now time to look at the consumers.

Notes

1 At www.gratefuldeadarchive.org.
2 LOFI/DIY – "low fidelity"/"do it yourself".

6

CONSUMPTION OF MUSIC

Introduction

This chapter considers the specific analyses economists provide of the demand for music starting with the neoclassical approach and moving on to more socially embedded treatments. At the end we look at some specific aspects of the economics of music collectors and "fans".

All demand must come from some underlying notion of utility or value in the objects or activities. A number of elements have been identified in music (see Chapter 1) which provide utility, such as mood enhancement, catharsis, excitement, physical effects of rhythm and spirituality. Some music may satisfy only one element for consumers who choose it. Some consumers may only be seeking a small sub-set of elements. It might be argued that some genres of music expressly forbid the inclusion of certain elements. Music which aspires to the state of being high art or *avant garde* may be required not to contain too much excitement. White music critics and fans who idolize such forms as the blues, soul, r'n'b (and going further back its gospel origins) seem to claim that these idia can encapsulate all the elements simultaneously and are thus, in some sense, superior to other genres beyond being merely more personally preferred. Conversely heavy metal and rap or boy and girl band teen pop may be demeaned outside their fan groups, due to the lack of spirituality, an over easy form of melody and too much aspiration to excitement.

The most recent attempt to elucidate a fuller categorization of the elements of value (utility) in music for consumers is from marketing scholar Holbrook (2013) in a case study of jazz musician Gary Burton. Burton is said to embody eight types of consumer value:

Efficiency
Excellence

Exhibitionism
Elitism
Entertainment
Esthetics (spelling as original)
Ethics
Ecstasy.

Holbrook also attempts a genre hierarchy argument. In the end, this seems to collapse into the idea that "high" and "low" culture can be demarcated by size of audience. High culture has small audiences and low culture has large audiences. He seems to say that Paul McCartney cannot ever produce high art, if the work generates a mass audience. The distinction is however asymmetric. Some work with low audiences may simply be mass market music which has failed to sell. But, the thesis seems to be that if a large audience is reached then the work cannot be high art. Elements of such disdain can be seen in some of the reaction to the unexpected and atypical success of Gorecki's Third Symphony. This was initially an obscure work which took off to sales of over a million copies which were not repeated by Gorecki's other works despite them containing the same elements and him now having a reputation which brands his works.

This is effectively the well-known historic pop phenomenon of the "one hit wonder".

Consumers could decide to simply make all artists one or few hit wonders by taking only their most loved works or they could be more generally omnivorous. Or they can specialize in the consumption of just a few suppliers. The limit of this is the obsessive fan who borders on being a musical hyperunivore which we come to later.

How do we measure music consumption?

Most economic studies of markets (like music) do not actually use the word consumption but rather the term "demand". Economists however use the term consumption (as in consumption function) in macroeconomics to look at aggregate household spending on all goods and services. Demand may be seen as the narrower term as it usually relates to observable units of product sold in the marketplace without much reference to consumer interaction with the product, or their style of use of it, or any meanings they attach to it. One could consume a lot of music with very little expressed demand through the long-established medium of radio listening, or through later innovations in duplication. Online streaming effectively constitutes a resurrection of music radio but with the presenter concept of DJ emasculated.

The narrower term of demand has dominated the heated discussions on downloading which display a fixation with sales of physical product. It seems appropriate, for cultural and entertainment goods, to talk about consumption rather than demand due to their psychological and social complexity. However, it is logical to begin with the standard economic theory of demand so that we can see exactly what it does and does not contain.

Following the exposition and contextualization of the narrow demand theory, we will then move on to consider the degree to which there can be economic models of wider issues which have been typically dealt with in marketing and anthropology.

Simple economics of individual consumer choice

The standard introductory economic approach to decision-making starts from an isolated individual. They have a fixed utility function which is maximized subject to constraints of price and income. The utility function is a mathematical representation of the individual's preferences. One way of dealing with this in the context of music is to suppose an individual who does not attend live music, or create music themselves, but simply chooses between two goods M = aggregate stock of music recordings and X = aggregate of all other commodities such as food and clothing. If they created music themselves we would have to consider the question of substitution between their own musical efforts and those of others.

In this framework we are concerned with substitution between other goods and music which is heavily focused on price in the economic model. The other key determinant is income. Music would be seen as potentially what some (misleadingly) like to call a "luxury" or "superior" good. In economic terms this can be defined as having an income elasticity of >1 so that the share of income spent on the good, on average, will rise as income rises. Conversely, the share will shrink as income falls thus leading us to expect that recessions will have a severe downward effect on music sales. This possibility is overlooked in many of the discussion about downloading, streaming and piracy. A more complex treatment is where we have ML = aggregate consumption of live music and MR = aggregate consumption of recorded music. Here we would have substitution between live and recorded music influenced by their relative prices. We can subdivide this further into different types of live and recorded music such as festivals, arena events, intimate club gigs, genres of music etc. In all decisions the individual is assumed to act rationally. The contradictory evidence on income effects, for live music, has been noted in marketing reports on the buoyancy of the music festival market in the face of major recession (see Larsen and Hussels, 2011). An econometric study of US time series data by Mortimer *et al.* (2012) has a graph (Figure 1 on p. 4) showing a symmetric rise in *numbers* of concerts performed, plotted against the falling sales of albums from 2000–2003. This choice makes them match almost exactly in slope. However, there are issues of the relative prices and revenues. The detailed econometric work in this study looks at P2P sharing, in the Napster era, and concludes that there is substantial compensation for lost recording revenue in increased performing revenue.

If we were to assume just two types of live and recorded music, the utility function may be written as:

$$U = f(ML1, ML2, MR1, MR2, MX, e)$$ (6.1)

where e is a random disturbance to allow for all other factors. This is a very restricted categorization but it sufficiently encapsulates the empirical studies discussed in the next three chapters which look at the "omnivorousness" of musical taste.

A univore sticks mainly to one of the two types of music and an omnivore regularly tries both. This can be simplified even more if we assume that the two types of live music are simply the two types of recorded music being performed which still makes them different products.

This could still lead to outcomes such as consumers who choose one type of music solely on recordings and the other solely in the live arena. The rate of substitution between the four choices should be determined by their relative prices, if income is given in the short run. The live music literature, especially on festivals, notes that price of festivals and live music may well be rising not just staying still. This might seem contradictory to the basic model. However, the "price" of a unit of festival is a difficult item to precisely pin down as the range and quality of products in the bundle may be rising more than a global price rise, in any period. Thus, we would not rush to the conclusion that festivals could be an example of a Giffen good (see below).

Maximizing utility subject to constraints is the core of the economist's definition of rationality. The fixity of the utility function comes from the assumption that tastes are inherited from somewhere outside the choice making environment. The lay person is likely to object to this as unrealistic. The defence is that of "positivism" endorsed by Friedman (1953), of generating accurate predictions of human behaviour. In the extreme view expounded by Friedman there is no time for ethnomethodology. There is no point in interviewing actual consumers about their motivations which would not necessarily agree with the assumptions of the model.

As indicated above, the usual state of affairs is that the optimizing consumers can be used to derive a market demand curve which for a "normal" good is negatively related to price. As in any scientifically styled field of knowledge, anomalies to this "normal" state of affairs do crop up. The major anomaly for demand is to find that the demand curve slopes upwards instead of downwards. This *cannot* happen in the conventional individualistic theoretical model except for the so-called "Giffen good", which is a very strong inferior good, on which consumers are spending a very large part of their income. Giffen goods have never been deemed to be relevant for the field of music due to their discretionary nature. It is not essential to life in the way that food is. Music is not like the potato which is the original example of a Giffen good. We might observe that people, *ceteris paribus*, demand a different bundle of types of music when income is higher. This might suggest that some types of music might have the negative income effect which is a prerequisite for Giffen good status, as their demand falls as income rises. However, this raises the problem that income may well be related to other things, including changes in tastes which are assumed away in the basic individual choice model.

The theory of consumer choice assumes that people have exogenous given wants which (along with prices and incomes) form the constraints on their utility maximization. Firms exist to satisfy the wants of consumers. Wants are shown in the form of tastes/preferences. These preferences give rise to the individual and market demand curves. Hence, the demand curve is regarded as showing "revealed preference". It is assumed that people know their own preference completely or that they can learn them efficiently. Further, it is assumed that there is no conflict in preferences, i.e. people are not subject to the influence of preferences which they would prefer not to have. In practice, wants may come from a number of places such as advertising, influence of other consumers, deep seated genetic desires endogenous to consumption such as addiction or acquired tastes. The discussion of J.S. Mill in Chapter 1 highlighted that his musical wants were severely attenuated by his depression and nervous breakdown. It is obvious that hearing decline (see Chapter 7) may reduce music consumption. This would be regarded as a deterioration in music appreciation capital.

Conventional microeconomic theory takes a different view of advertising, to that just implied, in which it serves the useful function of providing information to help consumers make better decisions on the basis of their given exogenous preferences. It follows that consumers should be happy to pay for advertising in the form of higher prices.

We can expand the basic model into what we may term the Becker–Lancaster approach combining Becker's model of household production and Lancaster's good characteristics theory.

In the Becker–Lancaster approach, utility is derived indirectly from the "characteristics" that inhere in goods. Becker proposed that goods are combined with the time of the consumer(s) to make "commodities" in a household production function.

The household can be one or more unrelated or related people. Time of individual members can be used in different proportions. In a multi-person unrelated household (such as flat-sharers) one member could specialize in being the finder of recorded and live music events for the others to enjoy whilst the others specialize in other activities. In a related household the presence of children may have a substantial impact on music as the availability of time and money income for such discretionary spending, and leisure, is reduced. The impact of this factor is little studied in empirical work on music consumption. Studies looked at, in the next chapter, tend just to use marital status and child presence dummies, of a fairly broad grain, that are available in the secondary datasets. There may, of course, be a transfer of music-related spending towards investment in human capital in the child such as violin lessons or the purchase of instruments.

Time is scarce as it cannot be increased even by technological progress. Technological progress can increase the marginal productivity of time and it can increase the volume and quality of goods obtained with the same resource input. We can refer to goods as more or less time intensive. A piece of music would seem to take the time it lasts to consume. This is not strictly true. Live music has attendance requirements. Recorded music also has transactions costs. More importantly, repeated listening is a time use that is of significance. If we take the stereotypical view of high and low culture (espoused above by Holbrook and often found amongst cultural economists), there may be a broad division of how this works. The highbrow/less popular music requires repeated listening because this is a form of study to invest in appreciation capital given the complexities and difficulties of the music. For the popular/lowbrow music, the repetition of listening may be in terms of the "stupefaction" concept of drug affinity implied by Stockhausen's remarks in Chapter 1.

There is a straightforward wage substitution effect away from time intensive goods in proportion to their time intensity. Thus, rising wages throughout society would lead us to expect a shift from the more time intensive to the less time intensive music. However, the impact is indeterminate due to income effects which will reduce the degree of time reallocation. If the income effects of wage rises are strong enough, then the more time intensive goods may even increase relative to the less time intensive. This is leaving aside lexicographic taste constraint barriers which might prevent someone from choosing "easier" music to listen to (or play for leisure consumption) just because their time has become scarcer. They may prefer no music to easier music, if time is scarce, just as a keen amateur sports person might prefer not to play at all if events of a sufficient standard are not available.

In this model, goods are no longer "just goods" but rather factors of production which households purchase, in order to combine them to produce utility. For example, utility from a musical recording is a function of a production process in which it is combined with equipment and the time and level of attention the user is able to invest in it. For live music, the presence of significant others (friends, family) or ambient strangers (such as at festivals) contributes to the output from the raw input supplied by the performers.

The social features of live music give it the quality of a club good in the sense of Buchanan (1965). Many people will experience a loss of value if the venue is very sparsely attended. This is normally attributed to lack of "atmosphere" but there are other economic factors that can explain this. Lack of attendance is a proxy for low popularity and it may have a detrimental effect on the performers and the self-esteem of the consumers, who feel that they have made a choice which is not socially condoned. They may feel the stigma of having deviant tastes when this was not their stated aim. This may spark vicious spiralling domino effects, in that an initial decline in attendance for specific artists may push marginal attenders out of the market for their next performances. Thus there are even fewer people, and less ambience, pushing more marginal attenders out and eventually leading to cancellation or non-booking.

Standard economic logic would suggest that some form of price discrimination is used here. The extreme case of this is where some free tickets are surreptitiously given away to improve the atmosphere. There are some barriers against such price discrimination such as the institutional practices of ticket agencies.

There is assumed to be continuous sustainability between characteristics in the individual's utility function. For many goods, the optimal solution involves combining different "brands" of the same good. This implies that giving producers freedom to proliferate brands will be welfare enhancing, providing other conditions are favourable. In musical terms, the first stop in brand terms is genre. The genre of heavy metal contains characteristics that may not overlap noticeably with those of country and western. However, we find fusions in other genres. Popular music, to some extent, began its process of fusion which would be deemed "crossover" by firms in the late 1960s and 1970s. The ailing sector of jazz entered into "jazz-rock" fusion, the emergence of prog rock to major sales may have accelerated the decline of classical music sales.

The Eagles, took the crossover category of country-rock to massive sales in the 1970s. Black artists, like Michael Jackson and Run DMC, would implant metal elements in their work but it would still be marketed as of its source genre. Michael Jackson proclaimed himself to be the King of Pop not the king of soul or r'n'b or dancing.

Figure 6.1 illustrates the consumers' goods characteristics choice with respect to the country-rock genre in the 1960s and 1970s, using the Lancaster goods characteristics model. In the UK in the twenty-first century, we could make a similar

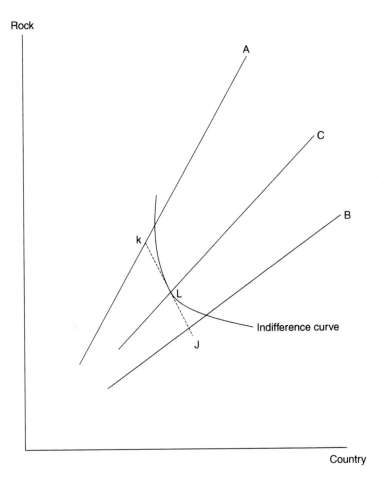

FIGURE 6.1 Lancaster goods characteristics model.

point with respect to the emergence of a somewhat folk rock genre such as Mumford and Sons. It is assumed that there are initially just two major suppliers (A and B) who keep their product approximately rigid. Thus, each song may differ in various ways but its combination of rock and country stay the same.

In Figure 6.1, the music has two elements, country and rock. Supplier A is relatively rock–country and supplier B is relatively country-rock. Assuming convex indifference curves, of which one is shown, the consumer can achieve higher utility by combining the two goods to reach a point such as L rather than K (only A) or J (only C). A third supplier can emerge offering a more evenly mixed form of country-rock, such as C but this should, in theory, be irrelevant depending on pricing. Each ray represents a fixed amount of country and rock in the units of supply. The amount available depends on price. If A, B and C set prices which take us to the points K, L and J then the point L may be an optimum attainable by choosing either A and B in a combination, which equates to L, or simply by choosing the point L directly and only consuming C and none of A and B. This only applies for the specific indifference curve shown. For other indifference curves, which are not tangent to K, L or J then the consumer may optimize by choosing combinations from the set of A, B, C to reach the desired point. In this scenario, it is irrelevant to the consumer whether they pick A, B or C as it is only the characteristics that count.

Thus they do *not* have any loyalty or fanship despite the sometimes found claim in textbooks that this model "explains" consumer loyalty. Those claims are simply based on the revealed preference of consumers not leaving a product when prices become less favourable relative to close substitutes. If there are significant transactions costs, they may prefer the single supplier option in the situation where they would otherwise be indifferent between this and a combination.

In theory, A, B and C could remove each other from the market by cutting prices. However, as discussed at the end of Chapter 2, this is an extremely rare approach for recorded music. They could alter their bundles of characteristics and thus move into a more beneficial part of the product space. However this will only work if genuine loyalty can be engineered in some way and/or there is the "millionaire shortbread" effect. The "millionaire shortbread problem" is as follows. Many chain coffee bars now sell what has been known as millionaire shortbread which is just single successive layers of shortbread, caramel and chocolate. Each of these can be bought separately and consumers could, in theory, be better off by sticking optimal combinations of each of the constituents in their mouth at the same time. That is, if the prices of these are comparatively cheaper and the transaction costs are low enough. But of course its not the same. There may be complex synergic effects of concurrent combinations of characteristics.

There may be a synergistic effect of the way the manufactured combination has been structured that produces gains in utility. Further, not all consumers may have the same style. Those who are less omnivorous (foraging even) in seeking out music will be marginal to a specific sector, Hence they could drop out altogether if a suitable hybrid(s) does not come along to make the product space in Figure 6.1 more dense.

In terms of practical examples, in the country-rock vein, we may liken A and B to the Byrds and the Flying Burrito Brothers (FBB) who could be deemed respectively more rock-country and more country-rock. The FBB emerged from the Byrds' "country" record "Sweetheart of the Rodeo" (1968) (SOTR) which was unpopular both with the mainstream and the traditional country music fraternity. Authentic country colouration was attempted by working in Nashville with sessions musicians and playing the "Grand Ole Opry". A similar authentication of product, by process, route was later taken by Elvis Costello in his country phase.

In terms of good characteristics, we may see the Eagles as solving the "millionaire shortbread" problem for the consumer, by a more fitting combination of the characteristics.

We can subdivide the characteristics into elements like the vocal harmonies, the pedal steel guitars and so on. This is too many characteristics to fit on a simple diagram but could be mathematically modelled. For some cases, even non-musical elements will be important; for example, hair and beards. Currently, the beard is more socially ubiquitous than it has been for a long time and it seems to be a core motif of the rootsy/folk/country fusion music. Facial hairiness accelerated in the country rock bands that emerged – the post-SOTR Byrds, FBB and Eagles all tended to have beards and/or moustaches. The Band came to some prominence at this time as the epitome of back to grassroots authenticity (what now tends to be called "Americana") with a fair tendency to facial hair. In heavy metal and prog rock, lack of head hair in members can be an impediment to the consumer's well-being due to credibility issues. The imperfect substitute, in the production process, of a wig could be used. Attractiveness and weight of the artists may also feature in the consumer choice in a similar way in many genres. The increasing importance of these, in recent times, in operatic and classical performances has concerned purists. Attractiveness could even become a negative factor if it reduces the perceived credibility of the artist.

These matters highlight the crucial subjective element in the economic theory of demand.

We have to presume that if appearance, hair and even things like political opinions, matter to the consumer then their utility should evaporate if they discover that the musicians are sequestered within a wig or harbouring unacceptable political views. That is assuming they do not reject it via an act of cognitive dissonance.

The impact of unacceptable political views is documented in a film about the Dixie Chicks (*Dixie Chicks: Shut Up and Sing*) covering the aftermath of their throwaway anti-Iraq invasion remarks, in 2003. In the USA, there was a concerted call to discard their music including an invitation to people to bring CDs to be crushed by a bulldozer. They suffered loss of income from lost sponsorship, TV advertising etc. This did appear distinctly to impact their ticket and record sales, in many parts of the USA, leading to an increased focus on the Canadian market. It may have led to the career hiatus that they took in the wake of these events. It may also be no coincidence that their decline was followed by the meteoric rise of more anodyne corporate country crossover act, Lady Antebellum. Their social activities correspond neatly to the accepted corporate responsibility model. For example, they are partnered with a charity for disabled orphans in Haiti. This is an extra-musical goods characteristic that can hardly fail to add to the consumers' welfare.

The same political topic brought audience discontent to Crosby, Stills, Nash and Young in 2006's "Freedom of Speech Tour" when they nightly criticized President Bush's Iraq policy, from the stage. This was also turned into a documentary film. This was a much more extreme case as anti-Bush songs and visuals were presented. When the tour reached Atlanta, a significant audience share protested and marched out. This is a very curious case of irrational consumer behaviour, as it seems many people bought tickets not realizing what they were coming to.

This kind of problem has long vexed consumers of classical music in connection with composers like Wagner, and composers and conductors with Nazi sympathies. Standard economic theory would argue that this should *not* be a problem so long as the product space in the goods characteristics space is dense enough as there should be a substitute good to which the worried consumer can move. In the manner of diet Coke and low fat spread, consumers can search out a Nazi-lite, or pro-war, or anti-war free close substitute to the good (factor input in the household production function) they desire. We can push the logic of economics even further. In a system of patronage, or the modern development of crowd funding, the consumer could seek actively to induce composers with less negative baggage to compose substitute works.

In the case of "high" culture music, this faces the additional problem that the consumer values the experience of engaging with works by members of a canon of greatness. The canon means that one is adding an extra constraint to one's consumption choice based on the accumulated views of respected taste formers. High culture consumers also value evolutionary progression, so it is difficult to accept a modern recreation of a past style of work simply to avoid dealing with the creator's unpalatable aspects. Thus there are severe limitations to substitution effects from new entrants into the product space.

Lipsey and Rosenbluth (1971) developed an extension of the goods characteristics model where normal goods may have inferior characteristics. This may give rise to some discontinuities in the demand function. Demand for the good will still rise as income rises up to a certain point beyond which the weight of the inferior characteristic causes a shift. Going back to the 1995 Stockhausen remarks, in Chapter 1, we could give the example of music that one likes, for being interesting in its ambience and sounds, but dislikes, in terms of its rigidity and repetition.

Rational addiction

Both live and recorded music have properties that might be conveniently situated in the context of the theory of "rational addiction" in economic theory. This model needs to be set in historical context. Prior to Becker's promotion of this model, from 1988 onwards, the approach was either that addicts are totally irrational (in that they accept no substitutes), hybrid models or myopic models. A hybrid demand curve model has vertical segments of zero price elasticity, but is downward sloping when prices fall below or above certain threshold prices due to income and substitution effects. Myopic addicts have a stock of addiction habits which is a function of their past consumption. They are myopic because they do not take into account the fact that their current consumption is changing the stock of addiction habits in the future. Thus they are missing out by not maximizing lifetime discounted utility. The vertical demand and hybrid models are not consistent with the convex indifference curves of textbook microeconomic theory. The myopic model should not be deemed to represent irrationality, in the normal sense of the word, but it is incomplete rationality.

Becker's rational addiction model makes a number of assumptions including the obvious one of life-cycle utility maximization. Addiction is defined only in terms of the time separability of the marginal utility of goods. That is, for a non-addictive good marginal utility in the future is not influenced by the quantity of that good consumed in the past. For an addictive good marginal utility in the future is influenced by the quantity of that good consumed in the past due to tolerance, reinforcement and withdrawal effects.

The key conclusion of this model is that the long-run price elasticity of demand may be considerably greater than the short-run elasticity. Becker also made a big deal out of the fact that there can be "good" (beneficial) and "bad" (harmful) addictions. Becker would tend to include music in the beneficial addictions as he gives learning to play the piano as an example, in his exposition. Having said that, we can clearly identify groups of people typically of strong religious views (such as Tipper Gore and those who brought the legal case against Judas Priest in 1990 for causing their son's suicide) who would wish to term addiction to some types of music as harmful.

One thing needs to be made clear. Although Becker's rational addiction model is applied to drugs, it would not treat music as a "drug" in the sense portrayed by Stockhausen in Chapter 1. The key musical implication of Becker's approach is that if we took two identical individuals (including in their capacity to enjoy different things) we could find very different levels of demand for music due to stocks of appreciation capital. Musical consumption could be an addictive good for some individuals at some points in their lives but not so at others (see the next chapter). It must be addictive, by definition, if it is not time separable in the utility function. When there are no learning/appreciation capital formation effects it is likely not to be addictive as the utility does not carry over into the next period.

There may be exogenous shocks which cause discontinuities. Nostalgia (see next chapter) may arrive unexpectedly and thus lead to a new cause of rational addiction as the individual "tops up" their "nostalgia capital". It is difficult to fit nostalgia fully into a pure rational addiction model, as individuals would tend not to anticipate the onset of nostalgia and factor it into their choices. That is, in a pure rational addiction model, one would make choices well ahead of the onset of nostalgia in order to maximize the benefit from it. This seems implausible.

Socialized individual choice

Extensions have been made to basic economic theory to allow for the influence of other people on choice. In the 1950s, American economists such as Harvey Leibenstein and James Duesenberry began to introduce social comparison effects into economics, in the wake of books like the *Lonely Crowd* and *The Organisation Man*. Leibenstein introduced three types of consumption externality. The bandwagon effect is a positive externality in that your utility rises when other people's consumption of the good rises. The snob effect is a negative externality because the reverse happens. The Veblen good is a situation where price enters *directly* into the utility function rather than simply operating as a constraint on achievable utility as in the conventional model. According to Leibenstein it is the "conspicuous price" which is the price which you think other people think you paid. In the case of the Veblen effect, the consumer values a good more the higher is its perceived or "conspicuous" price. This serves the function of ostentatious display and is a flag of the status or wealth of its purchaser. This is not to be confused with the use of price as a quality signal which may also be present. In the case of music, the use of price as a quality signal is highly prevalent in the purchase of musical equipment and instruments but not in live and recorded music.

In the Leibenstein version of the Veblen good model, the usual conclusion is that the demand curves for bandwagon and snob goods will still slope down but the long-run slopes will be different. The Veblen good may have upward sloping segments *but* this cannot be so throughout the range of demand curve as conventional income and substitution effects still operate (in all cases) meaning that the income effect would force the curve to bend backwards at some point. For the snob effect it would be somewhat inconsistent to have relatively large negative income effects for a snob good hence there should not be any independent tendency towards an upward sloping demand curve from that source.

Gisser *et al.* (2009) correct the widespread mistaken impression, stemming from an article by Becker, that bandwagon goods can have upward sloping demand curves contrary to the original Leibenstein work. We also find, in arts marketing literature (Patmore, 2013), the idea that a high price might encourage demand, in the context of bundling, for the supposedly more "high culture" (=less popular) musical genre. However, this is slightly different being really just an example of the "bargain offer" effect (as in BOGOF). The potential consumer of a bundle, say four concert tickets in a season, is said to be more interested if the price of an item separated from the bundle goes up because the bundle then looks like a better deal. This is inconsistent with the standard rational choice model of demand, if the person would have bought the bundle anyway, as the actual price has not changed for the bundle. If a person was going to buy one or more elements of the bundle it may tip them over into consumption.

There are few empirical studies by economists of music consumption in terms of Leibenstein's additions to the model. There are some slight incursions of bandwagon effects in some of the studies discussed at the end of Chapter 4, but the most overt attempt to apply Leibenstein style elements in the context of music is by Moe and Earl (2009) who analyse chart placings in Norway. Their focus is exclusively on bandwagon effects. The data covers the official Norwegian music chart, "VG-Lista", or VG-Chart and is based on record sales from 100 of the highest-selling retail outlets in Norway. The study looks at cross-sectional data for all 170 artists represented on the VG-Chart during year 2000. The model includes a reputation effect as well as the bandwagon effect as predictors of highest chart position reached. These are measured by first entry position and change in position from first to second week. Reputation is estimated by the artist's previous performance using a "previous top 10 or not" dummy variable.

Some support is found for the bandwagon effects in both singles and album charts.

The data in such a study is too aggregated and vague to allow in-depth study of any bandwagon processes. Further, it becomes increasingly difficult to use chart data for such analyses after 2000 due to influences discussed in Chapter 4. There is now also the factor, discussed with respect to the "Sleepify" album, of strategic fan behaviour which disrupts the time profile of activity in charts.

Snobbery and Veblen effects

Social positioning effects such as these (trying to be "superior") are well documented in music journalism. However, these are not generally related to price of tickets or pre-recorded music in any analytical treatments. These effects may well be present in the hardware used to play back music, as very expensive reproduction equipment is well suited to serve as high-status consumption display. The revival of vinyl records may impact on this, as quality turntables now have not only retro chic but comparative scarcity to elevate their status.

Behaviouralism: beyond satisficing

Discussion thus far has been predicated on the optimizing consumer. Even if they are being swayed by vanity, and the desire to impress others, they are still seen as utility maximizers with, subject to the limitations of the costs of information, perfect knowledge. One alternative is to take the *satisficing* approach where consumers stop searching once they think they have crossed a threshold of satisfaction. So, they may think "I want some music, I will try that, it seems good enough, okay, I shall not look for any more that might be better for me until my next search point." In terms of the market, satisficing will create sclerosis and lack of variety in sales in that the consumers will tend to cluster at fixed choices for long periods of time. A very successful musical product, in economic terms, may lack the symbolic meaning and emotional content, to the consumer, so beloved of writers in cultural and media studies. The genre most likely to illustrate this would be the "easy listening" music of such performers as the James Last Orchestra. The type of bundling provided by music festivals may help break up variety stasis as the satisficing consumer will get the chance of a "buffet lunch" type exposure where they have not made significant pre-commitment to the new experiences.

The core notion of satisficing has been elaborated in more complex, essentially behavioural economic models. These models are variously described as models of *Multiple Utility, Bi-utility* or *Meta-Preferences* (Thaler and Shefrin, 1981; Shefrin and Thaler, 1988; Camerer and Thaler, 1995; Schelling, 1984; Etzioni, 1987). The term metapreference means having "preferences about preferences" as the word "meta" means "beyond". These are relevant to the notion of the canon. People may feel they should like "better" music than the music that they do prefer.

This would require investment in their appreciation capital. They may also suffer from backsliding or tergiversation where they become "weak" and fall back to their less preferred preferences. This creates the opening for such classical music crossover packaging as "Classic FM" stations which broke with the convention of presenting a composer's work in its entirety.

Beliefs are also a component of individual welfare. Maintaining beliefs that conflict with the environment impose further costs in the form of the strain of reconciliation. For example, someone who aspires to "improved" tastes needs to be convinced that this is what they have achieved.

Cognitive dissonance was first propounded by psychologist Leon Festinger in 1957 and has been incorporated in economic models by some fairly mainstream economists (see Akerlof and Dickens, 1982; Gilad *et al.*, 1987). Dissonance is the opposite of consonance, or harmony between the elements of one's life. A music consumer may like to think that their choices represent "good" choices possibly not just for themselves, but also for their reference groups. This need not be that their taste is of a higher culture but it could be that it is in some sense "cool". Attribution of inauthenticity and dangerous ethical values, to the artist, is a source of utility that could bring dissonance if information arrives to challenge it. For example, if they discover that their working class hero is from a wealthy background or that they did not sing or play significant parts of their recording (or have a wig). In the case of Metallica, their fans have had to accommodate a negative view arising from the band's lawsuit against Napster, in 2000, for damages with respect to unauthorized distribution of their songs. This was presented in the media as them "suing their fans".

Dissonance may trigger an information filter which selects in favour of information that confirms the wished-for belief that is otherwise contradicted by the world. The idea of filtering has been extended in a paper by McCain (1990), in which the notion of a two-tier preference system is replaced by the idea of an individual subject to a series of impulses. The significance of the filtering effect in terms of economics is that we find sudden jumps in demand when there has not been a significant change in the underlying information set. Perceptions may change due to snowballing effects where the more other people hold a view the more it impacts a random individual who may be denying the information held in that view. This may be the logic behind the spectacular fall in sales of the new release of Robin Thicke, in July 2014, relative to his previous work. His album "Paula" sold just 520 copies in the UK in its first week of release, less than 55 copies in Australia and 25,000 copies in the USA. In contrast his song "Blurred Lines" sold 1.5 million units in the UK alone.

His video for "Blurred Lines" attracted enormous media and social media opprobrium for the sexist treatment of women. His new video had yet more questionable content and his pre-release promotion had foundered in some disastrous social media interaction where he was targeted by those still hostile to "Blurred Lines". Such controversies have not, in the past, tended to have any impact on sales of an artist so this case may testify to the power of social media as a filter breaker.

Individuals could reconcile themselves to negative information merely by accepting the new view of the artist. Music is not dangerous in the way that a car or medication is, so new information about reliability and desirability does not necessarily have to lead to significant changes in consumption. Utility may have declined but there will not necessarily be a fall in demand for the product. The negative impact would have to be strong enough to cause substitution to the next product in line and that depends on the density of the product space in the goods characteristics space. Also, many individuals will have low attachment to a view of the artist so as information salience fades away misdemeanours will have little impact on them.

In the case of Robin Thicke, we could probably agree that there is no shortage of music with similar characteristics. Popular dance music consumers are unlikely to be constrained by adherence to the canon in the way that consumers of more "high art" music are.

Dissonance is reduced by the deliberate evasion of dissonant information. Individuals may play down the importance of potentially dissonant information or simply make sure that it is not received. It is also possible to dissipate dissonance by excess exposure to counteracting information. This is how firms would deal with PR disasters. The music consumer who may lose out from receiving negative information can opt to focus their attention in places where positive information is provided. This is one rationale for being a fan as opposed to a disinterested consumer.

When fans meet, physically or virtually, they essentially amplify the utility from the same piece of information by confirming the views people wish to be true. These can be a variety of things such as "our hero is a nice person", "X is a genius" or "we are a superior group of people because of this taste". The operation of this process is not intrinsically different between an inclusive group like One Direction fans and fans of, for example The Smiths/Morrissey who feel that some people, such as UK prime ministers, should not be allowed to like their music.

Collectors and fans: conformists or deviants?

Being a fan may decrease demand for some goods as love of X may set up in the person an opposition to Y as the antibody of the loved objects (Bryson, 1996). Hostile non-consumption may be seen as a form of deviancy in a marketplace –

criticism of others for their likes is an attempt to deprive them of utility in order to increase one's own. Collectors and fans would appear to be potentially "deviant" as they are not normal in the sense that most people do not share their activity. Often immensely popular artists, with legions of fans, appeal to a specific demographic group, so that fanship is "normal" within that group but not in wider society. In extremum, this is tending towards the status of a cult or religion.

Collectors and fans exist in many other spheres such as literature, drama, other media and sport. There are those who cross all these spheres most conspicuously, autograph hunters. The nature of the music market, under capitalism, allows for a very high level of involvement in terms of goods to a degree greater even than for sport (see e.g. Thorne, 2011; O'Reilly, 2011; O'Reilly et al., 2013).

We must first deal with issues of semantics and gradations. The word "fan" is a constriction of the term "fanatic" and thus straight away we are confronted with the idea that a fan may be someone with mental health issues (albeit fleeting in some cases). The word in common use has developed a trivial meaning as in "strong liking", such as "I am a fan of strawberry ice cream" = "it is my favourite flavour". We associate fanship most strongly with identification of specific individual(s) to follow. A fan is likely to be a collector, given their nature, but we can have collectors who are not fans. One economic reason for this is speculative arbitrage. Individuals can purchase collectibles in the anticipation of making a profit by re-selling them to fans.

There is some academic literature on the psychology of music collecting (such as Straw, 1997, 2000; Reynolds, 2004; Moist, 2008). Belk (1995) recounts the case of a man whose whole house was filled with vinyl records including a fridge and a stove. Giles et al. (2007) interview 20 people to find out how the introduction of CDs has changed people's relationship with their record collection. Studies like this also highlight that collecting puts a strain on people's relationships with their significant others. This is not surprising in an economic union (such as a marriage) as income, which could provide shared goods to the unit, is spent on what seems nonsensical to the non-sympathetic party. In the extreme the "shrining" of the collected goods sets up the fan target as a rival love object to members of the collector's family or union.

The above studies do not make any attempt to deal with the issue of the price paid as they are solely concerned with emotional and psychological relationships with the objects collected. There is some empirical work on prices of autographs and collectibles but it does not have a specific music focus. In some unpublished work, with my colleague Mike Reynolds we looked at prices, on amazon.co.uk in 2013, for 1,050 sale offers in the minidisc format. Price premia for these should reflect collectibility as the music thereon is available in "better" formats already at low prices. A fan will already have the music, in this study, and broadly speaking only fans should want these versions of the music. The regression equation showed significant death effects. Solo artists who had a tragic death commanded an estimate premium of around £28 (or 85 per cent price gain using the power function) with this being statistically significant. These results were statistically significant at high levels although the smaller premia for bands in which a member had died were more mixed. There was also a statistically significant premium for greatest hits collections of around £11 (46 per cent price gain in the power function version). As there is no additional music on a minidisc greatest hits that is not available already, this cannot be explained by song rarity. It would seem that a greatest hits collection may give a more warm "glow" to the fan collector as it validates the achievements of their chosen target artist.

The death effect is explored further in a marketing study by Evans *et al.* (2009). This does not look at prices but rather esteem value and liking of dead celebrities in the sample. The sample is essentially a convenience one of 161 undergraduate students in a southern USA university on one degree programme. The celebrities are general but include musicians. Bob Marley scores highest in overall popularity amongst the musicians with twice as high a score as Johnny Cash who is only slightly behind Kurt Cobain and is above John Lennon. Variables are constructed, using principal components, derived from the questionnaire instrument. It is found that identification of the celebrity with oneself makes them more popular. One feature of this is age of the celebrity at death. The variable of difference between this and own age is found to be negatively related to celebrity popularity thus supporting the "aspic" hypothesis that death has frozen the identity of the celebrity at a point in time where they can not disappoint the worshipper by becoming older and doing things that conflict with the wished for image. Clearly, Johnny Cash has very high esteem in the list which would seem to be an outlier given the aspic hypothesis. However, he was a very significant beneficiary of "Indian Summer" career rehabilitation which is discussed at the end of the next chapter. Social risk is found to be a statistically significant factor, in celebrity worship, in this study. Social risk refers to the fear of rejection and hostility when going into social situations. In economic terms reducing social risk by celebrity worship is effectively substitution of commodities. That is, replacing living people with dead ones because the expected costs of encounters with the living is higher. The same of course applies to living celebrities but these do have the mentioned problem of not being in aspic.

Not surprisingly, economics tends to focus on the "normal" pattern of consumption. There is nothing unusual about a consumer who declines to take any of a very popular work of music. They are simply at a corner solution where zero is the optimal choice given their preference and constraints. Likewise someone with a high consumption level of a specific musical item, or artist, may just have strong preferences or they may be rational addicts. If there are bandwagon effects, then we may think that there is some form of conformism going on. On the other hand, strong levels of collecting (such as autographs, rare items, limited editions) may be seen as a species of deviant consumption as the individual is behaving in an unconventional way.

There is a body of economic analysis on the degree to which individuals follow social conventions (for example: Akerlof, 1984; Axelrod, 1984; Banerjee, 1992; Bikhchandani *et al.*, 1992; Bernheim, 1994; Coleman, 1987; Gifford, 1999; Granovetter,

1979; Heiner, 1983; Hirshleifer, 1995; Jones, 1984; Kandori, 1992; Manski, 2000; Young, 1992). In Akerlof's formal model, the utility function has three arguments, in addition to the usual ones, social reputation (R), belief in the customary code of behaviour (B) and conformity with its conventions (A). Obedience of a code one believes in and disobedience of a code one disbelieves in are obviously the most expected of the four contingencies.

In extreme musical fanship groups, part of the code may be that you should not like certain other types of music. The conventions may include such things as manner of dress, hairstyle and other lifestyle consumption such as choice of vehicle. In some cases, these are mainly eschewed except in the case of collective rituals. Investment in symbolic displays may increase one's reputation in the group. This can involve making t-shirts, customizing other clothing and so on. Thanks to YouTube, there is also now the widespread phenomenon of the "fan video" where (usually) pre-existing media (like old black and white movies and stills of the artist) are created in homage. If comments are allowed, this permits a reputation utility glow to the creator.

The heavy metal fanship culture is probably the sphere where daily life is most imbued with code conventions. One constraint on such commitment is employment. Visual compliance with a fan subculture may limit one's job opportunities, or promotion in an existing job, simply because it represents deviancy in mainstream culture. Thus fans may ritually come together to engage in collective display activity. This can be of minor cost and effort – the country and music fan who simply puts on boots and a hat or the goth music fan who wears black clothes to the convention. In some cases, this leads to codes that threaten to be, under law, discriminatory – for example there are goth oriented clubs that do not allow people into concerts if they are not visually of sufficient subculture conformity.

We can see that fan subculture has high levels of stability. Individuals may have disputes and some may simply exit over time but there tends to be long-run adherence. The matter of why any particular musical act should attract strong levels of fanship rather than just liking is a difficult one to explore. Clearly it would require in-depth psychological profiling of the fans. Psychological literature on neuroses that may account for fanship is cited in the study by Evans et al. (2009).

In economic terms we can have the paradoxical case where two similar options result in one artist having all the full-on fanship and the other having none. If we go back to One Direction it should seem strange, to an economist, that so much of the demand for obsessive adoration should devolve on to one set of performers. This type of model has links to Becker's celebrated restaurant pricing analysis (1991). His example involved two fish restaurants which were similar in all respects, except for the one with the lower price having substantially excess demand and the other having excess supply. This arises because of information in this case.

People seeking the service choose the supplier who has already been chosen. This accumulates followers. In the case of One Direction, and their ilk, we also have bandwagon and club good effects.

The feature of loyalty in such affiliations may seem anomalous from an economic point of view. We can however regard it simply as another commodity.

Affiliation with others brings utility but the idea of loyalty will bring additional utility. Loyalty has an instrumental rationale in armies and sports teams but this is difficult to justify in terms of music fanship. Albert O. Hirschman (1970) provided the famous exit-voice model of loyalty. Normal economic market models do not feature loyalty. If the product declines in desirability the consumer can simply exit to a rival supplier. However, if they are loyal then they can seek to use "voice" to influence the supplier.

One classic problem for the loyal fan is when their target act delivers a poor quality work. One can be dismissed as possibly anomalous but further poor quality works would suggest they should exit to another fan group or cease fanship altogether. Loyalty may make it harder to leave the worse the situation is. Being "inside" the institution there is a degree of "locking in" due to emotional investments made over a period of time. Leaving involves letting everyone else down.

We now have cults of fanship over acts whose catalogue is now static or unlikely to increase by much. Such as 1960s/1970s rock bands whose fans regularly communicate digitally and often hold prolonged conventions to consecrate the work of their idols. Nostalgia is a factor here. The works which are accepted as the poor entries to the catalogue can, in this context, become a binding factor as the narrative of their causes, and their redeeming factors, unite fans in the celebration of the public good of their shared knowledge.

An interesting empirical explanation of the ramifications of fanship is provided by Halcousis and Matthews (2007) which is a case study of the band Third Eye Blind. In 2003, they went on a 20-date US tour for which the tickets were sold at auction via eBay. This gives us a chance to observe the marginal benefit valuation placed by fans which is usually hidden in consumer surplus under conventional fixed price ticket schemes. Under such schemes the surplus is partly creamed off by ticket touts. The authors estimate regression equations with the price as dependent variable. It is found that bundling of a VIP Pass, with the ticket, added around $40 to the offered price with this being statistically significant. This is probably not surprising, however a statistically significant *fall* in price was found for tickets bundled with autographed posters versus plain ordinary tickets. The point estimate was around $4.5. This may seem even more anomalous given the scope for retrading these items after the event. It perhaps confirms the negative result, as something other than just a freak of model specification errors, that the study also found that very little retrading of auctioned items took place after the event. No convincing explanation for this fall in price, when more is being provided, has been offered.

Conclusion

This chapter has explored the general issue of consumer demand for musical activities. In the following three chapters, I look at some specific features – age, gender and race/ethnicity. These chapters will also, of necessity, look more closely at the issue of music production and music labour markets.

7

AGE

Introduction

In February 2004, an anti-ageist hoax, on the British music industry, was perpetrated by issuing "45 RPM" by a non-existent band called "The Poppy Fields". The video used much younger musicians lip-syncing in place of the actual band. It was claimed that this ruse had taken the song into the Top 30, thus exposing the superficiality of judging music on the looks of the performers. This stunt was perpetrated by Welsh musician Mike Peters whose band the Alarm had its origins in the attitudes and stylings of punk.

In 1976–1977 disaster struck the established fraternity of UK "prog rock" musicians. A ritualistic "killing" of the previous generation by "punk" meant many would find their lucrative gigs on the university circuit cancelled and/or their fees greatly reduced and, in some cases, recordings would be left unreleased by their record companies. An acute symbol of this was the threat, in a club, of violent physical attack by the Sex Pistols, on BBC DJ/Presenter Bob Harris – one of the custodians of all that was "safe", "old" and proficient in UK popular music. Harris was saved by the road crew of one of the "dinosaur" artists under attack – Procol Harum. Fellow DJ, John Peel, would, unlike Harris, take a *volte-face* and shift to the new, young approach which was supposedly espousing lack of technical ability as a motif of authenticity. Peel proceeded to join in the derision of the once loved works as ponderous, dull and lifeless. Throughout the literature of UK music journalism, he has been acclaimed as a wise and constructive visionary with no one proffering the economic explanation that he saw which way the wind was blowing and was simply responding to demand for supposed "taste making". Indeed the BBC has seen fit to establish an annual lecture, in his honour, on the 6 Music station.

In contrast to John Peel, Harry Chapin's song "W.O.L.D", released in 1974, lamented the fate of an American broadcaster whose career was dwindling because he was too "old" to play music on the radio. We may note that this is long before webcams, but his need for a new toupee is mentioned in the song. Although this song is fictitious, it is reportedly based on a real presenter (Jim Connors) who was 34 at the time this song was released. The age of music presenter question has resurfaced many times. In the license payer funded, and thus market insulated, BBC, there was a purge of the old guard of character presenters, from youth oriented Radio 1, such as Dave Lee Travis (aged 48) in 1993 and, in 2012, Chris Moyles' exit from his Radio 1 show was widely publicly debated as an age issue (he was 38).

Unlike media presenters, in other areas there seems to be no tendency to take age discrimination actions in these cases. Often the presenters continue to be employed but are shifted to "more mature" channels or to off-peak late night shifts. It would be difficult for musicians to take age discrimination claims against radio stations, although we have had petitions from the likes of Status Quo about not being playlisted (see Llewellyn, 2010).

Let us return to the UK punk-rock age conflict. The situation of the victims was wryly summarized in the Jethro Tull album "Too Old to Rock and Roll, too Young to Die". So, what age were these fossilized musicians who were now under threat? Typically they were just past 30 years old. For example, let us just take the three musicians most hated by the insurrectionists, and two from second level "prog" ensembles. From ELP, the ages in 1976 at next birthday were Keith Emerson (32), Greg Lake (29) and Carl Palmer (26), from Caravan, Pye Hastings (29) and, from his own Camel, Pete Bardens (31). In academic life or politics these are the ages of mere striplings, the youthfulness of whom much fuss is made. Of course, like the original Young Turks in their revolution of 1908, the issue here is not mere biological age but the ossification of an established regime. In economic terms, the established regime of musicians and radio presenters constitutes a barrier to entry for the newer younger musicians. Specific taste credo, like the use of very expensive equipment and high skills, constitute further barriers to entry.

None of these age-related cycles of production and consumption are related to a biological decline in physical abilities although they could be construed as equivalent cycles in creativity. Or they may just be symptomatic of fashion.

Coming right up to date, on 12 June 2014, on BBC 6 Music's review (*Steve Lamacq's Roundtable*) of new releases programme, Simon Raymonde (former Cocteau Twin, record label boss and son of a film composer) was heard to say (*rough transcription by the author from podcast*) "I know an old bloke, who is like 52 being asked to comment on music by somebody probably a quarter of my age making music seems a bit strange." Not uncommonly, for musicians, his maths is wrong as poet/rapper Kate Tempest was not 13, but was in fact 27 (and-a-half), thus the more comfortable over half his age. He went on to expand, that her work is universal and thus accessible, as a consumer good, to all ages and social groups. It may however still seem strange that someone so well informed thinks that consumer–producer age gaps are in some way "weird" when we are now in such an amorphous market where it seems the commoditization of music and performers is complete and transcends any attenuation by cult, clique, fanship or tribalism.

The extreme end of the age achievement spectrum can be seen that Leonard Cohen is at the peak of his popularity despite being a very minimal live performer *and* he has had to come back for money which undermines somewhat his poet status. Tony Bennett, in 2011, had his first number one album in the USA at the age of 85, becoming also the oldest artist to attain this position. At the age of 88, "Dracula" star Christopher Lee released his first "full" heavy metal album although he had been working collaboratively in the genre for the previous three to four years. He became the oldest living performer to enter the Billboard Top 10 singles chart at 91-and-a-half years old (deposing Bennett).

It will be interesting, with reference back to Chapter 2 and forward to the next chapter, if we now look at the ages of the world's top ten wealthiest female "singers". This is indicated in Table 7.1.

Adele, Duffy and Joss Stone do not feature here, but this will be partly because of their comparative lack of age. Any successful earner will amass more wealth as they age provided they do not squander the earnings or have it misappropriated from them. Regardless of the sums or the rankings here, it is clear that the work of all these artists is still highly popular and highly regarded and has not been cast on the scrap heap of obsolete consumer items.

These singers have flourished in an age when there has not been a specific cyclical *fin de siècle* "attack" on the old artists as there was in UK punk. In that case, both journalists and the artists conspired to the point where some of the musicians later confessed to deliberately not admitting their liking of some of the older established rich musicians. I will come later to the question of the impact of age on output and productivity of consumers and producers but for the moment let us look at a specific "young kills the old" episode.

TABLE 7.1 Top ten female richest singers by age (in 2014)

		Wealth (net worth in $)	Age
1	Madonna	1.1 billion	52
2	Mariah Carey	250 million	42
3	Barbara Streisand	650 million	70
4	Celine Dion	600 million	44
5	Britney Spears	500 million	30
6	Cher	450 million	65
7	Ayumi Hamasaki	400 million	33
8	Beyonce	390 million	30
9	Janet Jackson	160 million	–
10	Tina Turner	350 million	72

Source: data from www.checktop10.com/top-ten-richest-female-singers-of-the-world-2014/ (accessed 3 June 2014).

Notes
Cher is mistakenly named as much younger UK singer Cher Lloyd. Barbara Streisand's name is given wrongly with the "d" omitted from the last name. The figures do not make literal sense as entries 2 and 9 have estimated wealth which put them in the wrong place.

Who did the Beatles kill?

Probably the first supposed killing off of the old in modern mass market music was the impact the Beatles may have had on finishing careers. Documentaries about UK music typically claim that any performer who was established at the time the Beatles came along had their career ended or seriously threatened. It should be pointed out, for historical accuracy, that the Beatles themselves did not champion any hostility to the status quo of British entertainment. Indeed they were friendly with many of the artists and quite willing to associate with them. To be entirely accurate it is not the Beatles per se that are in question here, it is the "Beat Boom" they under-pinned. Other Liverpudlian artists (such as Gerry Marsden and Billy J. Kramer) had astounding short runs of very high chart success, often using Lennon–McCartney songs which the Beatles did not use, which then evaporated. The UK record market was then left in a state of quite low sales. Subsequent youth oriented singles booms, such as psychedelia (1967) and glam rock (1972–1973) would likewise quickly flare up and dissipate leaving usually just one major sustaining act in their wake (Slade and Pink Floyd respectively – I am discounting David Bowie as being a glam rock act). These sharp cycles suggest that the market is intrinsically hard for older per-formers. Which is, of course, what Stockhausen was pointing out in Chapter 1.

If the "Beatles killed them" is a hypothesis, it is quite a difficult one to test; not least because small sample size and unique events (such as some artists dying at a time which biases the sample quite seriously) make it difficult to use classical statisti-cal techniques. We can only find a small number of highly established artists, with a long enough prior career, who might have suffered significantly. There is the problem that, at the time the Beatles arrived, the seam of output might have been drying up anyway. As we also see in Table 7.2, performance of output was also highly volatile (it is even more so if we look at all chart placings which are not shown here).

Table 7.2 shows a timeline of ten artists by year, from 1957–1963, and then aggregated from 1964 onwards. The numbers are the number of top ten hits in the UK charts with each asterisk representing that one of them was a number one. The artists have been chosen because they had enough success over long enough to make the comparison meaningful. They also need to be "vulnerable" to a degree that Cliff Richard and Elvis would not be. The majority are ballad singers who would also be considered "comfy" family friendly entertainers. The exceptions are Lonnie Donnegan, from the "skiffle" genre, novelty piano virtuoso Russ Conway and fellow Liverpudlian and pioneer UK "rock" stylist Billy Fury (Ronald Wycher-ley). Conway had a mild stroke and a nervous breakdown on stage in the mid-1960s but did continue as a successful live performer. There is perhaps some added irony in that Shirley Bassey's sole post-1963 hit was a cover of the Beatles' "Some-thing". Also, Ray Charles had two low scoring top 50 entries after 1963 (for which he scores zero in the final column) with ill-advised covers of Beatles songs.

The Beatles finally entered the chart in late 1962 (with the aid of some deft buying instituted by their manager Brian Epstein), the Merseybeat explosion took

TABLE 7.2 Who did the Beatles kill? UK Top ten hit singles and number ones, 1957–1996

Name	1957	1958	1959	1960	1961	1962	1963	1964–1996
Shirley Bassey	1	1	1*	1	1*	1	1	1
Billy Fury	0	0	0	1	3	2	3	0
Frankie Vaughan	4*	1	2	0	1*	0	1	1
Petula Clark	2	0	0	0	2	0	0	4
Ray Charles	0	0	0	0	1	2*	0	0
Perry Como	0	4*	0	1	0	0	0	0
Russ Conway	0	1	5*	0	1	0	0	3
Lonnie Donegan	4**	2	2	2*	2	1	0	0
The Shadows (without Cliff Richard)	0	0	0	2*	5*	3**	3	0
Connie Francis	0	2**	2	3	2	0	0	0
Total	11***	11***	12**	10**	18***	9***	8	9*

Source: data from Guinness (1997).

Note
Each asterisk denotes a number one hit.

off in 1963 and by 1964 they had achieved tremendous global market power. The aggregate and individual statistics here seem to support the idea that this timing correlates with falling recorded music fortunes of the artists listed. The average number of number one records per year declines very dramatically as we come to 1964. None of the artists concerned made an effort to specifically accommodate the new music in their output. Donnegan was stuck in a genre which was blowing out and has never had a significant revival of his music, of any type, even to this day. Fury would have liked to change, but was unable to break free from the shackles of his management who judged that the beat boom would pass and sentimental ballads would guarantee a secure future in music. The instrumentals of Conway and the Shadows wilted severely and were not compensated for by new entrants in this genre.

The economic thesis to be found here is that age may not necessarily be physically debilitating but it may lead to a performing sclerosis where artists and managers find it difficult to accommodate and absorb incoming trends. They are subject to elimination by incomers in a highly competitive market where few can be highly successful. We should however point out that ballad singers, identified here, may have faded somewhat in the Beatles era, but some relatively old ballad singers entered the market with success – to wit Val Doonican (38 in 1965), Ken Dodd had a top ten hit in 1960 but his greater success came from 1965 (when he was also 38), whilst Engelbert Humperdinck came to massive success in 1967, aged 31, when his "Release Me" famously denied a number one chart position to the Beatles. Dodd is better known as a comedian whilst Doonican's success was buoyed by being a family entertainer for more than just music.

The success of ballad singers, after 1965, also signals that the Beatles did not actually kill off the independent UK songwriter (usually a pair of men such as Mason–Reed, Cook–Greenaway, Callander–Mitchell). Artists could make more money by writing their own songs but they had to be able to write hit songs. Plus the quirks of the royalty system meant they could even hide their weaker compositions on the "b-side" and make significant money for something that may hardly ever be heard.

Economics, age and music

These are just a few examples but discussion of the relationship between age and music is omnipresent in popular discourse. It does occasionally crop up as an explanatory variable in individual sample-level studies of downloading behaviour. Economists have not shown much interest in the overall age profile of consumers nor have they said much about the role of age in the supply side or production of music. In terms of popular music, this is not surprising as there is very little work full stop, in economics, on the creative production side.

Age may be related to a number of passage of time effects. For individual musicians, creativity may increase to a peak and then decline for a variety of reasons. This is the general expectation about creativity in all fields. For collections of individuals, it may take time to seek out and assemble the right people. Once this ensemble dissolves it may not prove possible to create another highly productive organization. This refers not just to actual musicians but also producers, managers and all related staff.

In all statistical work on human behaviour, isolating a pure effect of age tends to be problematic as its impact tends to be confounded with other key factors. The first of these is experience. Experience cannot possibly be obtained without the passage of time and time cannot pass without the subject getting older. The producer may get more productive due to "learning" effects in experience and the same applies to the consumer.

Consumers may also have increased productivity (in the sense of giving themselves more satisfaction with the same resources) due to greater discernment arising from inspection of the range of options. However, even if this is not increasing, they may still benefit from accumulated knowledge of their preferences of the range of musical products through sampling them. These aspects could, in principle, operate without reference to social interaction such as snob and bandwagon effects. This is what is assumed in the rational addiction model (Becker and Murphy, 1988) where individuals develop a consumption profile over time purely from investing in their original fixed taste patterns.

Consumer income may also be prone to variation with age with this tending to depend on two main factors:

1   occupation;
2   likelihood of marriage and the production of children.

In occupations where physical capacities matter, and the labour market is able to adjust, the individual will eventually encounter declining income as time passes potentially through unemployment rather than a wage cut. Outside this, many individuals will experience a rising profile of income in the earlier part of their career. A standard static microeconomic theory of consumption would overlook the life-cycle pattern of income and treat current music consumption as a function of current income.

Essentially this treats the music collection, or use of music events, as a perishable good which provides a one-off bout of satisfaction, rather than a capital flow over a period of time. The recorded music collection clearly has such a capital aspect, as even a purely digitally owned piece of music will provide returns over time. The case of live music being a form of consumption capital is a little bit more of a philosophical issue. Individual live music experience perishes once its allotted time span is completed. However, the individual can derive satisfaction in the future from recollections, and it is possible that ritualistic consumption of live events can function in the same way as habitual consumption of recorded media. One can particularly notice this in the context of bundled consumption of multiple commodities in the form of festival attendance. This kind of factor is more prevalent now given the mania for people recording live events they have attended and posting them on

YouTube and other outlets. Eventually past live attendance may become part of a nostalgia experience.

There may be age-related substitution effects in the delivery media for music consumption. If technology stayed the same, and physically owned media had low obsolescence, then the older a person was they would have an increasingly larger collection with presumably less and less incentive to add to it unless they had some degree of strong addiction or omnivorousness. Further the less intense consumer, could increasingly switch to simply listening to radio (or now streaming services which are essentially presenterless radio).

Where the number of radio stations has increased, in the world, the content has to a largely extent been of much older music. This is branded as "classic" implying it has stood the test of time and is thus a high quality product rather than "nostalgia" a subject to which we return below.

The consumer may be subject to self-imposition of restrictions in consumption, due to the kind of social effects hinted at in the remarks by Ramonde discussed earlier. They may feel that they should not be consuming certain types of music or attending live events beyond a certain age. Older consumers' consumption can and has been piqued by technology. In the era of peak CD sales this came from the twin drive of improvements in playing equipment and the extension of catalogue. The diversity of catalogue repertoire greatly increased as many items not previously available were issued, especially the less well-known classical music composers.

Suppliers of music may experience similar effects to consumers but they are diametrically opposed in their relationship to the marketplace. The consumer does not have to consume music, but the specialized music producer has to either quit for another profession or change the idiom of music, within which they operate, if there is a persistent shortfall of income relative to their needs.

Statistical evidence

According to Nicholson (2005, p. 81), in his discussion of the possible death of jazz, in 2002 the share of consumers over 45 for all recorded music had doubled since 1992 to 23.7 per cent with buyers aged over 30 now being 36.1 per cent of the market (this is based on RIAA (Recording Industry Association of America) data for the US market). He asserts that Norah Jones' "Come Away With Me" sold 17 million units worldwide in 2002–2003 because of the ageing market, although he has no way of knowing the identity of the buyers of this specific record. This claim does make the point that sales do not follow the simple "consumer sovereignty" model of introductory economics. Major corporations made a conscious decision to push "old" oriented product. If they had shown inertia on this front, global aggregate sales would have been less. On p. 86 (ibid.) Nicholson makes a totally unsubstantiated remark "Generally speaking thirty plus consumers were past the point of wanting to be moved, or inspired by pop." Being pedantic, we should note we do not actually know the age distribution of Norah Jones buyers or indeed any other artist. One of the major problems with such a remark, bar the mind-reading aspect, is the definitional problem of genres – the category of "pop" is now a very problematic term as we have seen with respect to the discussion of blackness in Chapter 2.

We have established, in Chapter 4, the problem of all statistical data in the music arena, having a potentially wide confidence interval surrounding estimates. The more fundamental problem of whether any data exists in the first place also devils this topic. The long run of historical chart data, from a huge number of nations, does not convey any information at all about age of the consumers. This is the case whether or not it is based on sampling of retail outlets or on radio plays. It is thus not really possible to have a detailed historical analysis of shifts in the age pattern of consumption of recorded music. The shorter run of Nielsen soundscan data does not give us this information; we would require commercial linking information to the credit cards of consumers.

One could make certain inferences about age from the composition of genres predominating in charts, e.g. that the classical music or country and western audience may typically be older but genres against which they could be compared tend to be too broad to be of much use.

We can make inferences from some types of data about the ageing of the market. The chief dedicated historical evidence is to be found in the work by the RIAA cited by Nicholson. The older population share for this source is given in Table 7.3, which goes up to 2008 when the data provision changed. This does indeed give us very juicy headline figures if we focus on the period when CD was becoming king. The share of 45+ purchases rose from 10.1 per cent in 1989 to 33.7 per cent in 2008.

The aggregate figures do not readily allow us to cross-refer this by genre. We can note that religious music had increased at times during the period. However, rock fell from 40.7 to 30.8 per cent and it was, like country, quite volatile as a share. "Urban" music (rap and r'n'b combined) rose from 11.9 to 20.9 per cent. It is not very volatile although it had reached higher shares earlier. We can see that the combined rock and urban share has been about 50 per cent but it is difficult to be sure how much that tracks age of consumers.

This data is collected from telephone surveys of 3,000, or just over, people. It has been conducted by different companies in different years. It is therefore not a panel survey; it is different people every year. The figures are grossed up and discussed as if they were for the whole of the USA. When we break down to subgroups and cross-classify them (e.g. x gender, x ethnicity, x genre) we would get down to really quite small numbers. The most conspicuous quirk in these figures is that the series is fairly stable but there are two sudden huge jumps in one year, for 45+s. It is over six percentage points in 1999 and in 2008 it was almost nine percentage points. This is outside the typical figures for a 95 per cent confidence interval, based on the sampling error figures given in the reports. However it does not revert, i.e. the new higher levels are maintained. It is difficult to take these sudden ratchet swings at face value which does cast some doubt on the accuracy of the level estimates. There are several indications in the 2007–2008 notes of how the sampling was done to deal with changing habits of young users that suggest possible

TABLE 7.3 Share of recorded music consumption market value for the 45+ age group in the USA

Year	%
1989	10.2
1990	11.1
1991	11.8
1992	12.2
1993	14.1
1994	15.4
1995	16.1
1996	15.1
1997	16.5
1998	18.1
1999	24.7
2000	23.8
2001	23.7
2002	25.5
2003	26.8
2004	26.4
2005	26.5
2006	26.1
2007	24.8
2008	33.7

Source: data from telephone surveys conducted for RIAA (Recording Industry Association of America).

Note
Taken from various years of publications by RIAA.

inconsistency. It is, of course, possible that age differential trends reflect age differentials in not paying for music obtained digitally.

There is some recent one-off evidence. The YouGov "Music Consumption" report in the UK, in 2012, identified age decrements in own CD listening as the preferred delivery medium. For men over 40, greater than 75 per cent had this preference whilst for 25–39 year olds it fell to 59 per cent and for 16–24 years old it fell to 41 per cent. For women the corresponding figures were, >75 per cent, 62 per cent and 49 per cent. These are unlikely to be static cohort effects, that is as the younger groups eventually make it into the older groups their CD preference rates will be unlikely to rise up to their precursors' levels. This will offset any long-term "greying of the market" effects on overall sales depending on the relative take up of digital delivery in the long run.

I turn now to econometric evidence from the mainstream positivistic, hypothesis testing, paradigm which dominates cultural economics. Falk and Falk (2011) used ordered probit models for over 350,000 people aged 16+ in 24 European countries, in 2006, to look at the determinants of number of live performance attendances over one year. This does not specifically separate out the forms of entertainment being studied and thus does not provide specific results for music. They review a number of previous studies which have looked at the impact of age on live event performance. Of these only Favaro and Frateschi (2007) and Hand (2009) look specifically at music. The general consensus from all live arts studies is that age has a statistically significant and numerically large negative impact on live attendance.

Favaro and Frateschi look at the wider issue of "style" of consumption in terms of univores versus omnivores. An omnivore will consume a wide range of types of musical genre in a wide range of formats including live, recorded, broadcast, streaming etc. Their research is based on an Italian multipurpose culture and leisure participation survey. They find age to be a statistically significant predictor of segmentation with "snobs" more likely to be older. It also predicts decreasing consumption of both live and recorded music with age. The assessment of age, in this study, is more narrowly calibrated than in other studies. The "reference" group in the estimating equations is those aged under 30 with there being dummy variables for 30–44, 45–64 and 65+. These are very wide groups covering periods during which there may be dramatic changes in family events.

Hand (2009) follows a similar path to Favaro and Frateschi using the "Taking Part" survey of 28,000+ UK participants. His evidence suggests that there is a significant impact of increasing age on the likelihood of becoming a univore (in such areas as jazz and classical music) and, again, more pointedly becoming a "snob" consumer.

Falk and Falk's study finds statistically significant negative age impacts for 17 of the 24 EU countries studied. They also include a separate variable for pensionable age, in addition to a linear age in years variable. This is also statistically significant and negative. The impact of age is simulated in their Graph 2 which shows predicted probability of *no* live performance attendance, of any type, rising from 0.4 to almost 0.8 from the ages of 16 to 80 in an almost linear fashion. There is relatively little change in the high attendance categories (seven-plus attendances) past the mid-40 years old but these are already at a low base (probabilities of not >0.1 at any time).

They speculate (ibid., p. 13) that the absence of a significant age effect in some countries (Austria, Finland, Germany, UK) may be due to a greater dominance of "high" arts versus low arts in those countries. For music this may be taken to mean classical music and opera (or possibly also jazz) versus the nebulous category of "popular" music. They admit to having no basis for this extraordinary claim and suggest it requires further research. One has to infer what the basis of it is. It would seem to be that if we accepted a split into "high" and "low" we then have a two-sector model with potentially different rates of age decrement. If the "popular" sector has a more severe age decrement then we end up with the prediction offered. Even if this were correct, there would still need to be assessment of the relative size of the two sectors.

Favaro and Frateschi's specific study of music seems to be pulling in the same direction. On p. 217, they make the extraordinary claim that "popular music" is a "peculiarly juvenile enterprise". Given the crude grain of division of data, it is clear that they are not talking just about aficionados of S Club 7, the Bay City Rollers or One Direction but the whole sweep of mainstream music from Frank Sinatra to Bob Dylan and U2 and so on. This seems to neglect not only the descriptive data we began this section with, but also the long established embodiment of such artists into "serious" discussion by professors of Literature and Music and regular reviews and coverage in upmarket newspapers and magazines. Perhaps the cementing of the "adultification" of such music occurred in the boom in monthly music magazines taking the place of more ephemeral weekly titles. The repositioning in culture of rock and other popular musics as "serious" work worthy of deep analysis was documented in sociological writing a long time ago (Regev, 1994).

There are some additional factors that would potentially offset age decrement in the supposed "high" culture sector. These are hearing change and pricing differentials. As shown elsewhere in this chapter, individuals typically experience profound age-related hearing changes that do not necessarily have to entail any kind of deafness or hard of hearing categorization. The non-popular music concerts may tend to be less loud and have less of certain frequency content and more of others.

The pricing differential is hinted at, in some explanations, via the potential differential rates of subsidy to different genres in some countries. Popular music events are available in copious quantities at a wide range of prices. They are also sometimes subsidized in that local councils, in the UK, will underwrite festivals and even offer free events in the summertime.

There may however still be more older-age discounts on offer for the supposed "high culture" sector.

In Ewoudou's (2008) study of Canada, a similar pattern is shown to the above studies. Using the raw data in Chart 2 (ibid., p. 10) (using 2005 data), we can see age profiles for movies, music, videos, books and magazines in terms of broadly defined cultural participation.

Participation here seems to mean any sort of activity other than the more narrow sense in which the person would be performing or producing. The music category declines continually from age 15 to age 60+ falling from 90 to 70 per cent. However, the comparative declines of movies and videos are much sharper.

In the econometric work, age is not treated primarily as a cultural variable but as a control for other things such as taste formation and health and employment status. It is found to have a statistically significant negative effect for music (as well as movies and videos) when other variables are controlled for, unlike theatre, historic, galleries and books where the opposite effect is found. One might be tempted to see this bifurcation of art forms as showing substitution from more intense and stimulus driven activities to more sedate and reflective ones. Thus, the limited econometric evidence on age would tend to suggest that its increase tends to promote declining live attendance, increases in snobbery and general univoriousness.

Montoro-Pons *et al.* (2013) use the 2010–2011 Survey for Cultural Habits and Practices in Spain. The sample size for the study is 14,486. Their focus is on attendance at live musical events in terms of whether people attend or not and frequency of attending if they do attend. The majority (typically 88 per cent) are non-attenders. They include a quadratic for age giving the rationale that this is for non-linearity. One presumes it is for non-monotonicity. In all forms of their equations, there are no instances of both age terms (age and age squared) being statistically significant. Either one is, or the other, but not both. This implies the absence of a quadratic effect. The impact is negative suggesting a declining participation with age as in other studies. This paper does not provide any indication of the relative magnitude of the effects.

There are however a number of critical observations which need to be made about these studies. Some revolve around the "grain" of data rather than its accuracy per se, some about the lack of more detailed exploration of age and some about the problematic nature of attributions of univorousness/omnivorousness in consumption. These problems are intertwined with each other.

The first main issue is that these are *not* longitudinal studies. They do not follow a panel of respondents through their life to assess how specific individuals change in terms of their music consumption as they get older. It is hard to imagine how such data could ever exist due to changes in tastes and other factors making it difficult to devise a set of questions four or five decades ago that would still be meaningful today. The data only measures a cross-section of people who are of different ages at the same point in time. This means they cannot track the kinds of factors that were earlier identified in descriptive statistics and commentaries.

Further we have the problem of the coarse grains of age and of musical genre category. That is, using very wide intervals of age brackets makes it difficult to address many of the questions about diversity of voracity, snobbery etc. The use of dummies for age groups does allow for such possibilities as we can have coefficient sign changes as we move up in age. However the use of a coarse grain of age makes non-monotonicity more difficult to detect as it may be hidden within the broad age bands used. The quadratic form used by Montoro-Pons *et al.* (2013) is limited by the imposition of symmetry.

The datasets used in such studies are limited, to a large extent, by the fact that they were not designed for the purpose of exploring music consumption. They are general purpose cultural activity studies which yield some musical data more as a by-product.

There is a clear suggestion, in the literature, that increasing age leads to a decline in omnivorousness and an increase in snobbery, these two not being necessarily coterminous. However, we must finally face the issue of how applicable food survival analogies are to musical choice. Apart from the data not being longitudinal, it is also general purpose data which has not been explicitly designed and collected for the express purpose of performing economic analysis of cultural consumption.

We are also well aware the sheer number of musical genres has been mushrooming which makes analyses divided merely into, no more than, classical versus popular versus jazz seem all the more quaint. Claiming (as some do by inference) that some of the small range of categories are "high" (i.e. better quality) culture and others are "low" (worse quality) seems to rest on even more shaky ground. Someone could be a solely classical music listener who might be regarded as very omnivorous or not omnivorous at all.

There is, despite these reservations, a clear implication in the research cited that music consumption in terms of actual spending declines with age. This may seem contradictory to the claims that markets are "greying" but this depends not just on propensity to consume but the weight of the group in the population.

Consumer decline

Leaving aside social aspects, there is one central aspect of age in relation to music. This is the physical decline in individuals that may matter more or less in other areas in certain respects. The issues are not quite the same for consumers and producers. But each requires sufficient hearing to receive audio signals and appropriate mental faculties to process the signals. To listen, the only physical prerequisite beyond this is the ability to turn on equipment and search for sounds although someone else can do this. Attending live events will be impacted by physical decline as it will be more difficult to get to, and endure, the performances. Loss of memory will impair both producers' and consumers' performance.

Hearing decline will not be equal at all frequencies. In theory, this could lead to a rational economic switch of genre choice that is not due to other cultural and taste changes. Different genres of music tend to show different preferences for the density of use of different sound frequencies. Human hearing is usually enumerated as ranging at maximum from 20 Hz to 20 kHz although some sound reproduction equipment does emit lower frequencies and sound processing, in the digital realm, is carried out at higher frequencies. Even for the most gifted hearer there is a roll off towards the end of the spectrum. According to Moller (2006), humans have a maximum aural range that begins as low as 12 Hz under ideal laboratory conditions to 20 kHz in most children and some adults. The range shrinks during life, usually beginning at around age of eight with the upper frequency limit being reduced. Women typically experience a lesser degree of hearing loss than men, with a later onset. Men have approximately 5 to 10 dB greater loss in the upper frequencies by age 40. The general consensus on gender differences in age-related hearing loss is that much of it would be explained by differences in occupation as historically men have been exposed to significantly more workplace noise.

Deaf or death? The risks of musical labour

Performers are subject to the same physical ageing processes as consumers. For someone involved in making music it might seem that their long-term future is jeopardized by the data just presented but, are there additional problems not faced by consumers? Subjective well-being research would tend to suggest that music benefits consumers. However, some research leads us in the direction of wondering whether a musician's life puts one on the road to hearing loss and/or an early grave.

As an occupation, being a musician exposes one to risks and diseases that are found in many occupations including electrocution. There are specific problems that may be heightened by the marketization of music in terms both of standard economic competition and of performance competition. These divide into two main areas – hearing related and repetitive movement related. In the latter case standard RSI (repetitive strain injury) and musician's dystonia – for example curled fingers from prolonged piano playing. In the case of hearing, there is general hearing loss, frequency specific hearing loss and disturbance due to excessive concentration in precise listening (acusis, hyperacusis). In a fully (socially) efficient labour market, wage differentials and insurance premia would adjust to reflect these – for example, in theory there should be wage premia for the more "at risk" instrument skills. In practice, employers of musicians will not necessarily be driven to the market to offer such compensations in wages.

Musicians themselves may also under-insure due to myopia, tergiversation or excessive optimism. They may also operate in a world of denial about the onset of these problems because of the fear of declining employment and earnings. In economic terms, there may be a perception issue in employer behaviour as regards productivity. If an orchestral musician ends up with a medical diagnosis of some significant hearing loss, this would not necessarily diminish their productivity as this is routinized in a way that does not inevitably require minutely accurate monitoring of all aspects of sound. And we have to mention here that there is a prominent solo deaf musician (Dame Evelyn Glennie).

The main interest to us is hearing loss (HL)-related aspects. Some of the recent research on these strives to separate musician specific effects from normal age-related hearing loss (presbycusis). However, it is surprising that many studies pay relatively little attention to age as a factor. In some cases, this would be difficult in any case because the samples are so small.

Sometimes age is taken into account but only as a control factor. It is not investigated in its own right to any great degree. The effects being discussed here are not generally pure age effects but rather "passage of time" effects.

Research in the area comes from occupational health and medicine scholars and has tended to base its metrics on general occupational health work which uses noise levels in industry as the base line. The simplistic approach is to determine that a musician is at risk, if the decibel level of typical and peak experiences exceed the prescribed numerical values in industrial settings. Not surprisingly, attention to musical noise risk emerged in the mid-1960s with the perception that the unprecedentedly high levels of amplification used in rock music would wreak havoc with tender ears. It should be noted that the academic studies, such as Speaks *et al.*'s (1970) study of ten rock bands (54 musicians) refers to the music played as "noise". The general thrust of such early studies was that amplified guitar band music did not typically exceed threshold danger levels but there might be a long-run risk.

It is perhaps ironic, that the balance of evidence seems to suggest that the risks for classical musicians (generally in orchestras) are much greater than that for rock and pop musicians. This is not contingent on the increasing trend for rock/pop musicians to wear ear defenders on stage as this is a comparatively recent phenom-enon. Palin (1994) reviewed the literature for classical music and noted (p. 135) that ear defenders will be ineffective for some instruments due to vibration.

The problems of classical musicians are different from those of musicians who work primarily with amplification or electronic instruments. The proximity of loud acoustic instruments to the ear is potentially more damaging and there is also docu-mentation of the problem of asymmetry – that the significant hearing loss is in the ear on the side of the instrument. It has also been shown that there are significant hearing facility drops in different frequency bands according to the instrument played. These issues are strongly linked to the large amount of time spent in per-sonal practice (Behar *et al.*, 2006). Orchestral musicians are also effectively forced, by their employment, to sit through loud passages generated by their colleagues. The impact of this is mediated by the physical layout of where players are on the stage. This may explain the surprising finding that percussion players suffer less than wind and string players. They have louder instruments in terms of individual one-off exposure but they are further away and are generally inactive for longer periods.

The most interesting rock-pop specific study was conducted by Axelsson *et al.* (1995) who remeasured 83 Swedish and British performers 16 years after they had first been studied in 1975. This found next to no evidence of any hearing deteriora-tion despite continuous exposure to high dB levels. They offer some unexpected explanations. Specifically, that positive attitudes may have helped and that there may have been endogenous muscular contraction for the purposes of self-protection.

The most comprehensive sample study of musician hearing effects is by Schink *et al.* (2014) who used German insurance records, from 2004–2008, using a sample of 2,227 musicians with over two million non-musicians. However, this can only document reported HL and subcategories thereof. It has no additional measure-ment of the environments the individuals operate in (which includes the type of music) or their circumstances beyond basic demographic data. It may also be biased due to musicians being in denial and concealing their losses. Age is used as a control variable in the multivariate analysis used to construct incidence ratios for musicians versus non-musicians. There is consistent evidence of more pronounced incidence of HL amongst musicians by a considerable margin.

Although age is specifically taken into account in determining incidence, there is a shortage of investigation of how the age–HL profiles vary between types of musi-cian and musicians versus non-musicians controlling for other variables. There is some suggestion in some studies that musicians, because of their developed hearing, have better resistance per se to presbycusis than others (Zendel and Alain, 2011).

Age-related deterioration highlights the need for insurance. In Thomson (2010), the Future of Music Coalition (FMC) conducted an online survey of 1,451 USA musicians' health insurance coverage: 33 per cent said they did not have health insurance which was nearly twice the estimated national average rate. This might be expected due to greater self-employed status and lower income. A total of 86 per cent of respondents without coverage said they could not afford it, however FMC discovered that some musicians who think they cannot afford coverage may not be fully aware of available public options.

It is perhaps not surprising that musical employment may contribute to whether or not one is increasingly deaf, and underinsured, but death is a more unexpected matter. The idea of "living fast and dying young" is a cliché within pop-rock circles. Bellis *et al.* (2007) seek to quantify this using data on 1,064 famous/successful European and North American rock and pop "stars". The sample is selected primarily from a list of the top 1,000 albums of all time, compiled from the opinion of 200,000+ people in the year 2000. The study identifies differences between the population of stars and the general public's mortality rates, and between Europe and North America which change as the individuals survive to an older age. Calculations are made, based on years since achieving fame, and age and gender standardized mortality rates are used to compare with the general population. Both territories show much higher expected mortality for the musical stars, than for the general public, in the first 30 years after fame. But, after 25 years of fame, the European stars actually start to have better survival rates than the *general* North American population and come close to matching the *general* European population. Survival rates for the American stars decline rapidly from year one of fame onwards; from 100 per cent to just above 70 per cent which is over 20 percentage points behind the European group.

These are very striking results. Unfortunately there is no actual use of explanatory variables to try to account for the differences in the study. The explanations that are offered are untested and indeed almost untestable. They amount to speculation about the differences in pressure in different societies and quite a lot of suggestion of peer group effects. For example, that certain sectors of the music market in the USA in the 1960s and 1970s set a template for dangerous drug abuse that others would seek to follow. There is no specific discussion of suicide in this paper.

For classical musicians from the vintage nineteenth century crop, Borowiecki and Kavetsos (2011), also present evidence that their life expectancy is impacted by peer effects that they cannot actually measure. A total of 144 composers are studied. The results of the regression equations suggest that locating in a hub or nodal centre, for their trade, actually reduces life expectancy. At one point, they suggest that a composer's life expectancy will be reduced by three years if just one more rival comes to inhabit the centre of production they are in! It is difficult to identify the direct factors that may explain the measured impacts. Speculation is made about the impact of stress from the environment but there is, of course, no meaningful measure of individual stress available.

Nostalgia and Indian Summers: the market position of age

The gist of the above and our next discourse is that the named artist (i.e. not just a jobbing player) may have a U-shaped career from fame if they do not die at some point along the U. That is, early success followed by decline with a possible upturn in later years. For successful recording artists, the upturn may come when an old record resurfaces perhaps in a film or advertising campaign. For jobbing musicians in more niche areas they may be fortunate to experience an upturn in fortunes of the niche.

One problem with age is that one's IPRs are also getting older and subject to the laws of extension in the territory. These vary by country and between composer and performer in some instances. In the USA, the Sonny Bono Copyright Term Extension Act 1998, raised sound copyright terms to 95 years thus meaning the owner would receive income through all their lifetime and there would be some inheritance. European Union law has been under debate since 2005 with some in the UK not happy about harmonizing with its 50 years as opposed to the USA's 95 years. The 50-year term by 2005 would begin to take income away from living artists from the coming of pop-rock dominance. Thus we had lobbying not just from the BPI (British Phonographic Institute) but also such people as Ian Anderson (Jethro Tull) and most notably Cliff Richard for a 95-year term.

An analysis of the various arguments can be found in Gowers (2006, pp. 48–57) and a technical economic treatment of the subject of droit de suite can be found in Solow (1998).

Many of the arguments are not related to this chapter. The chief one which is, the "Cliff Richard pension fund hypothesis" which was extensively discussed in the House of Commons with reference to his extensive lobbying. MP Michael Connarty provided the case for low income musicians outside the charts. He cites the specific case of Tommy Whittle relying on income from old recordings with the BBC orchestras and other jazz big bands to sustain him and his wife, who was a singer, in their old age. Shorter terms of protection mean that work passes into public domain and can be issued and broadcast without paying royalties to those who previously had rights. For an economist, the pension fund argument is not a satisfactory one as it seems to be using the wrong instrument to tackle a policy target. Musicians face risks of age poverty by choice of occupation therefore either they should quit or if we wish to support the non-quitters some form of general income transfer should be instituted.

The upturn may be the market phenomenon of an "Indian Summer", where an artist is rediscovered and/or otherwise experiences increased demand at a late age or is even subject to their first burst of market success at a late age. Surprisingly there is no conventional statistical research specifically testing any hypotheses about the impact of high age on the careers of performers. The analysis of Billboard chart hits by psychologists Pettijohn and Sacco (2009a) refers to "mature" performers in its title. However, they are not using the term as a euphemism for being biologically old but rather in terms of *not* having a juvenile appearance. They use pictures to compute physical measures of aspects of eyes, chins and lips as the measure of maturity. They even go so far as to average these across individuals where the lead singer of an ensemble changed. Actual age is not considered in this analysis at all but they suggest taking it into account in the future.

The "Indian Summer" may or may not be connected with nostalgia. The connection with nostalgia is not necessarily a simple one-to-one explicit mapping. That is, we cannot guarantee that once successful artists can expect a "windfall" of nostalgia income at some unspecified age. As nostalgia has only been mentioned once before this section, it is time to give it a more explicit economic consideration. The connection of age with nostalgia is axiomatic. The longer you live, the more opportunities you have to be nostalgic and the more past things to be nostalgic about. This does not prevent quite young people from being nostalgic, nor does it force old people to be so. In theory we could have a 17-year-old who is more nostalgic about their music than a 70-year-old, who is equally keen on its consumption.

We could regard nostalgia as a characteristic inherent in certain goods, or as a commodity in its own right, which is produced using inputs of other goods. In the former case, consumers may have induced nostalgia from certain sounds, instruments or styles in music.

For example, I have heard fairly recently reviewers express nostalgia over the use of drum machines like those found on Marvin Gaye records. There is no specific pining for a lost or better world of "real" sounds here just simply association with something that is in the past. The household production of nostalgia can be found in full scale where people add to the musical inputs by such things as dressing up, and engaging in other period specific consumption, such as in the case of tribute acts. The study of celebrity worship by Evans *et al.* (2009) discussed in the previous chapter, showed statistically that nostalgia was a strong factor.

In terms of rational choice consumer theory, nostalgia is essentially of a capital good nature and could, therefore, come under the category of addiction. There is an incentive for sellers to capitalize on nostalgia by consolidating it into specific products which target this emotion. Nostalgia is subjective and can be enhanced by a consumer, without generating any extra revenue for sellers – they could simply get out their old records, or concert tickets, or phone videos and watch them again without spending any more money. The explicit monetization of nostalgia therefore tends to require social network effects. Specifically that people are sharing a common bond with "their" generation. This tends to lead to the live arena as the place where nostalgia is minted into money.

As an emotion, nostalgia is specifically linked to ideas of loss as in the past being a time when things were simpler, better etc., or one had more hopes, prospects, a better physical appearance and so on. It could also simply be a reliving of certain experiences which were pleasurable thereby rebooting this capital asset in the stock of consumption. But even this has a sense of loss aspect. We may briefly cite some specific cases. The tribute band scene (see Chapter 5) links heavily to nostalgia. However, tours by Bob Dylan and the Rolling Stones would seem not to be primarily nostalgic but rather museum events where people flock to see these musical dinosaurs consecrating their canon. There are two factors mitigating against heavy nostalgia in those cases:

1   They are not reunion tours. The Rolling Stones have never formally split up and a solo artist cannot split up.
2   Both have maintained a high level of success.

A lull in success may precipitate nostalgia at return or reunion as the fan may identify themselves with the star thinking that some of their former youth aspirations and achievements could, likewise, return. These factors are antagonistic to the peaking of a collective feeling of a lost shared past experience. More pertinent cases are the package tours of semi-forgotten musicians which tend to focus on 1960s beat/pop music and 1980s "cheesy" pop and "New Romantic" music. The latter has become a successful franchise starting with "Here and Now" tours in the 1990s, continuing now as the "Rewind" package and also consolidated in some local two- to three-day music festivals in the UK. These market bundles do *not* major on authenticity as often a phalanx of session musicians provide the input. So long as some key personnel are present, the packages are deemed acceptable. Some of the local festivals actually mix reunion acts, with original stars, with tribute acts to those who are still successful on the same bill (such as Take That).

In contrast, the real money in nostalgia is to be made from the middle-aged who crave authenticity and revelled in hedonism during the peak period for the acts such as the Happy Mondays. The Stone Roses reunion of 2012 provoked a storm of economic activity that would have Stockhausen turning in his grave muttering about musical drugs. Newspaper reports suggested that they would make £8.25 million but, with the addition of an extra show (making three gigs in total), it is estimated that they earned £16.5 million with approaching 25 per cent of this from merchandise alone.[1] A staggering achievement without issuing a note of new music.

To be fair, this case had the added factor that their early career was severely attenuated by various factors thus meaning there was pent-up demand for performances and recordings that never took place which might reasonably have been anticipated to occur. Also the acrimony between the members prior to the reunion adds a tinge of soap-opera-esque life affirmation to the narrative. Reunions of such diverse acts as Madness, Take That and Duran Duran have whipped up a storm of renewed activity in their products which has even proved sustainable to some degree. In contrast, reunions of female acts have proved problematic. The Spice Girls' return and their "jukebox" musical have both flopped dismally. The stunning case of an outlier in the reunion stakes is Bananarama who were record breaking successes in their heyday (they still hold the record for most chart entries in the world by a female ensemble) but have come back numerous times with recordings that were not released or sold little. Their career is now largely confined to the nostalgia package tour.

The Indian Summer refers to artists making money in older age because they are discovered, or rediscovered, and held up as worthy of consumption, by those too young to remember their earlier work. Rehabilitation probably began with the case of Tom Jones which was masterminded by his son and initially involved him working with Art of Noise on songs by Prince. The doyen of rehabilitation was Rick Rubin whose highest profile case was Johnny Cash.

More recently Jones has followed the Rubin style in his latest work (2013) "Praise and Blame" where he goes for a stripped down bluesy "authentic" style that his record company would not have allowed in his heyday.

For cases with no prior success, we may notice the reluctant success of British singer Bill Fay, which finally came in 2012, and the curious emergence of Seasick Steve who will be considered first. Seasick Steve released his first album, at the age of 60, in 2001, after a life often spent busking. His popularity exploded in the UK, following a television appearance on Jools Holland's annual *Hootenanny* BBC TV show on New Year's Eve 2006. He won the Mojo award for best breakthrough act at the age of 66. His UK sales by age are shown in Table 7.4.

He has gone on to numerous awards, tours and popular exposure. We may well ask why?

Did his productivity suddenly shoot up after a lifetime of investment in experiences and musical craft? Harking back to Chapter 2, he attributes his success to "magic", specifically his three-string "trance wonder" guitar purchased for $75, is clearly not a piece of high tech equipment of glamorous proportions. According to him a friend

> says to me, "I didn't tell you when you bought it off me, but that guitar used to be haunted". I say, – we'd leave it over in the potato barn and we'd come back in and it would be moved. You'd put it down somewhere and the next morning you'd come back and it would have moved. When you took that guitar the ghost in the barn left.

At the age of around 65–67 (one presumes as his age does not seem to be listed) Bill Fay, found himself seriously in the market, for the first time, in 2012 having been dropped by his record label in 1970 and dropping out of view. Fay was active in the music industry from 1967–1970 beginning essentially as a Bob Dylan-derivative artist. His 2012 album had major chart success in some key territories and rave reviews. He largely shunned publicity, performing and donating the money to charity despite not being wealthy.

The paradigmatic rediscovery case is David Bowie. "The Next Day" was released in 2013 (when he was 66) without any of the normal overt promotion of mainstream commercial work. Bowie had made earlier ill-received attempts to accommodate to new trends particularly his "Tin Machine" era (1989–1991). His

TABLE 7.4 Seasick Steve – UK chart positions by age

Age at release	Chart position at release
63	198
65	36 Gold
67	9 Platinum
68	4 Gold
70	6 Gold
72	14

Source: data from Official Charts Company (www.officialcharts.com (accessed 5 June 2014)).

2013 record majored on using his age and fragility as tokens of authenticity. Critics and fans latched on to this and it shot to success. It was number one in the independent record store charts, and the official album charts, in the UK. At the point of release it was the best selling album of the year in the UK. It actually debuted at number one in the UK, Belgium, Czech Republic, Denmark, Finland, Germany, Ireland, Netherlands, New Zealand, Portugal, Sweden and Switzerland and topped iTunes charts in 64 countries.

It would be hard to attribute such a blanket market dominance to nostalgia or simply to the work being of high quality in an era when the supply of quality is low (as some eulogistic reviews claimed). It would seem to be a global involvement bandwagon type of event where consumers felt left out if they did not join in. It clearly marks the power of pulling in consumers who are not regular buyers. It caps the trend for rehabilitation that would have been unthinkable when the Beatles may have been killing the grinning showbiz entertainers of 1960s Britain.

Conclusion

This chapter has considered the role of age in the music marketplace. We have looked at the physical and social aspects of ageing in terms of production and consumption. In the next chapter, we move away from the person-related matters of the last three chapters and look at issues surrounding musical trade flows between countries and regions.

Note

1 See www.gigwise.com/news/74210/stone-roses-%C2%A3165m-payday-from-heaton-park-gigs (accessed 21 June 2014).

8

GENDER

Role of gender

There are gender divisions in both consumption and production – some of which were hinted at in Chapter 2. There is comparatively little attention to gender divisions, in analysis of markets, other than bipartite male–female division so I shall concentrate on that.

Gender and the demand for music

Somewhat inevitably discussion of evidence will have to focus on simple male–female data differences. The aggregate published RIAA data, for the USA, which was discussed in the last chapter does identify if the consumers are male or female but it is of limited usefulness. The male/female share is quite volatile within a narrow range. If there is any distinct pattern, it is from the late 1990s. Before then the female share was prone to drop as low as 46–47 per cent but after 1997 it seldom falls much below 50 per cent and sometimes goes above it. Some newspaper discussions, at the time of the first Lilith fair (which is discussed below), got rather carried away with this late 1990s shift going so far as to suggest that the music buying market was becoming female dominated.

There is little research which deals with household as opposed to individual behaviour. This is partly because the conveniently available datasets are collected on an individual or household basis without couple matching. A rare exception is Upright (2004), which is a general study of attendance at arts events with limited grain in the music data (only musicals and classical) using a matched spouse sample of 1,147 people in 1992. The basic descriptive statistics show live event attendance with and without partner. Women's overall attendance is higher for classical music and musicals. This is said to be consistent with theories of a gendered division of

cultural labour, men's attendance is more strongly influenced by spousal characteristics than is women's attendance. I should point out that even this data is concate-
nated from individual responses – it is not actually collected using joint observations
of couples.

There are a number of studies of aspects of consumption which simply use a
female/male dummy variable without taking any account of relationships, other
than also possibly adding marital status and children dummies. These studies control
for a number of other important factors the most important being level of education and past musical education.

The Spanish study by Montoro-Pons *et al.* (2013) of live music attendance, discussed in the previous chapter, finds a female dummy to be statistically significantly
negative in most of the equations. One of their estimation methods also finds consistent statistically significant positive effects of children. This is an anomaly in terms
of expectations but no explanation is offered, in the paper, other than to express
surprise and note that there is some reverse effect of younger children (under ten
years old).

Dejean *et al.* (2014) use a male dummy variable which shows a statistically significant greater likelihood of attending local and international concerts, for males, in
a sample of just over 2,000 French internet users. However there are no significant
male–female differences in the purchase of classical CDs or the total amount of
music streamed. Nor is there any gender effect in the likelihood of ever having used
paid downloads to obtain music.

Turning to the issue of differential omnivorousness which was introduced in the
previous chapter, there is some evidence in the papers discussed there. Falk and
Falk (2011) find women are more likely to attend live events than men, but this
varies widely amongst the 24 countries studied. Favaro and Frateschi's (2007) Italian
study uses a gender dummy (female) and some marital status and age of children
dummies. From the estimated equations, females are more likely to listen to
recorded music "often" versus "infrequent" listening. There is no gender difference for the separate categories of "only listen to classical music" and "only listen
to popular music". For live concerts the results are strikingly different. The all
music result is the same, as for recorded music, *but* for "only classical" women are
more likely to fall in this group while the opposite is found for the only popular
music group. My indication of difference here is in terms of statistical significance.

In Ewoudou's (2008) study of Canada, the "sex" dummy is actually 1 for male
and 0 for female (as was DeJean *et al.*) so in terms of more normal nomenclature it
is a "male" dummy and it is the opposite way round from the gender dummy used
by Favaro and Frateschi. The raw descriptive statistics show little sign of male–
female difference. Their estimated equations reveal a more complex gender effect
for music listening in Canada. Men are more likely than women to be occasional
listeners. But, when women listen, they are more likely than men to be regular
listeners. Regular listening rises when a conjugal partner's education rises, which is
consistent with the work of Upright cited above. Probably the most interesting
gender result is that the effect of the respondent's father having tertiary education

qualifications exceeds that of the mother's equivalent by 83 per cent for regular music listening. Being married increases the likelihood of listening occasionally and decreases the probability of listening regularly, as does being widowed or living common law, in comparison with being separated or divorced.

White (2001), using data from the 1982, 1985, 1992 and 1997 Survey of Public Participation in the Arts shows no notable difference between men and women in the raw descriptive statistics in terms of "core likes" from the 12 or more genres of music enumerated.

In the multiple regression using race, class and age variables the gender dummy consistently finds some statistical significance for the hypothesis that the female audience is more omnivorous. There is no significant difference in the male–female age profiles.

We might wonder *why* there is a hypothesis that females are more omnivorous than males. This is motivated by work showing that, in various settings, males and females use music in different ways in terms of its degree of "being in the background" and the extent to which it binds a group together. These kind of cultural differences do not necessarily generate predictions about differential omnivorousness. They are about meaning and meaning is not measured in this data. So there does not seem to be any coherent hypothesis about male–female omnivorousness.

Besides this, we need to go back to the issue of numerical significance versus statistical significance. If we look at her Table 10, the largest result is for 1997 (the rest are much smaller) with the point estimate being 0.558. The intercept is 5.528 so the upward shift is only about 10 per cent in the predicted value of a discrete variable which can only take values of 0, 1, 2, 3, 4 etc. For 1982, the coefficient is less than half the size for 1997 and for the other two years the results are statistically insignificant. So, even if there is a statistically significant effect it has to be deemed to be small in size. This is on top of the fact that there is not really any strong grounding to the hypothesis of differences in male and female omnivorousness.

None of these studies look at differences in male–female consumption with respect to the difference in gender of the musical artists.

Besides regular music consumption, it is of interest whether women display different behaviour in terms of "piracy" and the counteracting spirit of altruism in terms of making gestures to support musicians. A study of the willingness to pay over the set price for music on the Magnatune website (Regner and Barria, 2009) found that the female dummy was not statistically significant. Hence women do not have a tendency to give more, or less, than men above the set rate. There is no clear hypothesis about why they should differ, *ceteris paribus*, from men other than vague notions of male–female caringness being different.

Overall, evidence on gender differences in music consumption is a bit mixed and messy. This may be because gender has not been a specific focus of the research but simply one variable looked at along the way. Perhaps the most interesting result was the influence of father's education being a much bigger positive stimulant of musical consumption than mother's but there are no follow-up studies on this phenomenon.

Discrimination in the labour market

Music is certainly one of women's oldest professions. In the eighth century, Jamila, an Arabian songstress, conducted the first touring orchestra of 50 female musicians who regularly made the pilgrimage from Medina to Mecca.

The most common idea about gender in music is that women have been discriminated against. I should point out as this book has an economic root I will not be discussing sexism, per se, in the music industry nor its current shocking manifestations in social media. Where economic discrimination declines, and we encounter very high earning female artists with control over their work, the criticism is made that blatant sexism is a factor particularly in terms of music videos.

I now consider the economic theory of discrimination which is also relevant to the next chapter on race. In economic theory wages are mainly determined by marginal productivity. In perfectly competitive labour markets, wage rates should equal marginal revenue productivity.

The marginal revenue productivity therefore provides a benchmark figure. If workers are paid below it we may deem them to be "exploited" by the employer. If workers are paid above it, we may deem them to be exploiting the employers. Wage discrimination in economic models means differences in wage rates by marginal productivity differences *or* differential rates of exploitation. That is both a man and a woman may be being exploited by the employer but the latter more than the former. Such discrimination may be unintentional as it is a by-product of the market, for example in a monopsonistic labour market differently sloped supply of labour curves by demographic group would result in wage differentials.

Actual wage differences for successful musicians will depend on bargaining situations. It is not likely that the top ten women shown in the last chapter will be on lower royalty rates than men or lower concert fees. At the other end of the spectrum, there is an "equality in poverty" as PRS from such things as YouTube and streaming will be the same whoever you are. However, it was reported that UK "manufactured" child-oriented boy–girl bands (such as Steps) had lower pay for the female members.

We can distinguish three different types of intentional discrimination in terms of what causes it to exist. The dominant model in economics follows Becker in regarding "taste" or even "distaste" as the driving factor. Such tastes manifest in consumer discrimination, employer discrimination and co-worker discrimination. In the perfectly competitive model, employer discrimination cannot exist in the long run as any firm that tries to discriminate will be driven out of business due to non-discriminating rivals being more efficient. The non-discriminating employer may be forced to discriminate if their customers or workers demand compensation for working with the "out" group or require separation from them.

There is no clear evidence of how consumers might discriminate against women in music.

It may be a factor underpinning some of the genre case study material elucidated below. There are few "quasi-natural" experiments in popular music genres to allow us to see what happens if a woman takes a traditional male position. The Northern Ireland rock group Ash brought in a female bass player in 1998 with no apparent consumer response. Her eventual departure was not attributed to any gender-related reasons and they did not replace her but simply continued as a smaller unit.

There is clear evidence of gendered specialization in music markets. Female presence in the rap market has been very slight with rare exceptions such as the group Salt'n'Pepa. There are male acts aimed almost exclusively at female consumers, such as boy bands but also individual "boys" like David Cassidy and Justin Bieber. There are male genres with heavily male audiences. The exclusion in these cases is self-exclusion via tastes not any kind of forceful exclusion.

Cowen (1996, 1998) puts forward four hypotheses: specific to evidence of discrimination against women in specific visual arts labour markets. He does not focus on music per se. These are:

i   the genetic hypothesis;
ii the maternal obstacles hypothesis;
iii the parity hypothesis;
iv discrimination hypothesis.

The parity hypothesis is more of an observation than a hypothesis. For example, the above claim about rappers. The genetic obstacle is the claim that women are, for biological reasons, simply not suited to certain activities and are thus destined to fail compared with men. The classic view can be found in the notion that it is "not natural" for women to play rock guitar as alluded to by Robert Christgau in the following passage:

> It is possible to argue – as a function of cultural deprivation, of course, not innate disadvantage – that women have little bent for instrumental improvisation. As rock exists now, that may be true, although if so, it is even more so of jazz. But the deeper truth, I think, is more unpleasant than any cant about cultural deprivation. First, women cannot play rock guitar because men won't listen to them, and there is no need to belabor phallic analogies to explain why. Second, women cannot play rock because they cannot and/or do not want to create in blues-based male styles.
>
> *(1970, p. 367, of reprint in Kureshi and Savage, 1995)*

There are currently young women, of note, in the blues-rock guitar style but they are often playing to largely older male audiences in small clubs. They are not attracting legions of admiring female wannabes.

Similar phallocentric themes lurk in the history of jazz. Piekut (2010) discusses the position of Carla Bley within a male radical jazz movement. At various points, Piekut notes that critics' reviews of male horn players would identify their weaknesses in playing as being feminine characteristics. It could also be argued, from this evidence, that a continued emphasis on improvization as being more important than composition was a strategy to marginalize Bley whose strength lay in composing. Piekut's article also claims that a husband–wife duo working together would often experience the inference that the more important contributor was the man.

For classical music, the virtuoso show off instrument is the piano, and here, a prominent composer expressed similar views to Christgau: "Many women play much more beautifully than men, but men can provide more of the physical excitement that any audience, however sophisticated, comes to share" (Schoenberg, 1962). In classical music, a surprisingly strong statement of the genetic obstacles position comes from Mabel Daniels, a twentieth century American composer of many full-scale orchestral works. She believed that women "were naturally rather too weak for the hard work involved in composing large-scale works" (Fuller, 1994, p. 102).

Like rock guitar, there is not necessarily a genetic obstacle in playing many acoustic instruments but dominant beliefs may impose this status on them. Musicologists Porter and Abeles (1978) asked musicians and non-musicians to rate orchestral instruments in terms of masculinity and femininity. The rank order of the most feminine instruments was flute, violin, clarinet with the most masculine being drums, trombone, trumpet. The piano occupies a sort of neutral position as the view that it does not look right or is unfeminine to play the piano has never been expressed; indeed, piano playing was long deemed to be a lady-like virtue.

A study by Kuhlman (2004) explored whether gender stereotyping of instruments influences choice of instrument. This was based on asking a set of American school-age students about their preferences for the timbre of instruments and looking at whether this correlated with their choice of instrument to play. Out of 632 third-grade students, boys ($n = 312$) most frequently preferred the oboe, English horn and bassoon timbre (35.6 per cent), followed by tuba (27.2 per cent) and flute (24.8 per cent): least preferred timbres were trumpet and trombone/baritone. Girls ($n = 320$) most frequently preferred the flute timbre (39.6 per cent), followed by double reeds (24.8 per cent) and saxophone (24.8 per cent): least preferred were low brass timbres. In fourth grade, the instrument choices of 232 of these students were examined. Results indicate that even though boys' timbre preferences did not conform to typical instrument gender associations, their instrument choices do: 83 per cent of all boys ($n = 117$) chose to play the saxophone, trumpet or trombone, yet only 28 per cent demonstrated a preference for these instruments. Nearly 80 per cent of all girls ($n = 115$) chose to play the flute or clarinet, yet only 40 per cent preferred these timbres. This suggests choice of instrument is constrained by gender-based expectations.

Abramo (2011) studied original composition processes in a school where bands were formed to facilitate learning. Three same-gendered rock groups and two mixed-gendered rock groups were observed. It was found that boys and girls rehearsed and composed differently. The boys combined musical gestures and non-verbal communication whilst the girls separated talk and musical production. In the mixed-gendered groups, tensions arose because participants used different learning styles that members of the opposite gender misunderstood. These are fundamental tensions due to cognitive differences which, in the real-life band situation, are further exacerbated by sexual tension.

Moving on from genetic factors, the maternal obstacle is the expectation that women may be expected to withdraw more of their musical labour time than a man will when children have been produced. This would be consistent with the Arrow–Phelps model of "statistical discrimination". Children may be a severe hindrance to creative activity as the necessary periods of concentration required may be punctured by the needs of the child. They are an even more severe burden on the workaday life of a jobbing musician who may have to travel and attend lengthy rehearsals and learn a variety of pieces at short notice. Further, traditional family structures have tended to feature an orientation towards support for the male career taking priority over that of the female. This is indirectly suggested by studies of earnings functions in the general run of occupations (e.g. Waldfogel, 1998; Cameron and Ward, 2000), which find that there is a profound earnings deficit from children for working women but not so much for men.

Cowen (1996) says the spread of effective contraception should facilitate a reduction of maternal obstacles. In classical music, the general impression from Fuller (1994) was that women composers had either no children or small families, unlike some of the visual artists referred to by Cowen (1996). There does not seem to be any substantial evidence of women deliberately finding a rich husband as a means of internalizing the need for financial patronage. In the early and mid-twentieth century, the typical female "serious" composer was a performing musician who married another musician (or arts person) and subsequently reduced their performing activity with an attendant shift to composing on a piecemeal basis.

The existing evidence does not allow one to reach clear-cut conclusions on the impact of children on "serious" composition. The biographers of Lutyens (Harries and Harries, 1989) swing both ways: claiming that they were an impediment and at other times a stimulus. There is a point where Lutyens makes a conscious decision to get married and have children on the grounds that musical compositions are not adequate substitutes for children.

Applicability of discrimination theories to musical markets

I look now at empirical work within the mainstream paradigm of economics. Schwartz (1991a) claimed to show, from aggregate data, that discrimination at the point of hiring could not account for the disproportionate representation of men in US symphony orchestras. He attributed most of the differential to human capital differences without going on to draw the conclusion that this may indicate pre-entry discrimination. Goldin and Rouse (2000) employ the "blind testing" method, finding a statistically significantly lower likelihood of a woman musician being hired by symphony orchestras in normal labour markets. This is deduced from the elimination of female bias with the introduction of screens so that recruiters cannot tell the gender of the applicant from appearance.

A paper by Albinsson (2013) uses Swedish performing rights income to establish determinants of the income of contemporary "art music" (i.e. highbrow/classical work). Female composers are found to earn statistically significantly less *ceteris paribus* than men. It is difficult to establish what the sources of this are. It is unlikely to be consumer discrimination but it may be point of hire (commissioning works) discrimination in an elite market.

There are many general studies of artistic labour markets which although they do not focus explicitly on music, do shed some light on male–female differences in outcomes in arts labour markets (Wassall and Alper, 1998; Filer, 1986, 1990; Throsby, 1992; Throsby and Thompson, 1994; Heikkinen and Karhunen, 1996). Several of these studies, estimate Mincerian earnings functions and use a simple 0–1 gender intercept shift dummy formulation. This gives measures of residual "discrimination" against women that are very large in comparison with general labour market studies. In contrast to this, the verbal responses in surveys such as those of Throsby and Thompson and Heikkinen and Karhunen indicate that women, in the arts, do not particularly perceive themselves as being subject to discrimination.

We could fall back on the chart statistics, and record sales in terms of landmark gold records to look at differences in male–female performance. Giles (2006) finds that being a female solo artist is not statistically significant in terms of Billboard number one records compared with the overall sample of those who charted, i.e. not versus all records released. Fox and Kochanowski (2007) look at USA Gold records. Women are statistically significantly less likely to get Gold albums but more successful in singles/entry markets. The same caveat applies about the sample. Ceulemanns and Detry (2008) look at Billboard performance of 514 songs from 2009. The female solo artist dummy is statistically significant for chart success (position reached) but not for survival (length of time on chart) or in critical appraisal. This study does include songs that were not already in the charts selected from other measures of popularity.

These studies cannot tell us anything about discrimination as such. They document the widespread extent of successful females in popular music. The use of recent data by Ceulemanns and Detry highlights the present prevalence of supposed "duo" or "guest" records. Cooper (2010) gives a fuller account of the evolution of this phenomenon on the Billboard charts. Statistical classification as a duo is very simple – if there is one named female and one named male on the credits of the performance. However, the nature of the duo has changed. Mainstream pop duos like Donny and Marie Osmond and the Carpenters, do not feature now. The current duo vogue in terms of chart success is of the "featuring" or "versus" type best exemplified by the ubiquitous Pitbull who appears after a standard female vocal entry to rap and gesticulate in the videos. Or it is a mainstream white rock band teaming up with a black/ethnic female singer to expand their market reach. Musically this is not really a "duo" performance which would feature unison and harmony singing. This style is rooted in folk and country music where there have been romantic partners, like Ian and Sylvia, sisters and brothers and platonically paired unions like Parsons/Harris and Plant/Krause.

There are many journalistic and sociological studies of women in rock and to a lesser extent jazz, blues and country music: these tend to consist of fairly unstructured interviews (see Bayton, 1993, 1999; Bufwack and Oermann, 1993; Evans, 1994; Gaar, 1992; Greig, 1989; McDonnell and Powers, 1995; O'Brien, 1996, 2002; Reynolds and Press, 1995; Shevey, 1972; Stewart and Garrett, 1984). The major equivalent text on classical composers is by Jezic (1989). There is also a recent book of set format interviews of female dance music DJs derived from the pinknoise website but this lacks any sociopolitical or economic structure. The lack of quantification in such work makes it difficult to bring them to bear on the economic models of discrimination. In particular it is difficult to assess the labour market hypotheses that would be applied in more regular jobs. Specifically, the crowding effect of discriminatory exclusion. We may find many ethnic migrant taxi drivers in some countries because of barriers in other job markets but with women it is difficult to test whether the heavy skew towards singing in many markets is due to exclusion or preference.

In the next section I construct some historic quantitative data from qualitative sources, and draw inferences from broad patterns.

Case study evidence from classical music and jazz

In his entry on "women" in the companion to twentieth century music, Lebrecht (1992) writes:

> Although women's rights advanced, their status barely altered in music. There were star singers and soloists as ever before and a rising number of orchestral players from 1920 on, but no woman joined the front rank of conductors and none was counted among top composers. Social expectations unquestionably retarded the progress of women in music. Many like Elisabeth Maconchy put family before career. Those who did not like Elisabeth Lutyens were condemned for mannish callousness.

This of course contradicts some of Lutyens remarks made above.

In June 2014, in the UK, Judith Weir became the first woman to hold the post of "Master of the Queen's Music" in its 400-year history. This is not symptomatic of a massive shift in lack of parity in the classical music sector. The quip of famous conductor Sir Thomas Beecham that there have been no women composers was patently untrue. Long before this as the *International Encyclopedia of Women Composers* (Cohen, 1987), listed 6,000 women composers throughout history and the compiler amassed 7,500 recorded specimens of their works. A moment's simple arithmetic reveals this to be 1.25 records per composer.

As a proxy for the female share in recordings on readily available labels I examined (Cameron, 2003),[1] the 1992 Penguin Guide (March *et al.*, 1992) which ran to 1,206 pages of A–Z of recordings listed by composer. Of these, an astonishingly meagre one-and-a-half pages were devoted to female composers consisting of seven disks from Lili Boulanger, Hildegard of Bingen, Maconchy, Fanny Mendelssohn and Clara Schumann. This gives a female share proxy of 0.1244 per cent which is a considerable deviation even from parity with respect to output as Cohen (1987) estimated that 8 per cent of the world's classical compositions had been by women. None of the female authored works recommended, in the Penguin guide, are symphonic, being rather at the lighter weight end of the composing spectrum.

If we look at composers in more modern times, the survey of 500 composers by Collins and Morton (1992) showed similar absence of parity as only just over 8 per cent of those listed were women. Apart from there being fewer women composers published and recorded there is also a problem of the length of the works. Even a full-time lifelong composer such as Elisabeth Lutyens failed to produce much symphonic work: amongst her hundreds of pieces the only one given as a symphony "Symphonies for Solo Wind, Harps and Percussion" is a mere 17 minutes long and the vast bulk of her work was pieces of 15 minutes or less. Looking at perhaps the four best known dead female composers of modern times: Amy Beach lived to be 77 and produced only one symphony and one concerto; Nadia Boulanger lived to be 92 and produced no symphonies or large-scale orchestral works; Clara Schumann lived to be 77 and produced one concerto and no symphonies; Elizabeth Maconchy lived to be 87 producing two symphonies, two ballets and five operas. All of these women had a large general output. The symphonic or full-scale orchestral work level is very low compared with men.

The tendency of these women composers to produce short works, may be part of a nexus of factors which result in "blind" discrimination against the performance of female works. That is, mainstream concert programming tends to focus on about three moderate length (30–50 minute) full orchestral pieces or a longer very well-known (and hence inevitably male) piece. This inflicts a double jeopardy on women which may lead them to choose to work on short pieces. Short pieces may also reflect having to rely on minor sources of commission funding. There is also a historic bias towards male compositions which it is hard to imagine being restituted due to the lack of copyright in the works of the dead composers (all men) which dominates the small and stagnant market for classical recordings and concerts.

Disparity in length of compositions may reflect discrimination in training as access to some of the relevant capital for symphonic composition was, for a long time, denied to female music students. For example, at the Munich conservatory women were not allowed to attend counterpoint classes until 1897. Mabel Daniels caused consternation, in 1902, when she was the first woman to take part in the score-reading classes. Faced with such a historical deficit in composition-related human capital, women's writing would be expected to show a tendency to shorter works as the composers would be either self-taught in composition or rooted in their own instrument as a voice in writing.

The main leadership function within the orchestra, namely conducting, is a heavily male preserve. The entry "Conducting" in the *Concise Oxford Dictionary of Music* (Kennedy, 1980, p. 144), said: "There is no explanation, beyond the obvious one of psychological personality, for the way in which a conductor can, often with a minimum of rehearsal, impose *his* own style on an orchestra he may not have encountered before." There have been notable women conductors, such as Imogen Holst and Nadia Boulanger (who was the first ever woman conductor in 1937), and there are currently women conducting major orchestras but they have not been in the elite of superstar conductors. To be fair, the age of superstar and wunderkind conductors has probably passed with the collapse of the classical music industry.

No one is likely ever to reach the mammoth sales of Karajan by endlessly recycling the canon.

Another heavily cartelized position is the virtuoso pianist. Only six of the 37 pianists featured on the CD sampler (Phillips, 1998) from the project of "classic" twentieth century piano performances are women and even then they were the less well-known names.

The broad overview of classical music is that women have been subject to overt discrimination in the more distant past which continues to influence their position in the present. In theory countervailing action could through lobbying raise the position of works by women in the canon of "great" work. The practice of this is discussed below.

Jazz

The foothold of women in this sector is largely through the emergence of singers in the 1930s who overcame the initial obstacle, of the male bandleaders, to carve out solo careers. Examining the *Guinness Who's Who of Jazz* (Larkin, 1995) shows a total of 75 separate female entries.

However, a rough estimate of their share in the total text of the book comes out at around 6.66 per cent. Within this, around 56 per cent of the female entries are for singers in the "traditional" (i.e. verging on blues or cabaret) mould. Only three of the 75 women received text entries of at least one page and these are the archetypal chanteuses: Ella Fitzgerald, Billie Holliday and Sarah Vaughan. To some extent the Amy Winehouse, Adele etc., style, discussed in Chapter 2, has absorbed this into the mainstream.

Scarcity of prominent females in the instrumental areas of jazz has been a distinct feature. The women interviewed in Dahl (1984) were at pains to point out that once they had demonstrated their ability, that initial male objection evaporated. However, Piekut (2010) paints a less rosy picture, with respect to Carla Bley, in terms of the acceptance of a woman as a jazz composer.

Pop/rock markets

At the dawn of rock and roll, there were notable female songwriters particularly inside the almost literal "factory" of hits, the Brill-Building: Carole King, Elie Greenwich, Carole Bayer Sager and Cynthia Weil, who tended to work with their marital partners. The major pop-rock exception to this syndrome, in the 1960s was

Jackie De Shannon who has had her own compositions widely performed, often to great success, by a range of artists.

The epitome of the male directed female has been the "girl group". In its classic early pop form (see Greig, 1989) they tended to wear similar clothes and have distinctive dance routines, but no direct musical input to their work. The girl group can be seen as an unstable formation prone to turnover and the pushing of one member to the fore (as in the case of Diana Ross and the Supremes). There have been some very popular revivals of the girl group concept, such as the Spice Girls, who made a point of them wearing *different* clothes. At no point were they seen playing instruments and it would appear that several of them could barely sing (in some cases by their own admission). They were followed by some more competent singers such as Girls Aloud who nonetheless still are not seen playing instruments. It should be noted that boy bands have also been styled typically not to play instruments. Those who want to have had to fight against their grooming. We may note also that not playing instruments is partly dictated by the centrality of dancing to music aimed at a very young audience.

The classic autonomous unit is the rock "band" of usually four to five instrumentalists with singing who record their own compositions in a mode of production pioneered by the Beatles. Despite its amazing endurance and powerful record sales for the all-male, this has been a problematic modality for female and mixed ensembles. A number of factors conspire to make this so. One is the aforementioned opposition to female instrument playing in some spheres. Hence, a more viable alternative modality has emerged of the female lead singer with male backing where the woman may have some songwriting and general creative input. In the UK in the 1960s there were a number of "girl singers" who had male backing bands who were basically frustrated blues musicians. The pivotal outfits in breaking this barrier were Blondie and the Pretenders whose leaders were clear role models for the next wave. This product line of a desirable female plus anonymous male members has endured. Whilst this might be seen to be some step up for female autonomy in music it does tend to be stereotype reinforcing to some extent and record companies see the long-term viability of such artists in launching a "mature" career for the female leads which is likely not too far removed from the traditional blues/jazz/show music chanteuse.

This leaves us with the mixed ensemble. Fleetwood Mac (Mk II) are one of the all time biggest selling artists and were unique in featuring two female and one male songwriter who all wrote separately and had featured vocals. Both women played frequently on instruments. We also have Abba, and UK Abba clones (Brotherhood of Man, Bucks Fizz) and teen oriented groups with a mixture of males/females tending to come from television talent shows (Liberty X, S Club 7, Hear'Say, Steps). In the case of Abba, the songwriting and playing is a male preserve. In the clones and teen oriented groups no one plays an instrument. The basic workplace problem with these ensembles is the possibility of disruption and loss of output/profit due to sexual tension. One solution is to appoint resolutely gay male members. Where there are couples, within the unit, it may lead to a long-run increase in output by providing serendipitous material for more successful songs (Abba, Fleetwood Mac). The fallout of the discord will benefit all the parties concerned but where the men are the writers (Abba) their economic gain will be proportionately much greater.

Let us return to the issue of the all-female writing-playing-singing ensemble. In the *Guardian* "Weekend" magazine for 14 November 1998 a picture was shown of a never-heard-from-since ensemble called the Ladybirds in a New York club in 1967. They are visually like a 1950s Spectoresque vocal girl group apart from the fact that they play guitars and have their breasts fully exposed. There were, in the USA in the 1960s, some determined assertive female guitar bands who stood out against record company and managerial pressure to be groomed into more traditional female submissive archetypes such as She, the Sveltes and the Luvd Ones. These bands had few record releases let alone substantial sales. A slightly bigger splash was made by the American group Fanny (a renamed version of the Sveltes), touted somewhat falsely by their record label as the "first all female rock group", who seem to have been the only all female band with a sustained recording contract, at that time (about 1971). Their career only lasted until 1975 but they have left little trace in the form of sales, critical plaudits or songs that anyone remembers: their biggest achievement being two small US "top 40" 45 rpm hit singles. Following their demise, a standard four-piece guitar lead band of teenage girls, the Runaways, were launched in a blaze of publicity. They played instruments, wrote their own songs but, apart from the Japanese market, achieved few sales of their three albums released from 1976–1978. There were conflicts with the male management and record company people. The standard element in accounts of the Runaways is their manipulation by svengali figure Kim Fowley.

By the late 1970s, the insurgent climate in the "independent" music sector, consequent on punk, allowed women from non-musically oriented backgrounds to start playing as a gesture of defiance and subversion of the traditional "girlie" musical stereotype. The main commercial successes, after the passing of this era, were the Go-Go's who quickly fell apart under the pressure of fame and the Bangles. They had an era of commercial success from 1986–1988. These bands played their own instruments in the basic guitar-bass-drums format largely eschewing the male fetish of soloing. However, their successful songs were largely male compositions. The Bangles only had one large self-written hit composed by their principal member (albeit with outside collaboration). The exception is that the Go-Go's did write their own songs. Canadian band Heart, a mixed ensemble, were led by two songwriting sisters, but their major successes, helped by the primacy of video promotion in the "MTV era", were written by outside writers. Their videos do feature elaborate mimed guitar histrionics but the actual parts seem to have been played by the male member.

In all the more "popular" areas of the music spectrum, the historical tendency has been to see women as singers if their entry into a musical career is to be acceptable at all. In the popular areas of music, overt discrimination in training has not really been possible as the intuitive nature of production has meant training is really through personal or group practice with an instrument. Given that reasonably usable instruments have been relatively cheap for a long time there is likely to be little indirect discrimination through denial of access to an instrument. The main source of discrimination in popular music areas is likely to have been via sexism in all its forms including attitudes of major record companies to the positions which women can occupy in the industry. Sexism in all areas of the music industry is well documented and sexuality is an intrinsic element of music particularly in the pop-rock genre. However, despite persistent efforts in that direction, it has not been possible to shift musical product merely by marketing it as a joint product with sexual titillation. In the 1990s, a blatantly sexually exploitative (non-instrument playing) outfit called Fem2Fem released a couple of CDs to few sales despite appearing in *Playboy* magazine, "lesbian bondage" poses elsewhere and manifesting considerable nudity in their live shows. Many topless models have been optimistically called into recording studios but only one of them (Samantha Fox) has ever gained any commercial success. Nevertheless the failure of the Fem2Fems of this world does not imply the removal of barriers to female musical achievement from a sexist undertone in an industry in which production and distribution channels are in the hands of men.

Countervailing activity

Women have, not surprisingly, been concerned and disturbed by the presence of discrimination in musical markets. When market forces impose obstacles on an identifiable demographic group it is logical for them to form bodies to embark on countervailing action. There are various types of countervailing action that have been observed as follows:

Enclave formation

A disadvantaged group may be organized in some kind of separatist economy which I am calling an "enclave". If we took the extreme case where all women consumers and producers of music boycotted all male musical activity then this politicized reverse discrimination might well reduce the observed outcome disparity by a considerable margin. This is unlikely to happen but some enclaves have been generated in the form of specialist record labels and strictly all-female performing units. A number of companies, such as Leonarda, a nonprofit record label founded by Marnie Hall,[2] specialize in female oriented publishing and recording but the catalogue is small and the sales likewise.

The Women's Philharmonic Orchestra was founded in San Francisco in 1981 to perform only female works in its seasons. It disbanded in 2004 even though it was not in debt. The Community Women's Orchestra, founded in 1985 as an adjunct to it continued. This takes us back to the position where there were women's orchestras in the past but mainly not of full professional status or designed primarily to promote female musicians rather than female works.

There have also been, since 1970, all-women jazz festivals. These are often regional such as the Washington (DC) Women in Jazz Festival founded in 2011 and the Seattle equivalent. The Melbourne (Australia) festival is an international event but it is really a small set of one or two concerts on sequential days and thus lacks the archetypal full-on festival features.

The annual Lilith fair (see Spencer, 1999), was a travelling music festival founded in the USA by singer-songwriter Sarah McLachlan, which featured only female rock-pop-folk artists (albeit with male backing musicians). It ran from 1997–1999 and was revived in 2010 with the word "fair" deleted. Its founding was rooted in anger over the gender restrictions in radio play and concert promotion. Lilith originally raised large amounts of money.[3] Audiences were reported as being 60–70 per cent female. This was not an exclusive enclave type activity and was allegedly nonpolitical. Its venues gave prominence to nonprofit organizations active in women's issues. The tickets raised an extra $1 for local women's organizations.

However, the 2010 return tour became a financial disaster with cancelled dates and artists withdrawing. The concept was then laid to rest. Failure was blamed on the media and the state of the economy. McLachlan split from her male manager (who was blamed) who had promoted the events and the Lilith pages have been removed from her website despite there being links to them on other well-known websites. In interviews, at the time of the 2010 tour, she put forward additional non-economic arguments that things had changed and the time was no longer right for the concept. This contradicts the initial claim that it was not politically motivated and was just a good time with good music. There is plenty of internet speculation about why the package failed so badly including that McLachlan had too little recent market visibility. A popular view is that the focus is now irrelevant. The issues it sought to address have not receded but the target audience has lost interest. Younger females are not motivated by female specific events and Lady Gaga's rampant market orientation is seen as being one slayer of the concept. No one has attempted to systematically analyse whether the ticket prices were too high. Launching the revival at "too high" prices would seem like spectacular economic irrationality given the failure of the "alternative music" equivalent concept "Lollapolooza" revived a few years earlier due to allegedly too high prices.

It might be thought that "strictly" all-women groups are a means of overcoming obstacles such as male band member prejudice and apprehension about this by potential female band members. However, female jazz performers have expressed at least three reservations (Dahl, 1984): the impact of lesbian connotations on audiences, manifest gimmick or novelty value and a greater tendency for bickering between band members. The all-female jazz band has only been of limited success. The International Sweethearts of Rhythm, who lasted from 1938 to 1948, may be judged a success. However there were few others. The UK ensemble led by Ivy Benson ran for over 30 years but remained something of a novelty as instanced by their failure to release a record until the end of their career. There is an additional "economics of thin markets" problem in forming all women bands, which may be caused by past discrimination, in that the small total supply of women may make it difficult to find suitable quality replacements when members quit. Notwithstanding, there have been solidarist outfits such as the Feminist Improvising Group in Europe and Alive! on the west coast of America.

Economic theory suggests that enclave formation is not likely to be a very successful strategy for the remedy of minority misfortunes and indeed a number of writers on black political economy have been strongly against black-only businesses and black-only credit institutions.

Self-help

Women musicians face the same problems as other women professionals: lack of child-care facilities within their workplace and so on. One response to this is an interrupted career pattern which, according to conventional earnings functions studies, increases the outcome gap. Female rock musicians may wish to persevere with a career and children simultaneously rather than phasing their life-cycle activities.

To this end, a self-help/support group website appeared providing back up on such things as babysitting services whilst on tour (Motherrockstar).

Lobbying

Campaigns have been mounted, in the USA, targeting performance quotas for female compositions. The first attempts (Boone, 1995) centred on Title VI of the Civil Rights Act 1964 but were abandoned in favour of seeking an antitrust action against the National Symphony Orchestra on the grounds that it was purposefully mounting an "all-male season" being a restraint of trade in disbarring females from earnings opportunities. The US Department of Justice rejected this outright as it felt none of the prohibitions in Section 2 of the Sherman Act were being breached. Title IX of the Civil Rights Act was invoked, under a campaign led by Caspar Sunn against the Madison Symphony Orchestra. This has been abandoned and Caspar Sunn now appears to concentrate on organizing musical events for hospices.

There is an inherent problem that quota programming could lead to a loss of ticket sales and threaten orchestral viability as orchestral seasons are primarily of the time-honoured "classics" even in subsidized ensembles. This could have the perverse effect of depriving female musicians of employment. One of the arguments, of Caspar Sunn, was that women had established themselves as legitimate workers in the field of classical composition and therefore deserve protective employment rights.

Outrage/protest

Music is a communications market. Those who are not happy about its processes and outcomes can potentially deploy the industry to make their point – as we saw with the Mike Peters' anti-age stunt in the last chapter. Until the era of punk, in the late 1970s, women's output in popular music was as a traditional romantic figure or folk troubadour and confessional singer-songwriter. Even a female artist with a degree of autonomy, such as Kate Bush or Joni Mitchell, would have these roles pressed upon them and did not voice active critiques of the masculine order.

In the mainstream, females would play instruments demurely if they were not "just" singing.

The punk ethos opened the door to what is either non-playing an instrument or a challenge to what it means to play an instrument properly. The emergence of DIY record production meant that their efforts could be produced and distributed. This allowed women with little musical background to enter the market. The anarchic dress code also meant they could defy conventional notions of femininity. And so we get what are essentially sexual protest songs like "Up Bondage Up Yours" by Poly Styrene and X-Ray Spex, "Typical Girls" by the Slits and "Equal But Different" by the Au Pairs. These cases did however feature competent male musicians holding the fort. Gaar (1992) noted in her history of women in rock that the Au Pairs mingled male and female musicians in a revolutionary collaborative way, as part of its outspoken explorations of sexual politics.

In the USA, the riot girl movement emerged in the Washington DC region in the early 1990s (Marcus, 2010). These works expressly address sexual issues such as rape and lesbianism and male hegemony. The artists deemed to be in the genre often have provocative names. Unlike the above UK punk-rooted outfits they did not move to major labels where the music would be contoured into more acceptable market forms. The riot girl movement was also linked heavily to social activism.

Russian protest ensemble Pussy Riot goes further than any of these which is to be expected given the host economy in which they reside. They take their inspiration from the USA riot movement. They have not released any conventional albums of their music which so far makes no attempt at all to be anything other than basic pseudo punk rock. It is also unclear who is actually playing on these records. Their performances are said to last two minutes and have been carried out while masked. This is very strong anti-market activity but in 2012 the supreme economic irony reared its head. Their defence attorney (Verzilov) attempted to trademark the name in order to profit from Pussy Riot branded products.[4]

Verzilov lobbied Madonna, who at first associated herself with Pussy Riot, and then started selling consumer goods with the brand of the band. In particular, the singer's official online store offered t-shirts with the image of the band for about $20. It also appears that Verzilov was putting to the two on trial, the position that they had no chance of acquittal at all which may imply he was cultivating them as martyrs for exploitation. After release from prison, the two front Pussies turned up on an Irish television chat show (with interpreter) and quite palpably sneered derisively at the idea that Madonna was going to introduce them at a freedom event with the line that they were "freedom fighters like her". Footage of the actual event, with Madonna, seems to see them going alone with the situation quite demurely. They are not holding any musical instruments and they are not about to play.

The actual music of Pussy Riot seems to pass by almost unnoticed. The YouTube video of "Putin will Teach You How to Love" has pages and pages of the usual vituperation and response but no discussion of the music. It is unremarkable and could easily pass for a failed and forgotten UK or US band singing in Russian. Interviews with the makers of the documentary about the court case and imprisonment also ignore the music. If they relent on the trademark issue they could follow the Sex Pistols' economic miracle of generating a fortune from notoriety with music low down the bill of fare.

Their situation highlights some key features about music and the marketplace. Their music is not being discussed *but* if they had not come packaged in the musical field and had simply staged art events or performed plays the global social media attention would have been much less.

They are veering towards being commodities of packaged rebellion (like the unwittingly worn Che Guavera t-shirt and poster on the wall) embodying authenticity which has been a long-standing feature of seeking music to youths beginning with Elvis Presley. The Sex Pistols indicated that you could probably do better even by mostly taking out the music and the Pussy Riot case could be an even more elevated reification.

The two women in question would be deemed highly attractive by conventional standards so their position in the market is going to be propelled forward by this and notoriety. It is unlikely that they are going to inspire guitar wielding protest musician females around the globe rather than t-shirt wearing acolytes.

Conclusion

Women are strongly represented in musical activity as borne out by this chapter and also Chapter 2 but there is a distinct historical pattern of segmentation. In "serious" (supposed highbrow culture) music areas, the performance and recording ratios to publication for women falls markedly below parity with men. The entry to the high points such as conducting and major composition was usually via initial work at the rank and file of instrument playing where women do much better. Elements of the glass ceiling come from the policies of record companies and subsidy fund dispensers which create disincentives to go in for heavyweight composition. Whilst conscious discrimination at the point of trade seems not to be a large factor in music, unconscious discrimination in early musical capital investment sets in motion a chain of events which limit female performance in musical markets. Singing is doubtless the most accepted and perpetuated archetype of women in music across all genres. There are currently many high profile female artists in popular music who would seem not to be being exploited by male businessmen. They are almost universally singers, who do few other musical roles, for whom highly sexual presentation is a very important part of their sales strategy.

Notes

1 All figures from page counting are approximate as I have not taken explicit account of the small number of pictures which do have a female bias and I have also rounded up small entries to 1/4 of a page.
2 See https://www.leonarda.com/index.html (accessed 2 June 2014).
3 See http://edition.cnn.com/SHOWBIZ/Music/9807/28/lilith.fair/ (accessed 28 December 2014).
4 See http://english.pravda.ru/russia/politics/02-11-2012/122696-pussy_riot-0/ (accessed 28 December 2014).

9
RACE AND ETHNICITY

Introduction

It needs to be stressed at the outset that the availability of data, and any systematic analysis of it, is much weaker for this topic than any addressed earlier. As before, we shall review what there is and draw on case study material as appropriate.

There can be no doubt of the important relationships between music, race and ethnicity which also extends to religion. The origins of many forms of music are in religious celebration. National differences in "art" music, as opposed to heavily commercial music, to a large extent reflect these sources. To avoid cumbersome exposition, I shall generally use the term race in the rest of the chapter on the understanding that ethnic and religious differences are also implied.

I am not going to look at the markets for worship music which are quite buoyant.

It is probably wise to add some preliminary comments on how Jewishness is handled in the literature. Jewish music itself constitutes a distinct form which can be rousing and dance-oriented (Klezmer bands) but it seldom seeps into the mainstream. Its most visible presence is likely the droning cadenzas of Leonard Cohen, some aspects of Bob Dylan's work and the odd rogue event like the melody of the song "No Milk Today" (a hit for the Hollies in 1966) written by a young Mancunian Jew, Graham Gouldman. In contrast to this musical sparsity, Jewish businessmen have been very prominent in the music industry often managing and developing black artists. In this connection it is probably a little unfortunate that George (2008) refers to Ahmet Ertegun (Turkish) as a white man given that he would certainly have been treated as non-white growing up. Inflammatory anti-Jewish remarks by Professor Griff, in 1989, triggered his temporary exit from Public Enemy (see Ogg, 2002) not surprisingly given the strong Jewish presence in their record company. This company Def Jam featured a remarkable racial collaboration between Rick

Rubin and Russell Simmons which goes against the crude notion of whites (often Jews) exploiting the labour of black musical workers. In this instance, the more entrepreneurial element was the black man and the more musical element was the white man.

I have touched on material relevant to this chapter both in the previous chapter and in Chapters 2 and 3. Some features will be continued in the next chapter on international trade in music. Chapter 2 contemplated the "blackness" of the music of Adele. Chapter 3 dealt with critiques of "black" music forms – blues and jazz from those within those spheres, not with the specifics of discrimination and integration. Chapter 5 touched on the specific strategies of Tamla Motown/Berry Gordy in expanding their market. Gordy seems to have been driven by the brutal mathematical logic of the fact that the market of white consumers was much more substantial than the market of black consumers in terms of disposable income and accessibility.

Before the marketization of Little Richard and Chuck Berry (and others of their era) there was a strong historical bias against black music being played on white US radio. Billboard actually ran a "Race Records" chart from 1945–1949 until it was retitled Rhythm and Blues. The massive popularity of Elvis Presley allowed the elements of the race records to be integrated into mainstream white radio. The term rock and roll emerged from the 1950s to describe this hybrid although the term itself had been used in race records for many decades. At the time it may have looked possible to record companies that r 'n' b could be passed off in white imitations as had happened with various forms of jazz before. Hence there would not necessarily be an incentive for mainstream record companies to seek to develop black artists. This role before Tamla Motown was filled by the Chess label (see Cohen, 2005). However, Chess mainly distributed the work of artists it found with much less proactive developmental activity.

Overtly institutionalized racism across the whole economy will have musical consequences. In 1950s and 1960s America, black musicians continued to face acute problems with respect to hotel accommodation and treatment in southern states. South Africa provides an even more extreme case. According to Bradley (2013), the white South African Jazz pianist Chris McGregor "blacked up" using boot polish in order to fool the police from intervening as he travelled by car, with black musicians, to play in the townships. During apartheid, South Africa had few visiting white liberal musicians from other countries who might spread integrative ideology. This may have been because few were attracted to come. Visits proved a career blight when they did take place. It is still not entirely clear why the disastrous Byrds tour of South Africa, in 1968, took place. It backfired spectacularly leading to musicians union censure in the rest of the world and outright hatred in the South African media. This is even without the subsidiary members of the group being caught on ill-advised visits to the townships. Later, when there was economic apartheid, in terms of trade bans in goods and sports bans such as in cricket, other musicians incurred wrath for greed and complicity. Queen provide an example of this in 1984 by playing Sun City (Harris, 2005); they gave similar explanations to the Byrds for their visit but were blacklisted by the United Nations throughout the duration of apartheid.

The general issue is later enshrined in the song "Sun City" (in 1985) written by Steven Van Zandt and attributed to Artists United Against Apartheid. The artists involved (a wide range of luminaries in a range of genres) donated the money to anti-apartheid charity work and pledged themselves not to play the resort. This protest met with some opposition in the host economies and a significant number of radio stations refused to play it. It had some commercial success but did not become a cause célèbre global chart topper like the original Band Aid single. Resistance to it had taken place in spite of the fact that the militance of tone was significantly moderated en route to release. The demo version name checked offending artists, like Queen, who had played Sun City and not done anything to purge their guilt.

The South African apartheid economy also prevented black South Africans from even hearing commercial songs of protest about their situation. The late Gil Scott-Heron said of his famous anti-apartheid protest song "Johannesburg" (1975) that when he got to the actual place he expected the audience to shout its name at the "punch line" of the song but no one did.

The colour of music and race to the market

We encounter immediately the problem of how we can define music in ethnic or racial terms. At first, it might seem ridiculous to classify music based solely on the genetic composition (abstracting from gender) of the perpetrators. Indeed this is recognized in the British MOBO awards (established in 1996) which are for "music of black origin" and thus can be won by individuals who are classified as white or some other category than black. The NAMA (Native American Music Association) Awards (established 1998) likewise gives awards to those with no ethnic affinity who embody the "spirit" of the ethnic music. For example "outside" white lesbian acoustic duo the Indigo Girls were given such an award. NAMA have also honoured Jimi Hendrix (in 1998), due to his American Indian heritage which is quite a few generations back. The possible oddness of this is highlighted if we note that he has Irish heritage, not much further back, so could almost equally be given a spirit of Irish music award if there was a campaigning body seeking to stack up token bodies.

Nelson George (2008) particularly struggles with the issue of purity in the form of "blackness" in his "death of rhythm and blues" thesis. Talking about the 1960s "British Invasion" he remarks that white (English) singers could not hope to match the emotional intensity of artists like James Brown and Marvin Gaye. At the end of his work, he produces a strangely divergent argument when he argues that white artists in the slick adult oriented soul music of later periods (such as Rod Stewart and George Michael) are better at producing it than black musicians.

We must of course not forget that black is not the only colour. This oversight is quite common in both the discursive literature and the limited amount of empirical work. Around the globe there are a number of distinct ethnic musical styles outside the black (American or other idiom) – Australian Aboriginal, Native American Indian, Eskimo (Inuit), South Asian (which would be best known in terms of Bollywood stylings), Hispanic, Latin American, Irish, European folk traditions and so on. A very large share of work in these idia has not been significantly brought to a mass market audience in a consistent or continuous way. This is not surprising if they are left in their pure or semi-hybridized forms but many have also lacked significant mainstreaming exponents.

Latinate mainstreaming has come about through such artists as Ricky Martin and J-Lo who perform some concerts in Spanish although it is difficult to find much Hispanic content in the music of the latter. Other ethnic musics have had very limited mainstreaming. Hispanic music is not indigenous to the American continent. It is an imported form, as is the black gospel rooted soul music. This is essentially restyled African music. The indigenous musics of North America are Eskimo/Inuit and Red Indian. Their conspicuous absence in the market would seem to constitute possible discrimination. However it could just be that consumers are not strongly in favour of such music especially as it would lack some of the core elements of marketable music. Native American Indian music, in its traditional form, places little emphasis on melody which might limit its appeal outside novelty use such as in the song "Running Bear" (1960) although there were a few surprise "Red Indian" style hits in the early 1970s (Don Fardon's "Indian Reservation" and a band with significant Native American heritage, Redbone's "Witch Queen of New Orleans"). Perhaps even more of a novelty was the song by English artists Red Box, "Lean on Me" ("Ah-Li-Ayo") (not the Bill Withers song), in 1985, largely derivative of Native American rhythms which was a major hit. This was not a comedy or jokey effort but it did not blossom into a catalogue of continued success from this style.

The chief member of the band, Robbie Robertson, is of native American heritage but this passed largely untouched until his later solo work (similar concerns apply to others such as Rita Coolidge). The case of Cher provides someone whose ethnic heritage has slipped by almost unremarked, as far as musical identity goes, most of the time.

As we see repeatedly, non-white forms of music tend to get attached to the main tributary of black music (American soul and now hip hop and urban music in general) or (in the case of some British Asian music) the next most known form – reggae. The roots of populist reggae music are, in any case, in the main a black USA soul-gospel tributary. The most prominent Native American musician male, (1941–1992) Jim Pepper's career was in the mainstream of jazz, as a saxophonist, although he did produce works with significant indigenous content. As with Redbone, this is primarily through the use of chanting motifs.

We may also take the case study of Australian aboriginal singer Jimmy Little (1937–2012). He began with the Jimmy Little Trio in which the other three were also Aborigines. In 1963, after 17 singles, Little achieved a big hit with the gospel song, "Royal Telephone". Little continued to have mainly modest hit records until

1974 with "Baby Blue". He turned from his musical career to focus on his family. His music did not embody any specific aboriginal content nor did he absorb any incoming styles such as the work of the Beatles which (see next chapter) dominated Australia more than any other territory. Thus, Little had a significant medium-level career but his major breakthrough did not continue at that level, simply resolving to a level well above him being a "one hit wonder". In 1999, he was treated to a repositioning "Indian Summer" *à la* Johnny Cash (see Chapter 7) by the elite of Australian credible rock musicians, such as Nick Cave, on the album "Little Messenger" which peaked at number 26 in the national charts selling over 20,000 copies. It featured covers of well-known songs by Australian artists Nick Cave, Ed Kuepper, Paul Kelly and the Go Betweens and brought Little on to a number of Australian TV shows. Little's Indian Summer did not achieve any global impact nor did it trigger more aboriginal content in Australian music. As can be seen in data in the next chapter, Australian musical markets are very open in the sense that imported music dominates sales. This would be expected to curb indigenous diversity although the presence of a large home market does not necessarily encourage diversity.

There is a clear parallel between Australian aborigines and Native American "Red" Indians. Both are indigenous peoples whose lands have effectively been stolen by the incoming peoples. Broadly speaking the descendants of migrating races, or of those captured via slavery, have been able to make more impact on the music markets of their economies. There is no necessary economic imperative for this to happen. The "foreign" elements may simply be an additional attractive goods characteristics element which appeals to the consumer (cf. Chapter 6) which can be appropriated and absorbed by the host culture. This is illustrated in old pop hits like the Beatles' "Ob-La-Di Ob-La-Da" and Alan Price's "Don't Stop the Carnival" and white calypso like Lance Percival. This has long been discussed in terms of exoticism, in the musicological literature going back to Ravel and Debussy, and is regarded dismissively in Byrne (1999) in his attack on the use of the term "World Music".

Black music can be made by white or Hispanic or oriental people and vice versa. George Harrison could put a sitar on a Beatles record having taken instruction from appropriate Indian performers but this did not make the Beatles' recording any more Indian than that of other white groups, of the era, like the Kinks and the Byrds who used effects to make a fake sitar sound from conventional Western manufactured electric guitars. Or, to make things even more convoluted we could say the Beatles' recording is no more "Indian" than the black American soul records of the 1970s, which used the Danelectro "Teardrop electric" sitar which was not a sitar. No one in liberal regimes objects to virtuoso oriental origin classical pianists (such as Lang Lang) playing the resolutely "white" European repertoire.

However, there is one clear legacy, in musical markets, of the move away from formal institutionalized racism. This is illustrated tangentially in a specific case of the tribute band phenomenon that was discussed in Chapter 5. Gregory (2012) discusses extensively the humorous performances of the Hamsters, in their tribute to Jimi Hendrix tour in which they played exact facsimiles of his repertoire. It would clearly be hugely unacceptable for them to go for the lookalike approach by "blacking up", and donning an Afro wig, even if their guitarist was not of an entirely unsuitable build to pull off the trick. Nor do we find non-white musicians "whiting up" in tribute acts. Beatles tribute acts strive for extreme lookalike credibility and hence the UK bands in this sector are resolutely Caucasian. Nevertheless, there are non-white Beatles tributes, from countries of non-white provenance such as Japan, but these have the same ironic tone as the Hamsters. Beatles wigs (or hairstyles) are very common in global tribute acts but skin reorientation is not.

Labour market

I should start by stating the obvious lest it go unnoticed. As far as I am aware, there are no standard Mincerian earnings function studies of discrimination in the labour market for non-white musicians, in the economics literature. So, we must look at raw data and some basic observational and historical material on different sectors for the labour market. Generally, for pop-rock music this involves actual customer discrimination or employer discrimination as agents and record companies discouraged use of non-whites due to their belief (rightly or wrongly) that they were accurately gauging commercial potential by this.

The pop-rock labour market has been a fluid one where musicians themselves appear not to have been discriminatory. There has sometimes been reverse customer discrimination – Bradley (2013) reports some instances of people not being happy to see white UK musicians in funk bands in the 1970s. This only applies to live performances. Most people would be unaware that the organ, on UK reggae records of the era, was played by white Lancastrian Georgie Fame. In the UK, the 1960s and 1970s in movement was from the "Windrush" Caribbean legacy and the serendipitous arrival of Nigerian students. All black indigenous musical ensembles did not appear on UK television for a long time (until the 1970s) and the country also had the ignominy of the "Black and White Minstrels" who were whites in blackface make-up doing an Al Jolson kind of schmaltz. They were very successful with a career on UK television from 1958–1979. This is despite organized anti-racism protests against them from as early as 1967. Curiously, they did not have any hit single records. They had number one albums in the early 1960s but the chart positions of their albums slid progressively from the mid-60s. They were a very odd case of product substitution operating in the opposite way, for race, as in the tribute band market. There were no rival authentic black products of the same type.

Racially integrative music, and acceptance of all black indigenous music in the UK can be traced to record labels (Trojan for reggae (DeKoenig and Cane-Honeysett, 2003), Two-Tone records for the punk ska revival) and home-grown disco. "Rock against Racism", set up in 1976, was not a musical campaign, to promote non-white music, but rather a campaign by musicians against general racism. It came into being as a result of drunken remarks by Eric Clapton supporting the inflammatory repatriation policies of Enoch Powell. In so being, however, it would tend to promote supply and demand for primarily reggae music. Reggae/ ska was popular with UK punks leading to, most prominently, covers and appropriation by the Clash. Before these musical forms were popular with white skinheads which may raise the issue of paradoxical racism. However, literature on this tends to suggest there were factions of racist and non-racist skinheads. "White reggae" would, like white blues before it come to eclipse the commercial reach of indigenous reggae with the fairly centralist work of UB40 (a band with black and white members and a white singer) which is sold as authentic reggae in the Caribbean and the pop hybrids of the Police and Men At Work. The major reggae stars, who have come after this, and been signed to major labels, have frequently become enmeshed in campaigns against their violently homophobic material which eventually lead to some recanting.

Disco paved the way for UK black musicians who had struggled for a long time, in some cases. Liverpudlian ensemble, the Real Thing had enormous hit records, in 1976 and 1979, which were essentially substitute goods for the "Philadelphia Sound". The core members, the Amoo brothers had been active in Liverpool in the early 1960s and were even encouraged by the Beatles but to no avail. Eddy Amoo was a member of a vocal group called the Chants who met McCartney at a concert. The Chants auditioned for the Beatles who were so impressed with the group that they invited them to appear with them so they could provide the "backing" to the Beatles. Brian Epstein was persuaded by John Lennon to let this occur. The group grew tired waiting for Epstein to sign them and went with Pye records and entrepreneurial songwriter-producer Tony Hatch. The Chants toured for a further 13 years but with no record success. The personnel involved attribute their failure to the market "not being ready" for a black group even one from all conquering Liverpool. By the time of disco, we had an overall culture not just the music so titled, into which all black UK or multiracial UK bands were accepted. Disco also provided the lift off for the multiracial, but black fronted and toned, band Hot Chocolate to a high level of UK chart success with some global follow-up.

It seems difficult to attribute the changes to a decline in erstwhile consumer racism. There were also no significant changes in radio that can explain why black UK musicians broke through to chart success when they did. It may be that authenticity was the key factor as a music form arrived for which being black was a sign of authenticity. The hurdle of not being American also would have to be overcome. It is not entirely clear how this took place.

I turn now to the issue of classical music where the segmentation apparent, for women, is much greater in the case of race. Greene (2005) claims that there were over 300 classical composers of African origin. Before the mainstreaming of the CD market, very few of these would have been available in terms of there being many recordings of their works. Probably the most visible was Samuel Coleridge-Taylor (1875–1912) (particularly for his Hiawatha based works) although he was of mixed race and born in London despite him later being dubbed "the African Mahler". However, his compositions were devoted to incorporating African elements.

In terms of the labour market for classical musicians, in the USA, data from ASOL, the League of American Orchestras' 2006–2007 Orchestra Survey Report (OSR), showed the aggregate for African Americans in member orchestras to be 1.92 per cent. Carter (2002) looked at the population of black symphonic musicians in the USA, in symphony orchestras that receive public funding in New York and Texas. Problems of lack of appropriate musical education for young African Americans and lack of role models (the chicken and egg problem) are identified. Day (2008) listed the ethnic status of three UK orchestras' (the BBC Scottish Symphony Orchestra, the Ulster Orchestra and the Halle) core staff. Of the 225 people, one was Asian, one black Caribbean, one Chinese and 14 white non-British nationals. The same piece recounted that, in 1987, Edmund Reid successfully took the English National Opera, to an industrial tribunal after they refused to give him the title of co-leader, despite acting as lead violin for two years.

The article presents five short summaries of interviews with (fairly young) non-white active UK classical musicians. These confirm the overall argument that the profound disparity and segmentation of non-white UK classical musicians is difficult to attribute solely to post-entry labour market discrimination. Althea Ifeka is an oboist. She makes a very economically pertinent statement:

> What I have to say is probably very un-PC, but I'm going to say it anyway. The lack of black orchestral musicians is about money, not colour. It's a bad career choice. Norman Lebrecht has explored this very well. As a soloist and conductor you can earn a lot but orchestral musicians face many years of training followed by pitiful pay. I work mainly as a soloist and teach now but I did have a big orchestral career in the past. I have lots of African and Asian children in my teaching practice. First-generation immigrants don't want their children going into a profession that is uncertain and poorly rewarded.

Countervailing action, as with women, has been mild leaving aside Reid's action. Again, the logic of economics dictates that Reid's victory may be counterproductive, as its impact may have been to prevent hiring of non-whites for fear of further actions. There are several non-profit organizations seeking to bring classical music to (mainly youth) of non-white origin. This is cognate with general cultural do-gooding as a means to bring people out of gangs and drug culture – that is similar bodies seek to do this with playing cricket and performing Shakespeare and so on. The Sphinx organization, founded by Aaron Dworkin, seeks to increase participation of blacks and Latinos in classical music in schools, as professional musicians and as classical music audiences. The main tools are education in the art and attempting to persuade audiences over their cultural barriers.[1]

Gateways Festival was formed in 1992 to increase the visibility and viability of African American classical musicians and to heighten public awareness of their classical music contributions. This was to be achieved through presentation of "classical" music festivals featuring African American musicians from throughout the United States in solo recitals, chamber music concerts, symphonic concerts and lecture demonstrations. This is the benign enclave model, of the wilting Lilith fair, discussed in the previous chapter. It faces difficult problems of making inroads given the economic nature of the classical music labour market.

The awards of NAMA were discussed above. Their website contains the following quote:

> The music of the Indian is the spontaneous and sincere expression of the soul of a people. It springs from our own continent, and is thus, of all music, distinctly American. If Indian song be encouraged and recognition of it awakened among our own people, America may one day contribute a unique music to the world of art.
>
> *(Natalie Curtis, Musicologist)*

We could push this further and argue that country and western and bluegrass music are wrongly thought to be the "true" American "roots" music, when they are another derivative hybrid sprouted from largely Irish–Scottish origins. This places them in a similar vein to gospel-soul-urban music leaving the Native American Indian music as the true legacy. However, much of NAMA's work is not specific to music creation being directed at problems like flood damage funding and prevention of youth suicides on plantations. Direct labour market intervention is sought on day to day musical occupations – a cultural diversity programme to recruit Native American employees at MTV Networks was set up. They also sought to encourage native artist collaborations with mainstream artists. It also engages in heritage work with a national music archive and has become the world's largest Native American music archive with over 10,000 Native American audio and video recordings in all formats housed since 1990.

Heritage work is generally likely to keep an indigenous form consigned to a cultural appreciation "ghetto" rather than bring it into mainstream markets. However, NAMA claims to be succeeding in the aim of getting equal recognition for Native Americans as musicians. One alleged sign of this was the introduction of a Grammy Award for Best Native American Music Album in 2000. The Canadian Juno Awards also began to present an annual award for Aboriginal (i.e. Inuit not Australian aboriginal) Recording of the Year. On 6 April 2011, it was announced that the Grammy Award for Best Native American Music Album would be merged into a new category, Best Regional Roots Music Album.

This change does not seem to connote success in achieving high visibility, i.e. where the category does not matter anymore because it is so well established. Rather it seems to be vanishing into the amorphous mush of roots music which is folding in the amorphous mush of world music discussed in the next chapter.

Impact of race on demand for music

It is even more difficult to find standard econometric evidence for the role of race in the demand for music, than it was to find any substantial evidence for age and gender in the previous chapters. For example, I cannot find any studies from the countervailing NPOs (non-profit organizations) listed above which attempt to look at classical music, or any other music, listening in different ethnic communities. The situation compares unfavourably to the case of team sports where we can easily find economic studies which look at the impact on attendance of the presence of a player of "minority" race on attendance.

There is a historical data problem as far as "race" records in the USA goes, as there is no way of establishing whether or not white buyers would have discriminated against black records (which they were unaware of) as opposed to the white cover versions they were buying. The explosive success of Tamla Motown, in crossing over to white television and radio and charts, shows that there was an appetite amongst white consumers despite labour market and travel discrimination against the performers still being institutionalized. If white people have strong preferences for black music consumption and black people have weaker preferences for white consumption we might expect a long-run equilibrium where black music would come to dominate, subject to the comparative population weights. But this is difficult to explore, using data, due to the blackening of white musical idia and performance styles.

The paucity of regular data is not supplemented to any huge extent by one-off surveys of individual consumption. Certainly not those specifically directed to racial differences in consumption.

If we turn to the world of market research and consultancy we encounter a truly staggering claim. Gracie and Sinha (2012) present the "Gracie Management Music Consumption Model" (based on data collected in 2008 in the USA) which hits us right between the eyes with Point 5 in the summary:

> Ethnicity has no impact on music consumption. While in the political arena there might not be the post-racial/ethnic world people had hoped for in 2008, in the world of music consumption it has come already! One's race/ethnicity neither increases nor decreases one's consumption of music.

Point 5 in the executive summary says: "A better marketing plan is one that involves finding the white space that cuts across all people regardless of their racial/ethnic origins."

We need to point out here that "white space" seems to mean neutral, and thus is a potentially misleading term, rather than white as in "white" person. The study examined 490 people in the United States within the "core music buying demographic" which was seen as 18–34 years old, despite some of the claims we have encountered in earlier chapters about the greying of the market since the 1990s (i.e. that those aged 45+ alone may be 30+ per cent of the market!). Questions looked at uses of music, music consumption patterns, perception of music today compared to the past, sharing friends' musical tastes, styles of music discovery and, surprisingly, vinyl records purchase intent. Race comes within the seven demographic questions. The main questionnaire is ten questions but these often contain quite elaborate sets of statements to which the respondent must indicate their degree of agreement.

A statistical model was constructed with the aim of helping artists and labels devise their marketing strategy. This is a logistic regression which divides the sample into two groups – music consumers and "non-consumers" – and attempts to predict the contribution of variables to probability of falling into either group. This is a rather convoluted final model specification. The non-consumers are *not* people who never consume music (which as we suggested in Chapter 3 is almost imposs-ible) rather they are low in involvement. They are low to such a degree that we might conclude music is not a meaningful activity to them. None of this informa-tion is based on economic variables like amounts of spending. The division into the two groups is based on weightings of responses to different questions which are, to some extent, ad hoc. The reported model in the document does not actually show the statistical results for the ethnic variables, it is simply reported that they are sta-tistically insignificant in the verbal parts of the text.

Earlier work by Peterson and Simkus (1992) stressed that race was an important determinant of taste, as in genre of music chosen. We may look at a more recent application of this work in a sociological study (White, 2001) which looks at class, age, gender and race, in terms of the omnivore/univore which was critically explored in Chapter 7. It uses data from the 1982, 1985, 1992 and 1997 Survey of Public Participation in the Arts (SPPA) in the USA. This is based on "core likes" from the 12, or more, genres of music depending on year. These are likes in the old fashioned use of term ("what type of music do you like?") not the modern social media usage of the term. The race variable is simply a dummy labelled as black = 1 and 0 = else. There is thus no distinction between varieties of race. A number of equations and correlations are computed using different permutations of the "likes" measures. In all the statistical results, the coefficient on race is virtually always negative indicating that the white audience is more omnivorous. There are many cases where it is not statistically significant but the balance of evidence is clearly for a negative effect of being "black". In a purely descriptive graph (his Figure 5) the black "likes" show the same age profile as the white in terms of falling omnivorous-ness after about age 40, thus following what was said in Chapter 7.

This study might seem to be contradictory to the Gracie model. It cannot simul-taneously be true that race does matter and does not matter. The studies differ in date of data but we should not conclude that the differences are due to time passing. The questions asked in the studies are different and the data is differently framed, specifically the Gracie model reduces the data to a binary outcome categorization thus going to an even lower grain than White – indeed it does not look at omnivo-rousness at all. Ultimately we have to note that neither study really looks at con-sumption in any great detail in terms of music choice. They do not take us forward in knowledge of traversing (whites buying non-white music and vice versa) at all. Not only is the grain of data for music choice limited, there is a very crude use of racial categories. Above all else, they do not actually look at the amount of spending on music or length of time devoted to dedicated listening to it.

These are, of course, studies by non-economists, which are looking at meaning and taste rather than demand but, as this study has maintained, these issues can be encapsulated in a social economics approach.

Studies of chart success, which have been discussed frequently earlier, do include racial origin variables. However, this can give us little insight into consumer race preferences for the reasons given earlier. We can only see records in charts that already have some level of success so we cannot identify which music has been shunned totally by the buying public. There is also the problem of idiosyncrasy and crossover. Any given artist may have something unique that makes them popular and they may just happen to be black. In their different ways, Prince and Michael Jackson embodied different incorporation of elements of white music as did the Rolling Stones and Elvis Presley, in the mirror image case. There is no obvious way of scoring the mix to put in a regression equation.

As music is an experience good, consumers face problems of discovering new music if that is what they so wish to do. If media outlets either deliberately, accidentally or unconsciously screen out music for racial reasons, then consumers must rely on other forms of access. The alternate means of access have historically been direct marketplace activity in the form of simply visiting shops, radio, extra marketplace activity such as exchanging products without using money or word of mouth.

The rise of popularity in black rhythm and blues music due to the enthusiasm of UK consumers is well known due to frequent interviews with the surviving British musicians who encouraged this trend such as members of the Rolling Stones. However, the origins of increased black music content in the UK go back much further than the early to mid-1960s. Just prior to the blues boom amongst young white UK musicians, the frontier waves of music for the style aspiring young had been in skiffle and before that various forms of jazz. Here we had largely informal social networks enabling records to be heard. In some cases consumer club activity, via magazines, would be instituted to raise shared funds to support issues of certain titles.

Segmentation in the product market: the legacy of charts, radio and record labels

The extreme form of racial segmentation is a musical economy of "islands" that do not trade. If we simply have two groups B and W where Bs make music only with other Bs and Ws only with other Ws, all Bs only consume B music and all Ws only consume W music, there is no discrimination in the sense of individuals in the same production unit being paid different wages. For the total absence of overt discrimination we must assume that the Ws and Bs freely choose to consume only the output of their own groups.

Trade across these islands is promoted by the holy trinity of the charts, radio and major record labels. Digital technology may have put this into disarray but it still seems excessive to claim that radio is dead as a factor as its popularity continues to grow. Even if it, and the other two, were dead, their legacy still persists in shaping mass consumption and the possibility of survival for more specialist niche markets.

Before the need to introduce downloads and streaming, charts have generally been based on shop returns. So, it is clearly possible for something to sell well and yet be off the radar if it is not sold in chart return shops. The chances of being in chart return shops is much higher if the artist is on a major mainstream label. Music of African and Jamaican origin, in the UK, grew from sales in general retail outlets leading on to specialist shops (Bradley, 2013) which would not have featured in chart return shops thus meaning some possible hits for black UK artists have been lost in the sampling frame.

Such music suffered from a lack of exposure until regular live events were established and, in the case of reggae, the Trojan record label emerged. Some African music (such as Osibisa) appeared on "progressive rock" labels and the artists received exposure through this network. The Trojan label can be seen as important as it was effectively a trademark both for potential quality and for authenticity. Like most music brands it has been absorbed into the corporate structure through takeover and thus now has little to do with its origins being mainly a heritage brand. This leads to some degree of mythologizing about its nature and impact. Trojan was *not* an integrated structure of production at all levels like Tamla Motown. It largely licensed material from Jamaica which was also done by many other labels which were run by white English businessmen purely as businesses (such as Magnet records). I have not tabulated the data but I checked the UK hit singles of those on a list of 102 Trojan artists and a substantial number had either all of their hits when they were on another label or their main hits on other labels. As Trojan fragmented into many imprints due to the vanity of some artists, I double checked that this was not an artefact and it was not. The key trick to making the imported music palatable was to add further string arrangements to the records. The Trojan style records probably paved the way for Bob Marley to be launched in the UK. The keynote feature of this was his authenticity effectively watermarked by Rastafarian content. However, his band the Wailers, for the most part, did not play on his "global" records being replaced by white session musicians with no reggae background. We may also note that the most successful single charts reggae artist of all time in the UK was Judge Dread a white man albeit one who was genuinely enamoured of the genre and accepted by practitioners in it. His hits were also largely unplayed on the radio due to their risqué nature. The success they did achieve illustrates possibly the power of distribution that an ethnic imprint can achieve outside mainstream media exposure.

Despite its limited nature as a full-blown musical firm, Trojan helped establish a focus for reggae in the UK for the full music audience. This has not happened for British Asian music. British Asian music refers to what would in North America be called "South Asian" as it refers to people of Indian, Pakistani, Bangladesh, Sri Lankan origin. This experienced a significant potential of crossover in 1996–1997 with incursions into the UK dance music scene. This generated independent record labels who dealt in this music scene. Saha (2011) studies this scene, finding a general disillusion with the lack of continual mainstream success. He observes that Nitan Sawhney is the only British Asian musician from the club scene to have had mainstream success but, some would argue, only after he had softened his original club sound. He also reports interviews from label owners who are distressed by the temptation to submit to major label demands for creating purpose-built debased popularized versions of their music for the crossover market.

Free market economies obviously allow people to start specialist labels for ethnic music including those which are purely archival seeking to dig up works from the past from certain territories (such as African music). However such labels are constrained, not just by the power of major labels, and being statistically sampled out of the charts even if selling well, but also by the lack of outlets for exposure. The most valuable historic outlet has been radio. However, radio is a problematic medium for increasing the diversity of music. The commercial sector is intrinsically conservative with a tendency to risk aversion and relying on what has been successful in the past rather than taking risks with new sounds. Most potently, the use of playlists means the same songs are played several times a day thus blocking any kind of diversity leaving it to specialist stations.

As we have previously seen, nostalgia is a powerful force so we find many commercial stations have little interest in new music at all let alone new music that is, in content, not very new. The rock and roll revolution was the main force to reduce racial audience segregation in the USA. African American personality DJs performed flamboyantly on stations identified as black although virtually none were black owned or managed (Barlow, 1998). The issue of black (and wider ethnic) music broadcasting remains a problematic one especially in the UK.

The subsidized or not for profit sectors (such as NPR in the USA and the BBC in the UK) are subject to the whims of the taste makers who determine scheduling and the presenters they have appointed. Hence the disproportionate influence of the late John Peel in the UK. Like Andy Kershaw his programming of non-white music was part of the truly musical omnivorous idea that we should be open to all forms of music in all places.

Clearly such white liberals may fail to engage with the broader non-white audience. Pirate radio is the classic vehicle for breaking up the crust of ossified tastes and for "correcting" market failure by supplying customers whose tastes have not been satisfied by the granters of radio licences. Pirate radio, in the UK, was not originally conceived of, or a vehicle for, overcoming racial consumption barriers arising from the monopoly of state licensed broadcasters. Its focus was on what at the time was deemed to be "pop" much of which would now fall under the genre of "rock". Some promotion of black music would have taken place due to the immense success of Tamla Motown in marketing a global pop crossover.

However, since the 1980s in the UK, pirate radio has been an important driving factor in driving through emerging urban black music styles. Low costs of entry to the market were important as it was a relatively simple matter to rig up low powered broadcasting of FM signals.

Sustained efforts were made to eradicate this activity by vigilant policing. The government's prolonged campaign in favour of DAB radio, despite its lack of progress, also provided something of a technological threat. It would be much harder to run a pirate DAB station meaning shrinking audiences if FM radio had withered altogether and internet radio had not come along. Ultimately, this pirate radio music scene made similar transitions to the ship-bound piracy of the 1960s.

Taxpayer funded BBC introduced a service to meet the need – Radio 1 Xtra and some operators went legit. The legitimizing processes have left many unhappy about the outcome (Kenlock, 2013). Choice FM was the first successful radio station granted a licence to cater for the black community. It took more than seven years of continuous campaigning to win their bid for the 96.9 FM frequency for south London in 1990 and four years of campaigning to get another frequency allocated in Birmingham. The costs of complying with the greater complexity of DAB broadcasting led to the company being sold to Global Radio, in 2004, who turned it into Capital Xtra. The new owners sacked popular DJs and reduced the black music and community content to a level leading to its compliance with the licence conditions being monitored.

As with the failure of the Lilith fair, for female-only music, discussed in the previous chapter it may be that the era of black UK radio is largely gone. One of the key arguments of the supporters is the market failure one that we have a community who cannot readily get to hear "their" music on a regular basis due to its commercial limitations. The ability to stream music, steal music, listen to internet radio on PCs, phones, other portable devices and internet radio nullifies the accessibility argument. These forms of listening however do not tend to form communities in the same way but, as mainstream music becomes more of a homogeneous "one size fits all" product, the use of music listening (as opposed to forming choirs etc.) to coalesce communities is perhaps a thing of the past.

Given the concerns about the "sold out" nature of commercial black former pirate stations, it is not surprising to find criticism of the BBC's 1 Xtra as a token white-run act of political correctness. Radio 1 Xtra caused controversy, in summer 2014, over its Black and Urban Music Power list. (Number 16 on the list.) Wiley took to Twitter to denounce the whiteness of the list which peaked with Ed Sheeran appearing at number one. As Ed Sheeran is a white man, with receding red hair, who probably does not look that dissimilar to some members of the UK royal family one might think this ascends almost to the status of looking like an April Fool that migrated to the wrong date.

Perhaps what we have here is the dangerous politics of numbers in the hands of the non-statistical. There are other people in the top 20 who are clearly white or British Asian but if Jimi Hendrix can be given a Native American Music Award then perhaps they have every right to high acclaim in terms of black and music urban power. Indeed we may say they have more as they appear on this list because of working in the genre, even if it is not their primary or original style as with Sheeran, often with other people also on the list. However, Sheeran is not just on the list but is above Tinie Tempah (number three) and Dizzee Rascal (20) who have been the poster boys for the idea of a distinct UK identity in black urban music. This could be construed as perhaps racist.

Case study: British Asian musical assimilation

As mentioned, the British Asian diaspora did not germinate an equivalent of Trojan records to disseminate their cultural products nor, for a long time, did they have any specific radio licences. As with 1 Xtra, the BBC in the UK provides an outlet on BBC Asian Network which is however primarily a speech station with some music. Hence the launchpad for British Asian music was weaker than for reggae. There is the additional complication that reggae music is a form linked to a popular global music (American soul and r'n'b) whereas the traditional Asian music from which British Asian music derives does not have this linkage. There is also the problem that the younger generation of British Asians, like the Irish equivalents before the Pogues punkified Irish music, may see music of their parents' epoch as initially too old and dull and demeaning. British Asian music would seek its fusions with elements of reggae music and later electronic dance rather than rock despite the rogue presence of the isolated hit of "Brimful of Asha" by mixed race band Cornershop and the all-female all-British-Asian ensemble, Voodoo Queens.

As the matter can only really be properly illustrated by specific case studies, I now take a look at the careers of some specific Asians beginning with a migrant and then some UK born figures.

First, Biddu. In 2010, Biddu won an "Outstanding Achievement" award at the UK Asian Music Awards and was also awarded the "Lifetime Achievement Award" at the JD Rock Awards in India. He has been ranked at number 34 on *NME*'s "The 50 Greatest Producers Ever" list. His own views on his work can be found in his autobiography *Made In India*, perhaps a telling title as much of his music was not (although it is a reference to a work).

He began in the 1960s, singing in India before moving to England. Biddu was brought up in Bangalore and through shortwave radio (Radio Ceylon) he developed a liking for the UK pop/rock boom of the 1960s. He learnt to play the guitar and started a Beatles and Stones cover band called Trojans singing in English. By the time he came to Britain in 1967 he had already assimilated the incoming dominant global musical style *with the expectation of contributing in this idiom* not *perpetrating his indigenous music or a hybrid form*. In an interview with the BBC years later, he said "I didn't really know too much about England or anything – I'd just come here on the chance of meeting the Beatles and doing some music. Everything that I did had this danceable flavour." One may argue that dance elements are intrinsic to Indian culture but his mid-period dance music success was far removed from this. In his later career he would amalgamate a wide range of cultural influences and techno-logical changes in music production.

He was unable to become a singer in England which we may attribute to employer discrimination. He said "as an Indian in those days they were happier to hire me as an accountant than as a singer". Due to such segmentation, he moved to another part of the music sector where his appearance would not be a factor. From the beginning his work was extremely global in terms of collaborators and content. It was also both entrepreneurial and creative. He composed, produced and arranged. His first hit was with Japanese band the Tigers in 1969. He then began to work in film soundtracks and early disco. These elements combined in his work on the film *The Stud* (1978). In 1972 he produced with UK-based Jamaican-born musician Carl Douglas "Kung Fu Fighting" essentially a novel disco record, which in 1974 became a huge worldwide hit.

His mid-1970s career then began to parallel American soul musician Barry White who had his Love Unlimited Orchestra as well as his solo records. The crucial difference being that Biddu did not make any vocal records (he has finally returned to doing some singing when he is past the age of 50) after his initial rejection as a singer. This may well be because there seemed to be no opening in the UK market for South Asian singers as such. There were some broadly Anglo-Indian singers (leaving out Cliff Richard being born in India) such as Gerry Dorsey and Peter Sarstedt (whose two brothers also had success as singers) who had a massive hit in 1968 with "Where Do You Go To My Lovely?" He had quite an Indian appearance (as does Gerry Dorsey more famously renamed Engelbert Humperdinck) and his diction was in the region of exaggeratedly polite Indian English. The song though was in the idiom of French chansonnier complete with accordions and references to high class French places, celebrities and institutions.

These figures might be said to blend into the UK scene as per the Native American heritaged figures in the USA like Cher, Robbie Robertson and Rita Coolidge.

The first seemingly full "Indian" hit record in the UK was "Ever so Lonely" by Monsoon sung by Sheila Chandra in 1982. Chandra was the first (South) Asian singer to appear on the flagship television show *Top of the Pops*. The song was written by white English songwriter Steve Coe who married Chandra. The track had been floating around for three years originating from Coe's label "Indipop" records which popularized the term Indipop.

Biddu turned to making Asian music in the 1980s which was crossover in the sense that he merged indigenous music with disco. However although massively successful in native and diasporic territories it did not crossover into mainstream English speaking markets thus remaining a case of segmentation in consumer markets. In the 1990s, he popularized Indipop in several ways in the Indian market. He also worked in oriental markets such as J-pop singer Akina Nakamor.

In his later years he has shifted to presenting more of his own work of a spiritual and reflective nature. In 2014, interviewed on a visit to India (Kumari, 2014) he explained that he would not work in the desi music industry due to the excessive monopoly power wielded by Bollywood in giving composers spot fees instead of royalty payments. He went on to a "lay" explanation of the market failure argument, in welfare economics, that this was retarding the emergence of new work.

Biddu had arrived in the UK as a young adult migrant from India who did not have a diasporic market to sell his indigenous music to. He did not want do this in any case as his migration was due to a desire to participate in Western pop music. His later hybrid Indian musical forms seem to have been a product of accident and experimentation rather than ideologically or commercially motivated. Or they may be more appropriately situated in his general polyglot orientation as he worked in commercial music forms in many areas of the world and in many styles collaborating with people of a wide range of ethnicities.

It might be argued that Biddu's career stemmed from the market segmentation which kept him out of singing and performing as an isolated adult in migrant. When migration reaches significant levels, we eventually have not only a bigger audience for the relocated musician but also new generations who have grown up in the host culture.

By the 1990s the UK did not have an infrastructure for putting any kind of UK-Asian music in the mainstream. Media exposure was sporadic. A key figure was Apache Indian. He had eight UK top 50 hit singles (or EPs) between 1992 and 1995. Only one of these was significantly large. The rest peaked outside the top 20, with the exception of the one politically significant title "Arranged Marriage" which reached 15 in 1993. Four hits featured other reggae singers. The lyrics to "Arranged Marriage" have been perceived as provocative and controversial. For a pop record there is quite a large number of them and they alternate between English and non-English, some of it a type of patois rather than formal speech. In plain terms of what is written down, the lyrics seem to be really just a list of what the character in the song (if we assume this is an *auteur* work rather than a confessional one) wants from his arranged bride. It then refers to him sleeping with his (presumably white English) girlfriend. The overall tone is a portrayal of the character's sexism towards both women.

These records, with the exception of the first, and one due to licensing deals, appeared on a mainstream label, Island Records, who dropped him from his contract in 1997. His signing to Island might have raised hopes of a substantial "Marleyfication" of his work but this did not transpire. His best known, and widely used track "Boom Shack-A Lack" might be deemed something of a novelty record and thus affine with Millie Small's "My Boy Lollipop" (a 1964 UK reggae hit) as something which signifies a prescient rather than established market.

So we find there are some successes for this ethnic group, but they do not produce a major mainstream continuing act or high profile singer and they do not have a label brand to serve as a catalyst. These things do not matter so much now as we find ourselves in an age of high quality DIY technology and amorphous urban music. The British Asian pioneer of DIY music, White Town (Jiyota Mishra) had one surprise quirky number one UK single and international hit, "Your Woman", in 1997 but no further major success. His brief success was due to major label patronage (EMI/Chrysalis) but he was quickly dropped.

His hit was used in an homage by Naughty Boy who exemplifies the modern situation but also has parallels with Biddu. Shahid Khan (Naughty Boy) operates as DJ, songwriter, record producer and musician but not as a singer or live instrument player. In 2013, Naughty Boy's "La La La" was awarded "Best Song" and "Best

Video" at the 18th MOBO Awards. Naughty Boy was born to Pakistani parents in the UK. Khan started his career as a business using a grant from the Princes Trust in 2005. In 2012, he signed a publishing deal with Sony. His work is conspicuous for working with people of diverse gender, nation, background and ethnicity. These include people connected to television talent shows and those of supposedly more edge and credibility. The list includes Chipmunk and Wiley, Emeli Sandé, Leona Lewis, JLS, Cheryl Cole, Jennifer Hudson, Alesha Dixon, Tinie Tempah, Ed Sheeran, Gabrielle and Katy Perry.

His debut solo album, "Hotel Cabana", peaked at number two in the UK. We cannot assess at this stage whether Naughty Boy's success will continue. As he is primarily a production rather than front person (like Biddu) he will be less subject to the whims of fashion than singers/rappers. What we can see is that he seems to have been morphed into the black and urban music genre (he was number seven on the aforementioned Radio 1 Xtra power list).

Ethnic music, within the UK, has ultimately not been compounded in any systematic way. If we were blue sky thinking in the mid-1990s we might have speculated that black Asian and reggae labels would rise up as major businesses able to keep their artists out of the hands of majors and that their stars would contain some kind of high selling pop hybrid combos to rival Oasis or the Pet Shop Boys but it was not to be. Furthermore, there has been no significant polyethnic conglomerate independent business activity in the sector.

Conclusion

As we continue to see, research in the demographic dimensions of the economics of music consumption and production is somewhat fragmentary and unsatisfactory. For race, it is even more so than other areas. Work on race in music is overwhelmingly dominated by simple bipartite division into "black" and "white" music. It is difficult to pin down any pure forms of what these types are. Political and ideological elements render discussions both confusing and controversial. Black music often seems to be a shorthand term for the music of the black Afro-American culture and its identity becomes mixed up with political struggles. Some of this was made clear by parts of Chapter 3. Moving to the next chapter on trade will help highlight the wider racial dimensions of the world musical market.

Note

1 At www.sphinx.org.

10

INTERNATIONAL TRADE

Introduction

According to the IFPI (2013), global recorded music sales totalled $16.5 billion in 2012 being the first year of industry growth since 1999. Given that these are the years of wrestling with the problems of digital delivery and over a one-third of the above revenue is from digital sales, it might seem the corner is being turned from the great IPR theft panic. It should be borne in mind that these figures and those quoted below are based on recording sales (plus PRS etc.) and thus exclude touring income.

Music is a highly global economic phenomenon. The development of technology in travel, recording and broadcasting has helped this to accelerate rapidly in its nature.

The arrival of the internet takes the global aspect to its peak. Someone could make a recording right now and potentially have it heard, almost anywhere in the world, within a few minutes. Thanks to taste profiling and linking, by supply services, and the power of word of mouth, via social media, it is even possible that the global audience for this fictitious work could be a very large one in a very short time. Digital exports and imports could even reduce greatly the necessity of travel for musicians where travel is for the purposes of promotion rather than performance per se.

The balance of trade in musical markets is extremely uneven in terms of the pairwise relative exports and imports of different countries. A very open global economic market may increase or decrease such trade imbalances. In this chapter we need to consider also the "cultural balance of trade" as opposed to the traditional economic balance of trade. This is problematic but it highlights the very different kinds of figures we might come up with to buttress the argument, common in pro-music lobbying bodies, that the music industry is vital to the economy because of the fantastic contribution it makes to export earnings. This argument is usually dragged out to stake a claim for more government subsidy and support. Recently, the UK government has accepted this in terms of computer/video games but not music.

First, we have to consider whether the standard international trade theory of economics can be applied to music.

Trade theory and the cultural balance of trade

The ideas of the advantages of trade, between groups, have already arisen in our earlier chapters on gender and race. Race and gender groupings do not operate different currencies and they do not have their own physical national borders. The presence of such things does not fundamentally change models of the gains from trade.

International trade theory is one of the oldest and most venerable parts of the body of economic theory. Before the arrival of supposedly objectively neutral "scientific economics", the mercantilists of the seventeenth and eighteenth centuries argued that trade between countries was a simple matter, of buying cheap and selling dear, to make a profit at the expense of more gullible nations. Added to this, profits may be expanded by capturing other nations, in war, and using their resources. In musical terms, the slave owning nations could, for example, exploit the melodies and rhythms of their captives to make goods to sell on to other nations. This did not happen at the time as there were no recorded media and little scope for such touring events.

Following the later work of Smith and Ricardo, trade came to be seen as potentially beneficial to *all* countries even those who were poor in terms of resources and actual output at the time trading began. The free market would not condemn the resource poor countries to a never-ending life of poverty, as trade with the richer countries would raise the sum of output available to all. This is the broad theme of economic liberalism, as part of the wider idea of not interfering with markets.

In terms of trade theory, we have two basic ideas. The simpler of these, is sometimes confused with, or substituted for, the more complex of the two in popular discussion. The simplest idea is that of *Absolute Advantage* which says a country should specialize in the production of goods in which it is more productive than its (assumed single) trading partner. Thus, if one country is better in all sectors there is no basis for reciprocal trade assuming there are no other binding constraints.

In the case of musical product let us assume a simple two country, two goods, two factors ($2 \times 2 \times 2$) only model where the factors are melody and rhythm and the goods are melody-heavy music and rhythm-heavy music with there being no hybrid third good. If one country was more endowed or productive in the field of melody, and the other was more endowed or productive in the field of rhythm, then there is a basis for trade if the musical outputs could be owned and sold. The melody-rich, rhythm-poor country would export melody-heavy music to its partner and vice versa. In equilibrium, we might expect to see a corner solution of sole specialization as there should only be two-way trade if we introduce further specialization. All these factors would be constrained by transport costs. In a totally simplified pre-digital model, each country would manufacture its recorded media, in its own country, and export these by ship or plane.

Although it is not realistic, this can be clarified in terms of an example – let us say the UK exported heavy metal to France in return for ballads. One real world problem this example brings to light, is that singing in English is the dominant style in commercial global music even in cases where it might appear that the words are both unintelligible and of little importance or relevance. When the global pop music sector was coming to its market eminence, English speaking singers (including the Beatles) actually revoiced their hits, in other languages such as German and French, to increase sales in the export territories. Singers rendered the "foreign" versions purely phonetically due to not being able to speak the language. This policy was quickly stopped although there continue to be some bilingual artists (but these are people fluent in both languages). Although there have been jovial pieces of retrospective journalism about the export versions of 1960s UK pop, there has been no statistical study of how much revoicing contributed to export success. Economic theory would lead one to expect that non-English speakers would employ others outside the production unit to finesse their English language songs, to enhance their export potential. However, historical evidence does not support this. The classic example is Abba, for whom English language rendering was handled by their manager (not a specialist) with hilarious, and often mocked, consequences. It is also surprising that so few European language ballads have been retooled, with brand new English lyrics, for global success (as was the case with "My Way" by Frank Sinatra and one or two others).

Clearly in the music sector, there is a proliferation of two-way trade. A UK tour of Italy, or sales of CDs to Italy, of an Italian opera is an obvious example. Sometimes this is of the "selling coals to Newcastle" variety where one nation exports products derivative of an original product from the importer, e.g. the white r'n'b musicians of the UK in the 1960s. In this connection we should note that provenance protection is not available for music. For other goods, the European Union has decreed that a place name product (such as Cornish pasty or Provençal ham) has to be made in the actual place. For music, this is not possible. You cannot seek redress against someone making Italian disco or Chicago house in a different place. This limits the exclusivity of trade in music and can only be partially redressed by using first mover advantage to drive tourism revenue.

The more complex idea is that of *Comparative Advantage*. This says that there is a basis for trade, even if one country has universal absolute advantage, as the total output of the traders can rise due to specialization in the product in which there is comparative advantage. In the case of music, for example, we might posit the case in the simple two country case where one country is *comparatively more productive* (or endowed) in the field of rhythm and *also* in the field of melody so it is better at both the ballads and the heavy metal in the example given. But, if England is *relatively better* at heavy metal, compared with ballads in the example above, it should specialize in this allowing France to focus on ballads. We can thus have more of both genres in total (provided there are not constant returns to scale in both sectors in both nations).

In the cultural industries in general, there are cases of application of the simple theories expounded above often using gravity models. Within such studies we may find application of the traditional "infant industry" argument that free markets may not lead to the best possible outcome. That is, exposure to global competition might kill off domestic products that would, in the long run, have been successful. In the case of Australia, we could for example say, that allowing the Beatles free access to domestic markets in the 1960s, prevented home-grown groups from getting enough audience support to allow them to develop to efficient operation. The countervailing argument is one of "reverse engineering" that the home-grown talent would learn more proficiently if exposed to international competition. With trade restrictions, domestic musical labour would, like Biddu in the last chapter, have to resort to more obscure radio in pre-internet days.

In the long-run, in economic terms, the "learning from the imports" does not seem to have worked, for the genre of "jangly" Beatles-y pop music has failed to deliver antipodean artists (including New Zealand's "Dunedin" sound) with significant musical success. The premier artists in this field, the Go-Betweens, founded 1978, amassed numerous critical plaudits but were abject economic failures. Even in their own country they failed to produce any hit records despite eventually becoming such a cultural icon that one of their political leaders would give their works as a gift to leaders of other nations.

Modern popular forms of music are very heavily based on core technologies such as specific software packages (Logic, Ableton, Reason, Cubase, Fl Studio) and devices (external controllers, Akai MPCs etc.) available globally without prohibitive import tariffs. These enable almost anyone in any country to have the same resources to emulate the methods used in the imported works. The basic sound of an artist such as Eminem, or Lady Gaga, may be fairly easily copied anywhere and advice on how to do it is now copious and easily accessed.

The locational trade advantages that still remain are acoustic spaces and human capital. Historically these have been provided as market bundles in commercial recording studios. These have closed in rapid numbers due to technological advances eroding many of their functions. The acoustic spaces can be captured using the high-level mathematics of convolution to reproduce them digitally anywhere any time on a computer. In some cases this has led to visitors to famous studies being policed to prevent them from "capturing" the space covertly. Early enthusiasm for the results of convolution has dimmed in music technology circles meaning that there is still market value to the "real thing". There is also still some residual demand for working with specialist engineers etc., in specially designed rooms with properties that might be categorized in the "magic" category. The magic element in production might also be lurking in the idea that there is a "vibe" in the location therefore artists should go to Jamaica or Florida, or wherever to seek out the serendipity addition to the production function. Generally, this trade element seems to have receded with the advance of micro-technology and the increasingly clinical nature of music production. Even if people do go to high-value specialized locations they will do less of the process there than previously, as much preparation can be done on computers and other portable digital devices.

In terms of the financial theory of international trade, strong exchange rates will benefit home producers, in countries that manufacture little musical equipment as there is a vigorous market in retail technology exports. French and German music equipment warehouses, explicitly target the UK and other countries. Differential transport costs are not a factor and pricing in euros is usually not adjusted by these retailers to compensate for changes in the euro exchange rate.

Let us turn to the idea of a "cultural trade balance". It is convenient to think of the 1990s when CD albums emerged as the dominant commodity form for recorded music, to illustrate the issues. Imports could be measured by the physical number of CDs brought into the country from other territories. However, we might typically have an artist from the UK or USA or Jamaica, on a major record label which is Japanese (given their takeover of Anglophone businesses), where the CD is manufactured in another country. Let us say this was Mexico. Is this a Mexican import, a Japanese import or a UK/USA import? One could simply divide up the earnings by these territories of origin and apportion these shares to the respective nations. However the estimation of these shares in practice would not be simple as they would require accurate probing of the revenue components for different individuals and companies.

This would be a purely economic balance of trade which would not show us the direction of travel in terms of the contribution of culture or "creativity". A cultural balance of trade shows, at the basic level, the import–export difference in terms of the artistic end products. This could be broken down by genre, within music. Some genres may be more autarchic than others within a country. Although they do not directly show revenues, the record charts/hit parades can provide a useful illustration of this. Snapshots of these can now be readily obtained from such things as Android apps which show the "Top 20s" of numerous countries.

The official custodian of cultural product definition is UNESCO (see e.g. UNESCO, 2005). UNESCO (2005) defines trade in cultural goods and services as, "the exports and imports of tangibles and intangibles conveying cultural contents that might either take the form of a good or a service". Cultural goods and services include "the goods and services which are required to produce and disseminate such content, including cultural equipment and support materials, as well as ancillary services".

They distinguish between core cultural goods and "related cultural goods". In terms of music, the list for core cultural goods includes under the heading "Recorded Media" gramophone records, discs for laser-reading systems for reproducing sound only, magnetic tape (recorded), other recorded media for sound. In the "related cultural goods" category, for music we have musical instruments plus "Sound player recorder and recorded sound media". Typically in terms of revenue the related sector grosses four times more than the core category of music on its own.

However the ratios of profitability per unit will be much less as digital sound media have had very low physical costs of production compared to the retail price.

Leaving aside the remarkably arcane terminology, if we followed this and just used the core definition then the exclusion of musical instruments would give us a very different picture of the balances of trade, for reasons we come to below. Basic descriptive statistics, on the cultural balance of trade, convey a static picture. They overlook the long-run economic benefits which may accrue from impacts of exported cultural goods on trade in general and tourism in general as well as cultural good specific tourism (such as visiting a musical heritage site or music festival). General trade and tourism effects can arise because the cultural exports function as a type of advertising for the supplying nation. This will be greater if there is some national identity in the products – in the case of films, the movie *Crocodile Dundee* may have greatly increased American consumer interest in Australia. The generic product export will not have such an impact as importing customers will be oblivious to any national identity in the product, to the extent that they may not even know (or care that) the artist was from a different country. Staying with antipodean examples, the recent "out of the blue" success of New Zealand singer Lorde does not convey anything specifically New Zealand in its content whereas the setting of the *Lord of the Rings* films operates as an ersatz tourist information film by showing the locations. We should also note that she was, at age 13, signed up for development by a powerful global corporation (Universal Music Group) rather than being left in the weak infrastructure of indigenous firms.

This becomes a tricky definitional area in terms of statistics versus the perceptions of consumer and producer agents in the market. In the field of cutting-edge "urban music" English consumers and producers of the various "grime"-related genres would see their work as very English and thus very different from the Chicago house music of early times which is somehow "very" Chicago. Sales of such music abroad may not be perceived as such by the consumers. Thus, to the dispassionate economist this may be an instance of two-way trade. It is likely that ambassadorial promotion via interviews with the artist (if they become global enough) would be more effective in cultural trade terms. This may potentially create product differentiation by altering the subjective perceptions of the importing consumers. As emphasized, in Chapter 6, it does not matter what a good actually is but what people think it is. So someone may buy something they effectively already have because it's the English XYZ new sub-genre and therefore worth having.

Musical trade patterns: export failures and import substitution

Global music markets are heavily concentrated in a small number of countries as far as revenue is concerned. These are the USA, UK, Japan and Germany. The UK and Germany vie for third and fourth places. Some fluctuations may be due to the exchange rate adjustment used in the data. The recent higher position of Germany may also reflect that physical music sales are holding up better there.

Using IFPI data, Throsby (2002) shows shares of world sales growing, in 1991–2000, from around 30 to 40 per cent for North America, and declining from around 40 to 30 per cent for Europe. The Asian share is in the 20–25 per cent region. This leaves only about 5–10 per cent for the rest of the world. In terms of specific countries' overall markets, recent years' IFPI data shows very strong growth in Sweden, India, Norway and China, whilst other countries have been little above static or slightly declining.

Such sales figures only reflect legal trade and therefore the benefits to importing economies of "parasitic trade" are omitted. The enforcement of IPRs is much weaker in the 5–10 per cent rest of the world segment who may be consuming large amounts of product from the major markets either at zero or low price. This will benefit these economies, even those within them who do participate in piracy or approve of it, thanks to income effects. They have more to spend on all goods due to saving on their music consumption.

However the de facto "dumping" of musical imports creates disincentives for indigenous musical products. Collin (2001) espouses a specific hypothesis about Serbia that piracy eroded the indigenous music market because of the unfair price differential it brought to works by mainstream legacy artists, primarily British and American. Pirated physical recordings of these were much cheaper than the newly produced CDs of indigenous artists. As this is an essentially journalistic/historical work, it is not specifically stated as a hypothesis or subject to any statistical testing. It might be that indigenous artists would have struggled anyway to a degree where any substitution effect from piracy is negligible whatever the moral unpleasantness of the case.

In terms of cultural balance of trade, the IFPI data is incomplete for Europe prior to 2000 due to lack of data from some countries. In 2000, North America had only 10.8 per cent in imported sales share by artist. European import share was almost 60 per cent, Asian almost 25 per cent, Australasian just over 75 per cent. Thus the aggregate European and Australasian sectors are open economies in terms of cultural balance and the Asian and North American are much more closed. Table 10.1 gives a more detailed picture, for 2002, showing the share of domestic music sales in total recording sales, by country, in rank order from top to bottom bracketed into selected deciles. This is adapted from UNESCO (2005). More recent figures are broadly similar. A comment, in this source, appears to contain a typo; while commenting on the degree of autarchy question with respect to its growth in the 1990s it says the data, where the musical economy is more closed, does not necessarily show that "high" local repertoire is always produced. I presume this means high amounts and is due to the global problem of ownership of rights mentioned earlier.

We can see broad patterns here. The smaller Anglophone countries, and those with colonial links, are very open. The openness of the Australasian sector is extreme.

Apart from the UK, USA and Japan, other countries with high internal demand filling are those which are less culturally linked to the rest of the world.

TABLE 10.1 Share of home music sales in domestic market in 2002: rank order in selected
deciles

	Greater than 90%
1	Egypt
2	USA
3	India
	70–90%
4	Zimbabwe
5	Saudi Arabia
6	Japan
7	Thailand
	50–70%
8	Brazil
9	Russian Federation
10	Korea
11	France
12	Qatar
13	Lebanon
14	UK
15	Ukraine
	40–50%
16	Bahrain
17	Romania
18	Argentina
19	China
	30–40%
20	Mexico
21	Bulgaria
22	Pakistan
	20–30%
23	South Africa
24	Sweden
	<20%
25	Ireland
26	Chile
27	Australia
28	Malaysia
29	New Zealand

Source: data from UNESCO (2005).

The open cultural economies for music are inevitably importing a large share of
their imports from American artists, as is the case with the film and television
industries.

The population size is very different in different territories but this, by itself,
would not necessarily explain why there would be high degrees of openness in areas
of lower population. A smaller population, such as in Australia, does not necessarily

mean that the musical workers in the nation would be too few to supply a large share of the internal demand for music. One component of the degree of cultural trade imbalance is the power of global record companies which will seek to promote internationally established artists, in external territories, rather than promote the career of home artists.

There is also the issue, as noted, of a very strong tendency for the verbal parts of music to be in the English language if global success is to be achieved. Whether guided by government policy or not (see next section) a country could fall into various broad categories (see Rutten, 1991). The most basic one is neo-autarchic, or verging on self-sufficiency, where the majority of the country's music consumption is sourced from within. Exports of this music may be mainly diasporic being consumed almost totally by emigrants. This is clearly a logical possibility in many oriental economies. These do not require English language rendered music due to the large internal market. Similarly, India has a massive internal market which is to some extent dominated by Bollywood. If we follow the argument of Biddu, in the previous chapter, it may be that Bollywood is restricting the export potential of Indian music. There are some other enclaves in first language English countries, such as the French market in Canada.

The neo-autarchic situation might, in some cases, be more of a property of a group of countries rather than a single nation. Much has been made of "Hallyu" (a term coined in the late 1990s by Chinese journalists) in the K-Pop wave of surging Korean cultural exports especially in East Asia. This covers fashion, films, television and more but its source is traced to music as the precipitating factor (Kim and Ryoo, 2007; Kim and Ahn, 2012; Disdier et al., 2010; Park, 2014).

However, according to Park (2014), in 2011, music was only 4.7 per cent of the Korean cultural exports, to the East Asian region, by value compared to the towering 57.3 per cent share of the computer games industry. Given the pervasiveness and flexibility of use of music it may be that it has contributed to the sales of other goods in the cultural basket through operating as a kind of advertising for the overall style of cultural good.

Despite the central role attributed to music and the presentation of descriptive data on it, classical statistical research on this topic does not explicitly single out musical data although it will be part of the sectors in the regression equations. For example, Kim and Ahn (2012) compute TII (an index of trade balance which indicates advantage of exports over imports) for the cultural sector. For Korea's trade with East Asian countries, such as China, Indonesia, Japan, the Philippines, Singapore, Taiwan and Vietnam, the index, on average, has been at levels above unity. The results of their regression analysis indicate that Korea's cultural exports positively affect overall exports to the ten East Asian countries. From their point estimates, they claim that a 100 per cent increase in Korean cultural exports, to Asian nations, increases overall exports to them by 4.2–4.7 per cent, with a higher figure for reproducible cultural goods (i.e. media) 5.4–5.8 per cent. We might infer from this that music has quite a high spin off impact on general exports but we can not tell for sure. There is no guarantee that each type of "cultural" good transmits the same number of units, per dollar value, of cultural impact. Computer/video games have been defined as cultural goods but their export may have little spin off impact on goods in general.

The TI index is quite volatile in the data shown from year to year and for non-Asian (usually English speaking countries) there is some sign of a decline. Sales may be volatile due to very high impact of some individual releases. Sales to such territories is of a broadly diasporic nature. It is unlikely that K-Pop will appeal to older migrants as it is an integrative product which hybridizes local elements with global Anglophone pop culture. As such, it may appeal to younger and second generation oriental consumers, outside their place of origin, but they could over time secede to Anglophone formats (whatever the latest permutation of broadly electronic dance music and hybrids of it with heritage pop/rock styles is) in preference to K-Pop.

In theory, although it is unlikely, the UK or USA, could verge on autarchy (and the USA figures may be said to tending there) as there is a sufficient excess supply of home-produced musical works that they do not necessarily need to use musical end products of other nations. Self-sufficiency in music is much easier, than self-sufficiency in food or fuel. The opposite case is the totally open economy which receives exported music but is unable to generate much of a market for its own product or export this in significant amounts. This could, of course, be justified as a rational outcome of comparative advantage subject to consumer tastes. However, there may be an element of cultural trade hegemony where the domestic product (e.g. local rap or hip hop) is seen as inferior to the global (usually American) product. It has, for example, been claimed that for the middle class aspirational Latin American student the music of choice is US hip hop and urban music in general.

It is possible that a neutral objective measurement could determine that there is, indeed, such inferiority. In terms of goods characteristics models of consumer choice, authenticity may be attributed to provenance. That is, even given like for like, the consumer may not want to prefer the Swedish hip hop or Chinese heavy metal record unless they are a deviant, or omnivorous, style of consumer. There are some Western consumers who venerate Japanese and Mexican guitar and psychedelic bands but this is not a serious sector in terms of economic magnitude. The vogue for "world music" which began in the early 1980s (Broughton *et al.*, 1994) originally was strongly tied to a mapping of style of music to place of origin. Its roots are in the concerns of liberal Western musicians. Since 1982 WOMAD Festivals has travelled all over the world, bringing artists to numerous locations and entertaining over one million people. However, world music has mushed into a catch-all term and is likely to boil down further into roots music as per the fate of the NAMA music award highlighted in the previous chapter.

It has become a marketing term for all non-Western music leading to criticisms of the *inauthenticity of consumers, not* producers! Former Talking Head, David Byrne (1999) wrote an "I Hate World Music" editorial in the *New York Times* objecting to the use of the term, partly on the grounds that it promotes "insincere consumption" not a category I have yet heard on the lips of professional economists as to them it does not matter what the motives of consumers are. He also argues that other consumers may be put off. Part of such pejorative views on the world music genre labelling is that it embodies "tourism" not proper music consumption. The implication of this is tourism is just going somewhere and coming back unchanged whereas musical consumption is supposed to have deeper meanings and be life changing. But as we are dealing with markets, this is inevitably an attempt to "buy" meaning. Some (Kassabian, 2004, 2013) have classified the ubiquity of world music (in adverts, coffee bars etc.) as "distributed tourism" which is in some way a radical new form of listening (connected to the restyling of muzak in terms of using established artist work).

Crossover with mainstream musical idia, may be desirable, but world music hybridization (such as Polish or Egyptian reggae, or Balinese-Afghanistani crossovers) has not been predominant in terms of market influence. This disrupts the one to one mapping in which the consumer sees authenticity. However, the Polish reggae is quite a vibrant sector particularly among young musicians some of whom have gone to the Caribbean to record.

Given the freedom of world musical trade and the lack of provenance protection, there is no restriction on the generation of "fake" world music. It has often been claimed that many Pan Pipe CDs were the product of lone jobbing composers, in their bedrooms or garages in the UK, using digitally sampled versions of the original instruments. The zenith of such fake world music was the emergence of Incantation, in the UK in 1981, with their big hit "Cacharpaya". This band came from the musicians playing at the Ballet Rambert who had been asked to play in a work on oppression in South America. There was direct import substitution here as the band played the music in place of, using CDs, of authentic music from the region. This is nothing to do with the other Incantation (an extreme metal band) and seems to be a very rare case of shared musical names with no litigation.

At the level of genre and individual artists, we can also have exports which are not as popular in the home market, or may even be popular as an export but not popular at all at home. Size of markets might lead one to expect artists from smaller countries to target the major sectors without respect to their home market. This will contribute to cultural hegemony of the dominant markets as exporters to it will be under pressure to tailor their product contents to the customers there. This may involve dropping certain nuances such as singing accent. Northern Ireland musician "Duke Special" Peter Wilson has reported being ordered to sing in an English accent by bands, in London, to which he belonged. Such export-oriented stylings may be subconsciously absorbed, as in the case of male "blues" singers from the UK 1960s boom who developed in an imitative manner most specifically of Ray Charles.

As the core elements of popular music are so basic and easily reproduced, it would seem anomalous that very successful artists cannot be exported unless they have some very negative trait (such as an oppositional fundamentalist religion). If we look at some well-known UK cases, we can identify a number of artists who had very successful careers but virtually no, or only very isolated, USA success such as Cliff Richard and Status Quo.

Vocal stylings may be an element in some of these cases but we cannot meaningfully test this as a hypothesis. In the Status Quo case, the thin nasal voices are meshed into the overall sound. It is difficult to think of large American successes where the vocal element is not sculpted to be at the "front" of the soundscape. Even the more mumbled incoherent vocal stylings of USA "grunge" (e.g. Nirvana) to which Britpop may have been a reaction are a quite emphatic and forward element. The grunge boom and the Britpop boom did not show much sign of import substitution. Rather, the UK managed to export Bush (a grunge style band) to the USA for whom there seemed to be much less home demand. They had one large single and one large album hit at home (in 1996) with little other sales compared with five albums in the US accumulating $10 \times$ Platinum awards and positions from 1–22 in the Billboard charts. They had ten top 10 USA singles and several other hits.

The "Britpop" of Blur and Oasis might have been expected to penetrate the USA with its strong nostalgic echoes of the 1960s British invasion. Part of its product innovation seemed to be singing in more emphatic accents, than the precursors of the 1960s boom, which may even be unintelligible to some Americans. The comparative failure to export Britpop to the USA is shown in Table 10.2.

TABLE 10.2 Britpop at home and in the USA: Blur and Oasis chart positions

Oasis					
Albums	Top	Top 5	Top 10	Top 20	Top 50
UK	7	0	0	0	0
Cum.	7	7	7	7	7
USA	0	3	1	2	0
Cum.	0	3	4	6	6
Singles	Top	Top 5	Top 10	Top 20	Top 50
UK	8	11	4	2	1
Cum.	8	19	23	25	26
USA	0	1	0	1	3
Cum.	0	1	1	2	5
Blur					
Albums	Top	Top 5	Top 10	Top 20	Top 50
UK	5	0	1	1	0
Cum.	5	5	6	7	7
USA	0	0	0	0	0
Cum.	0	0	0	0	0
Singles	Top	Top 5	Top 10	Top 20	Top 50
UK	2	7	2	6	8
Cum.	2	9	11	17	25
USA	0	2	1	0	1
Cum	0	2	3	3	4

Source: data from Official Charts Company (www.officialcharts.com) and Billboard (www.billboard.com/artist/277052/Oasis/chart?f=379 (both accessed 23 June 2014)).

Notes
Live and compilation albums excluded. Cum. = cumulative total to that bracket including previous brackets.

The relative lack of success is very evident with the only notable penetration being early career album success, in the USA, by Oasis. Changes in radio, record promotion and the composition of genres dominating the marketplace may account for the lack of success in the USA. Mainly guitar oriented rock bands by this time were likely to be seen initially as "indie" album fodder. Thus they would find it more difficult than in earlier times to find breakout opportunities for mass market success.

Import substitution is a normal part of the process of trade. Foreign products can be manufactured at home by direct copying. If the copying is not 100 per cent direct, then the good may be an imperfect substitute. Textbook economic theory would argue that this requires a lowering in price, which will be proportionate to the degree of imperfection.

As we have seen throughout this work, price reductions are seldom a significant factor in competition between musical works. There may be fire sales of over-stocked works but artists do not compete in the normal economic sense in which a slightly bruised apple (inferior attempt at a musical style) would clear in the market because of a price differential with the unblemished item. Countries could enforce price discrimination via import taxes or subsidies to home produced goods. This does not happen for trade purposes. However, there are differential rates of commodity taxation of music within different countries (following different rates for goods in general). In the USA it varies by state. Europe is generally 20+ per cent. Hong Kong is zero and apart from China, at 17 per cent, the level in East Asia is low often below 10 per cent. This may encourage certain distortions in trade.

It has also been argued (Gowers, 2006) that national variations in droit de suite create distortions by encouraging indigenous artists to sign, in the USA, for example but there is (inevitably given the lack of many policy variations) no convincing evidence on this.

In previous epochs, where global cultural products encounter significant inertia of movement there are opportunities to profit from imperfect domestic substitutes. In the 1950s and 1960s the song itself, in UK markets, was arguably more important than the artist in terms of record sales. A "hit" in the USA market could be quickly copied before the "original" version could make the market. This could not really happen in the film industry which the UK government was trying to protect with levies, at the time, due to time needed to produce and relatively weak market power. UK record companies had a large degree of control, for the home market, and could rely on some possible home radio play preference. At this time musician union objections meant that recorded music was still limited to some degree in broadcasting. A classic example of this kind of import substitution is the song "Rubber Ball" by Bobby Vee in 1961. There were smaller UK covers by Marty Wilde and the Avons. In 1956, Tommy Steele copied the arrangement of Guy Mitchell's "Singing the Blues" but in this case both records reached number one spending a combined 35 weeks on the UK chart (22 for Mitchell and 13 for Steele).

These cases provide export earnings to the writers of the "foreign" hit although possible substitution effects deprive the artist of income they may have earned. Ad hoc and uncoordinated cartel activity mirrored the opportunistic copying of black records in the USA by white artists once they saw them "breaking" on the specialized race charts.

This kind of import substitution was killed off long ago leaving us with direct copying of artists' styles which cannot themselves be copyrighted. This has tended to be ineffective when 100 per cent copying is attempted (as in the USA group the Knickerbockers' "Lies" a complete Beatles style copy) leaving us with absorption which is part of the normal production process of popular music in any case.

We have already seen the high musical openness of Australia. Australia has the features of being an English speaking country which (unlike Canada) does not have an indigenous other language music industry of note. It has also had some interesting legal copyright and distribution issues. Australia is largely seen as a culturally thriving country. It has a comparatively small population, so in terms of performance one might expect to see it have less weight in the global music economy than the UK and the USA despite its English language base. In the 1960s a dispute blocked recorded musical works by overseas artists to a significant degree. It is claimed that the dispute opened the door for Australian artists to cover overseas hits whilst the rival original was not in the way (as in pre-Beatles UK). Once the blockage on competition was removed, it has been claimed, then Australian music fell back to infrequent levels of home chart success.

The arrival of rock and roll found the Australian consumer adopting very enthusiastically the most popular artists such as Elvis Presley. Indigenous hits were often novelty, or slightly folky, numbers like Slim Dusty's "Pub With No Beer".

The initial Beatles dominance in Australia was staggering even by the standards they achieved elsewhere (although we should note that in 1964–1965, as indicated earlier, a number of Epstein stable artists had huge hits with non-Beatles Lennon and McCartney songs). In Australia in one year alone they were number one for around six months.

Table 10.3 shows a summary of some more recent origin diversity data for Australia being a tabulation of the origins of the Top 100 singles in 2002. The share of American work is greater than the American share in world sales. The home-grown share is much higher than Australia's world music share. However this includes a substantial contribution from Kylie Minogue, a translocated artist whose key success came from moving to Britain. Big indigenous single hits in general depended quite heavily on some kind of television exposure in soaps or talent shows. In the actual titles/artists there is little sign of a foundation for long-run home growth in import substitution.

Achterberg *et al.* (2011) look at data for Dutch, French and German popular music from 1965 to 2006, claiming to find that there is some rise in import substitution over the period in terms of home-grown music.

The more prevalent type of import substitution in recent times has been due to the illegal "pirate" copies of CDs. This is not an import substitution policy and in some cases it would lead to loss of internal cultural revenue where there was mass bulk copying of discs in factories in other territories which were then shipped to

TABLE 10.3 Origin of Australian top 100 singles in 2002

Area of origin	%
USA	57
UK	12
Australia	15
Latinate	9
Spanish/Portuguese	4
German	1
Austrian	1
Swedish	1

Source: data from ARIA (Australian Recording Industry Association).

Notes
Aggregate non-UK European share is 7. Aggregate all-Europe share is 19.
Records with guest artist are officially listed by the primary artist – e.g. Dannii Minogue guesting is not reported as an Australian record. Country of origin is attributed as 50% of the performers being from the country. There may be other origin personnel in the works from any given country.

other markets. IFPI data for 2001 (Throsby, 2002) showed Paraguay (95 per cent) and China (90 per cent) as the most "piratical" countries in terms of estimated physical sales being illegal copies. This does not distinguish whether the pirated copies were domestic or foreign artists, or whether the illegal copies are home or imported, as the data are based on gross seizures of infringed material. The most recent high profile seizure of pirate CDs, was in Germany where the physical consumption of music is holding up more than comparable territories. These were destined for the home market. Given this, it is theoretically possible that this may improve the true value of the German cultural trade balance due to multiplier and redistribution effects.

Movements of capital

The trend in liberal democratic economies is towards greater freedom of movement in terms of labour and capital. There is no necessity for the balance of trade in end cultural products, and in cultural capital and labour to correlate strongly with each other. Trade theory suggests that a nation could dominate an end product market largely by relying on imported capital. The key labour issues will be discussed in the next section.

The Soviet economy, for obvious reasons, did not permit the importation of musical capital for a long time. As synthesizers became predominant in music production, the government took the step of instituting state production, often of what were broadly copies of Moogs which home musicians wanted. The most noted case is the Polivoks designed by Vladimir Kuzmin, who explained that these were often made in such places as tank factories and output was stepped up, beyond the needs of musicians to meet quotas, in five-year plans, because there was an excess of factories in existence (Reid, 2010). In interviews, he has estimated that about 200,000 were made based on the idea that around 20–25,000 came out annually during the production years of 1982–1990. Common internet sources are prone to quote an aggregate figure of about half of what he claims.

This results in the odd economic paradox of one of the world's most produced synths becoming a high priced scarcity item as the original Polivoks (which began to appear in outside countries in the late 1990s) is now a coveted item, of conspicuous consumption, amongst some musicians. It is now being replicated in raspberry pi type kit synthesizers and software emulations.

UNESCO (2005, p. 45, Box 7) showed the value of world musical instrument trade, in constant dollars, fell by 13.4 per cent between 1994 and 2002. English speaking country end products have been hugely successful in terms of export earnings (recordings, merchandise) and temporary labour migration (touring). However the hardware components of musical capital goods have predominantly been in the hands of Japanese companies whether they are acoustic or electronic end goods. Besides the dominance of such major prestige name brands, there is an increasing tendency for importation of oriental-sourced generic goods which are essentially non-branded or meaninglessly branded. The same microphone, for example, can be imported and sold by four or more different retailers under a fairly meaningless brand name of their own choosing.

Identification of the provenance of musical capital is complicated by the presence of Phoenix brands and brand buy outs. In the case of a Phoenix brand, the original company is long gone but the name has been repossessed because of its marque value. Someone else can resume production of the deceased products or can incorporate brand elements into new products. Brand buy-outs and phoenixing mean that the historical image associated with names may be essentially meaningless. Korg has acquired guitar brands such as Vox and Marshall. Piano (as in real acoustic or "grand" pianos as opposed to digital) manufacture historically became specialized in certain key countries especially Germany but with leading brands also in Italy and England. The main prestige pianos brands have been taken over (barring Yamaha which is already located in an electronics firm and besides this Yamaha had acquired a prestige UK brand) the latest being Steinway, bought by hedge fund billionaire John Paulson in 2013. The German company had for a long time been making models in American and German factories with some pianists preferring one provenance over the other.

The musical equipment market is dominated by three long-standing Japanese firms with a reputation for quality Roland (founded 1972), Yamaha (founded 1887 as a piano and organ manufacturer) and Korg (founded in 1962). The chief low cost firm in the market is the German Behringer (which has often used "copycat" issues of more expensive products) but this relies on low wage economy labour having a whole company town set up as Behringer city in China.

Of the high quality companies, Yamaha is the only one with a significant non-musical footprint due to its enormous activity in other areas, such as motorbikes, and the only one which makes acoustic instruments. It is also the only one with a long history in various acoustic instruments. The activity of these firms caters for the broad sub-markets of guitarists, keyboard workstations, recording and amplification equipment and DJ/performance. Effectively these Japanese firms have eroded European control of the music making market (formerly specialized in piano manufacture – see Ehrlich, 1976; various entries in Palmieri, 1996), thanks to capitalizing on mass, mechanized production due to, first, transistorization and then digital methods.

These companies also showed entrepreneurial flair in capitalizing on intellectual property that was generated, but not applied, in Western economies. John Chowning, of Yale University, invented the idea of FM synthesis in 1967 which produced musical instrument emulation using sine waves which modulated each other. The economic significance of this was that mathematical methods could be used to greatly reduce the cost of instrument manufacture as sound generation required much less processing. The maths are explored in Benson (2006). In 1973, his employer, Stanford University, licensed the discovery to Yamaha resulting, in 1983, in the DX7 synthesizer which (with its family spin-offs) was one of the best selling synths of all time. Allegedly over 200,000 were made (Pinch and Bijsterveld, 2003). This excludes the use of the technology in other products. For a while it became the dominant sound generator in computers and is heavily associated with classic early games. Stanford University, and hence the USA economy, benefited from the royalty income. It is not clear whether not manufacturing in the inventing country was harmful. Licensing the rights may have been a classic beneficial trade arrangement given relative labour, and other costs, and general comparative advantage. Similar factors apply to the development of other products. The "Rompler" based instruments which dominated the pre-software digital music area typically had their sample sets developed in USA branches of the Japanese companies.

Rival companies seeking to enter this market, in terms of hardware, were sporadic in Europe and the USA and have petered out or been absorbed. Such smaller companies face acute problems in terms of scale economies. Even if they outsourced basic manufacturing to oriental territories, the sheer number of units being produced was limited by the nature of the market and pricing tended to be very high relative to cost.

The most open market for musical capital is that for guitar effects pedals. Despite advances in technology and the convenience of digital multi-effects a veritable torrent of physical products come and go in this sector. The history of key manufactures and products is documented in Hughes (2004). Current non-major brands include basic items of around £20–30 (UK) value which can be seen on Amazon websites and typically come from oriental factories. Roland has also a significant brand establishment in this market via its Boss brand. For the purposes of this chapter perhaps the most significant exception to the oriental manufacturing supply was the presence of significant specialist USA companies. This may inspire some kind of provenance loyalty. The tribute website to Dod is americaspedals.net and the home page has a cartoonish stars and stripes incorporated logo. However this may be simply retro nostalgia as Roland/Boss eliminated the key American brands and their current existence constitutes phoenix brands and other specialist American owned brands are actually made in China. This tends to confirm the general picture of equipment manufacture being specialized in low wage countries even if the brand names are in higher wage economies to whom the profits will be returned.

When we turn to digital hardware and software, issues of labour costs and economies of scale in production decrease in importance. Specialization would be expected in a country where there is the appropriate intellectual capital. Software development requires coders so a nodal agglomeration of computer-related skills might be expected to raise export potential. Software that is not locked in dedicated hardware faces enormous problems of copyright protection. The dominant firms of Roland, Korg and Yamaha do not operate in software origination – their software products are mainly utilitarian applications used for managing and updating their hardware equipment.

The dominant country as a whole would seem to be Germany. Berlin-based Native Instruments, founded in Berlin in 1996, has grown to employ 400 people and moved away from initial freely reproducible software, has effectively eliminated rival software samplers from the market. Such companies also now make some hardware which is usually complementary to their software in such a way as to discourage copyright theft. This would typically be made in low wage oriental economies. None of the music tech companies (as with other information based companies) employ huge numbers of people so they are not a viable means of generating employment via export encouragement. The general area of tourism is more significant in this regard.

Trade policy: barriers and tourism

Mainstream economic theory argues in favour of free trade, so that a long-run equilibrium where the music and equipment of one or two countries dominate the music consumption of the whole world may, in principle, be globally optimal. It does not matter if some countries are effectively pushed out of these markets as they add to world well-being by making something else instead. Despite this there have been very notable restrictions on trade, especially for labour.

The most unusual case of trade policy is opposite to this. In Japan, Western classical music has been heavily encouraged. Japan probably has the most active concert scene, in this area, and the most investment in musical education of any country. This was political as the deliberate decision in 1868 to open up to the rest of the world was followed by the adoption of a heavy commitment to Western classical music in 1872. However, we now find many archetypal complaints about market failure (see Kurabayashi and Ito, 1992; Hewett, 2006; Oestreich, 2010). Japan has exported many star performers in the field, to the West, but much less in composition. However this may be inevitable as the market for new classical compositions is now so weak. There have been complaints about the rigidity of the playing styles of Japanese musicians and also discrimination against home-grown artists, in prefer-ence to overseas stars, in domestic booking.

In the limit, for political reasons, there may be a total ban on imports which may in some cases be just an aspect of a total ban on any kind of liberal or free thinking music. In such cases, the regime would also typically seek to underwrite state sup-ported music. Even in Iron Curtain Soviet Russia threatening Western rock music would find its way via an underground vinyl network.

Even without overt labour market interventions visa policies may be discrimina-tory in terms of trade due to the increased bureaucracy arising from growing con-cerns about covert illegal migration and the movements of terrorists. There have been numerous published complaints about this excluding African and other pro-ponents of world music from entering the UK (Appleton and Govinda, 2009). Those employed by major organizations, in the industry, have the resources to comply with the burdens and this further accentuates the difficulties of lower income musicians. Concern has been high about the "Schengen" visas (Di Federico and Le Sourd, 2012) with the EU increasing mobility within it but tightening movement in and out of it. The graphic on p. 39 of Di Frederico and Le Sourd indicates that Middle Eastern and North African musicians have the most com-plaints, in 13 categories, about temporary work visa problems. Musicians have also been completely banned for political reasons because of hostile relations between countries – see for example Sublette (2004).

There are three broad categories of overt labour market interventions. The three types are:

Prevention of entry of musicians to the country because they are taking the jobs of indigenous musicians

Musicians can migrate to a country which comes under general labour considera-tions. In May 2009, the UK's Migration Advisory Committee asked the government to exempt contemporary dancers and orchestral musicians from a new points-based visa system. The UK's Musicians' Union responded to this by noting that, while it was not opposed to foreign musicians working in the UK under certain conditions, "we do not agree with … the inclusion of orchestral musicians in the recommended shortage occupation lists, because we have yet to be convinced of there being a short-age of orchestral musicians in this country" (Smith, 2009).

This has the implication that the indigenous musicians can play the same type of music equally well (or better) otherwise the consumers of the country will lose welfare.

Musicians unions, throughout history have shown strong tendencies to oppose work visas, to tour, as well as full migration. Godbolt (2010) details the subterfuge employed by UK jazz fans, before 1940, to enable American jazz musicians to enter the country. In terms of trade, there is a "beggar thy neighbour" aspect to touring restrictions as global musical value may be lower due to the lack of cultural exchange. Free market logic began to prevail in the form of reciprocal exchanges (Cloonan and Brennan, 2013) between European nations in the 1940s. USA–UK relations were continually hostile with movement sometimes being totally unilateral (USA out, no UK in) amidst threats of strikes by the AFM (American Federation of Musicians). This is seen as becoming largely resolved by 1955.

Prevention of entry of musicians to the country on "artistic merit" grounds

Clearly this is a possible disguise for state control of what might be incendiary to the body politic in highly repressive regimes. However, the USA (not a totalitarian regime) has prevented musicians from entering the country on purely artistic merit grounds. This does not receive huge public attention because it is not applied to major highly successful star performers. On the other hand, it may deprive the workaday struggling musician of an important part of their livelihood. An illustration of such a case is the Anglo-Dutch group, the Legendary Pink Dots. No specific details were ever issued (as they are not in these cases) as to how the artists could try to improve to have their visas refused or why they were allowed soon after. As leader, Edward Ka-Spel put it in 1991:

> We got in two years ago.... Last year we were turned down for our visas. This year we must be of artistic merit because they let us in. I can just see them all in the immigration department bopping away under their headphones going, "Ah, those Pink Dots, they've redeemed themselves."
>
> *(quote in Sanner, 1991)*

It is impossible to determine the specific events of such a case. However, looking at the current USA visa guidance there is indeed a very clear indication of not just the use of "artistic quality" as a ground for refusal but even gradations of high quality to determine the type of visa granted. There are a number of different types of visa where international recognition is the main definition of quality. There are also requirements as to how long a threshold percentage of the ensemble has been with them. Overall this is not a transparent process. The applicant cannot tender some kind of expert witness document to "prove" their adequacy. It appears that the decision is simply taken on an ad hoc basis within the department.

Bad behaviour

Disqualification on purely *individual* bad behaviour grounds (such as for criminal convictions or comments made on stage during a musical performance) has no specifically musical aspect. The same broad rules are applied to non-musicians.

A number of noted UK performers have been prohibited entry to work in the USA due to drug use. This is typically triggered by recent home country convictions or charges, hence we also find others, whose similar behaviour is well documented even by their own hand at times, is ignored in visa granting.

Trade promotion

Opposite to these negative policies towards musical trade, is the policy of using music in a positive way to promote the economy of a nation. This can operate in both direct economic and more indirect long-term ways. Direct effects can be encouraged by subsidizing those with export potential or the use of trade missions to promote demand in target territories. Musicians may be part of trade mission activities directly but have also been sent on state sponsored cultural exchange tours.

The most pertinent indirect effect is the promotion of tourism. Tourism has the potential to redress some trade imbalances by increasing income to the weaker economies and can be part of a long-run economic development strategy. For a small island economy, significant development can occur from increased levels of economic activity, which are relatively small compared to the American contribution to the world music economy. However the net effect of music tourism may well not be equalizing as much of musical tourism as intra-country and many of the main tourist sites are in the dominant music countries.

Tourism may be induced by specific heritage or museum sites which have historic importance or by a more ambient factor of the belief that somewhere embodies the general "spirit" of a specific style of music. Sites may bring tourism by themselves or they may have associated festivals to give a focus to the visit (see e.g. King, 2004). Festivals may bring tourism spending independently of any musical site specific aspect.

The UK Music report "Destination Music: The Contribution of Music Festivals and Major Concerts to Tourism in the UK" analyses data from 2.5 million ticket purchases in 2009. This says (p.7) that only 5 per cent of the music tourists are from outside the UK, but they account for 18 per cent of the spending. Average reported spending per night by overseas visitor was £99, for music as a chief motivation, compared with £72 for overseas not motivated by music. In addition, p. 9 of the report says this is nearly a quarter more when it is in fact quite a lot more than a quarter more. It is probable, though not explored, that this differential might be due to the greater consumption of intoxicants by the musical visitor.

Most of the significant tourism/heritage sites are in the world's dominant music economy – the USA. These are ambient (or industry specific) sites – such as Chicago – as the home of "blues", Seattle for its grunge and Sub Pop label, Nashville and so on. Notorious or colourful person sites (Dollywood, Graceland) also operate. America contains many other cities which have had concentrations of musical activity and/or have had "sounds" appended to them (such as the Philadelphia sound) that do not have a tourism infrastructure geared around this.

Broadly, musical tourism to festivals and heritage sites will tend to redistribute income from poorer to richer areas or be simply neutral as with largely local festivals where most of the visitors are from within the region within the country. The most conspicuous case in a major music market where the music tourism can contribute meaningfully is in Detroit. This is the most notoriously economically declining area in the USA. It is typically quoted that 9 per cent of employment depends on tourism in general (as of around 2007–2008). In popular culture the city gave birth to Motown and techno music and is the original home city of Eminem, Aretha Franklin, Ted Nugent, the White Stripes and Madonna. The Motown Historical Museum sits in the original studio, known as Hitsville USA, and contains the studio and Gordy's apartment. An annual electronic music festival to celebrate the techno music heritage was set up in 2000 (there are now two electronic music festivals).

There do not seem to be any economic impact studies of the contribution Detroit music tourism makes to the local economy. However, this may not make much difference as the numerous studies for various other locales are limited as they tend to include double counting and mismeasurement of the net economic impact.

Small island economies have the possibility of net benefits from musical tourism. There have been many studies of the music sector in Jamaica and the Caribbean (Nurse, 2007; Rutten, 1991; Mitchell, 1996; Mundy, 2001; Burnett, 1996; Nurse, 2003, 2007; James, 2001; Wallis and Krister, 1984; Witter, 2002). These emphasize that interviews with practitioners find the collected data to seem highly inaccurate. It also appears that the music tourism scene is a largely sterile one where prefabricated bands churn out standard fare in hotels to tourists who do not venture out to "living" musical events. This is the antithesis of the USA blues region type of tour. UNESCO (2005) emphasizes (see Box 5 p. 40) that the majority of Jamaican musical activity is remitted overseas.

In general, the scope for musical tourism to resurrect disadvantaged and depressed regions seems limited. There is no clear evidence that the rate of return on putting public funds into this is greater than for more general economic activities.

Conclusion

There are significant disparities in bilateral trading in both music, musical making equipment and musical playing equipment. By itself this is not automatically a problem for any country which finds itself in deficit in any of these items. The exchange rate imbalance can be met by some other products which the country may follow according to the logic of comparative advantage. However, the remaining cultural deficit may be a matter of concern as, in the limit, we could tend towards sectoral hegemony and the effective elimination or museumization of some forms of national music. The ultimate fear in this regard is that everything outside the rock/pop/urban/country mainstream is boiled down into a mush of vaguely "roots" music.

We have now reached the end of the main body of this work. The final chapter will provide a brief overview and some further considerations.

11
CONCLUSION

I shall now comment on a few areas that were not covered and provide some recapitulation and clarification on those that were. The main focus for this book was to get away from the narrow theoretical and empirical approach to music in economic literature. There are three main areas which have dominated. The most preponderant in recent times has been the issue of downloading and streaming of music. There has also been a large number of papers on chart success and on specific problems of classical music – costs of orchestras, choice of repertoire and so on. There are very few papers outside these topics. There tends to be little explicit consideration of the social nature of music production and consumption other than empirically.

Much of the data used to study the economics of music is very unsatisfactory. You would not want decisions about your health to be made on the basis of statistics which are so far from accurately measuring the phenomena in question. There simply are no serious dedicated sources of data collection. Data is obtained "second hand" from general surveys and government and business data. This is not uncommon in many fields. In this one, it is probably worse than most and made considerably worse by people's insistence on reading too much into the results of using such patchy data.

I have not explicitly looked at the total social "value" of music as opposed to its mere revenue generation. This brings up the market failure problem. The market may supply too little music relative to the social optimum. It may also supply the wrong bundle. Too much of X and too little Y. From a purely mathematical point of view, it is logically possible that right now there is too much classical and folks/roots and jazz music and not enough hip hop and heavy metal. The case for market failure derives from the presence of significant elements of monopoly and the presence of both positive and negative externalities. In the latter case that music promotes violence and other bad behaviours. In the former, that it increases well-being, citizenship and even physical health. There has always been sporadic research on these issues – for example on the impact of music on Alzheimer's in terms of its ability to reboot memory in a way that might not be accessible in other forms of consumption.

There are acute problems producing monetized values of any accuracy for the impact of violence or the decline in severity of Alzheimer's. Apart from the intrinsic difficulties, short- and long-run impacts are hard to assess. Any figures produced will be subject to the very wide confidence intervals that public debate, and reportage, consistently overlooks.

The most serious externality problem relates to education. In Chapter 7, I did not discuss children and schooling as it would have been a divergence at the time. Outside Japan, few countries invest much in the musical education of children in compulsory schooling. Hence it is largely left to the free market, meaning that parents must decide to support children's musical education in competition with other uses of their income.

This will impact both consumption and production. A talented child may still compete for scholarship funds to further their studies or attempt to raise the money from social media or other campaigns. Or they might receive lessons from a benign patron who does not charge full economic cost. In terms of general musical production for a given country, there is such a tendency to oversupply of performers (as with acting) that it seems implausible that lack of investment in musical education is going to lead to a shortfall, in any area, for the consumer of music.

Perhaps more important is the argument about consumption. Studies of cultural consumption persistently highlight an increase in enjoyment and participation arising from childhood exposure to performing. Performing may increase the enjoyment to be had from consumption. It may also, in some specific cases, decrease it due to discontent at what was previously thought to be better than it now is. The cuts in musical education, in the UK, mean that children from non-musical backgrounds will not be exposed to musical instruments to a great degree. It could be argued that such musical exposure may be a foundation skill, like maths and literacy, which enhances cognition and functioning in other areas. There is a body of literature which seeks to demonstrate this. In the UK, for a long time the focus in education has been on increasing the computer literacy of pupils. This has led to awards for the composition software Sibelius. Musical education, via computers which are already in schools and pupils' homes is potentially very cheap. In principle, there is no reason why pupils could not be given music lessons, on tablets/phones which they already own given the cheapness of applications. The question that remains whether general purpose digital activity still provides the cognitive benefits to be found from engaging with physical instruments. I hesitate to use the term "real" instruments as digital pianos might provide the "look and feel" experience of acoustic pianos but they are not "real" in the literal sense that they are a digital simulation of something which provides sound by means of movement of physical parts. The external benefits of school musical activity may also be in terms of social capital. Ensemble playing (like team sport) is an activity in which people must learn to rely on each other and develop roles and structures which may prove useful in later economic life. We could set up ensemble activity with each member using phones, tablets, laptops or PCs concurrently but the co-ordination required will be of a different nature which may not bring the same benefits.

Returning to the general issue of value. One theme of the present work has been that narrow economic concepts of value fail to capture much of the dimensions of musical activity.

This is, of course, true for other areas (Douglas and Isherwood, 1979) such as food or team sport, which provide, in many instances, the most suitable comparison products. Recorded music, musical equipment and live performances are commodities. However, people have relationships to them which extend beyond price and cost. They may invest them with emotional significance which is not intrinsic to the item concerned in and of itself. They may self-exclude themselves from things which they might enjoy due to issues of identity and social affiliation. They may even choose to prefer goods that they are not enjoying (such as poor works by their favourite artists) due to concepts of belonging and assessing a collection of goods, as a whole, rather than discrete items. The analogy to team sport here is very complete.

My final remark is about what work might usefully be done in the future. Given the likely continuance of data poverty, economists might like to concentrate on some forensic exploration of the conceptual issues in analysis. The most pertinent one is the issue of costs. Literature on the music market throws around "cost" figures with careless abandon without seeking to identify clearly what a cost is. Generally these are not costs but expenditures. This is not the same thing in economic models of the firm. Traditional economic models of the cost function of the firm may not be appropriate here and it may be time for a more neo-Austrian approach to musical costs and entrepreneurship. Some studies of the costs of organizations, in the cultural field, even manage to jumble up cost functions with demand functions due to the tendency to treat expenditure as costs.

The other burning issue is the role of the record company. Depiction of the major record companies (like the detested bankers) as overpowered and overpaid fools, in some literature, may blind us to their economic role. At the other extreme, digital distribution and the emergence of crowdfunding have led some people to see a golden age of post-post-capitalist utopianism where fans and music makers live together in perfect harmony with no evil business getting in between them. This does not seem plausible. Like a dandelion or worm, depleted music capitalism will regenerate because large centralized organizations are the dominant mode of production in digital information economies. If musical capitalists subside finally, they would be replaced by total control from the other digital behemoths such as Apple or Google. If you want to be a small player focusing on quality and not excessively on profits then modern digital platforms facilitate this but it was something that can be done in any market system in any era.

BIBLIOGRAPHY

A

ABI Research (2011), Mobile Cloud Music Services: On-Demand, Internet Radio, Discovery, and Digital Locker Services, Research Report.

Abramo, J.M. (2011), Gender Differences of Popular Music Production in Secondary Schools, *Journal of Research in Music Education*, 59(1), 21–43.

Achterberg, P., Heilbron, D., Houtman, D. and Aupers, S. (2011), A Cultural Globalization of Popular Music? American, Dutch, French, and German Popular Music from 1965 to 2006, *American Behavioral Scientist*, 55(5), 519–524.

Adermon, A. and Liang, C. (2010), Piracy, Music and Movies: A Natural Experiment, IFN Working Paper No. 854, Uppsala Center for Fiscal Studies, Svealand, Sweden.

Adorno, T.W. (2002), *Essays on Music: Selected, with Introduction, Commentary and Notes by Richard Leppert*, trans. Susan H. Gillespie, University of California Press.

Aguiar, L. and Martens, B. (2013), Digital Music Consumption on the Internet: Evidence from Clickstream Data, JRC Technical Reports, Working Paper 2013/04.

Ahlkvist, J.A. and Fisher, G. (2000), And the Hits Keep on Coming: Music Programming Standardisation in Commercial Radio, *Poetics*, 27, 301–325.

Ahn, I. and Yoon, K. (2009), On the Impact of Digital Music Distribution, *CESifo Economic Studies*, 55(2), 306–325.

Akerlof, G. (1984), A Theory of Social Custom, Ch. 5 in Akerlof, G. *An Economic Theorist's Book of Tales*, Cambridge University Press.

Albinsson, S. (2013), Sound Earnings? Income Structure of Swedish Composers 1990–2009, *Review of Economic Research on Copyright Issues*, 10(1), 36–73.

Alcala, F. and Gonzalez-Maestre, M. (2010), Copying, Superstars, and Artistic Creation, *Information Economics and Policy*, 22(4), 365–378.

Alexander, P.J. (1994), New Technology and Market Structure: Evidence from the Music Recording Industry, *Journal of Cultural Economics*, 18(2), 113–123.

Alexander, P.J. (1996), Entropy and Popular Culture: Product Diversity in the Popular Music Recording Industry, *American Sociological Review*, 61(1), 171–174.

Alexander, P.J. (1997), Product Variety and Market Structure: A New Measure and a Simple Test, *Journal of Economic Behavior and Organization*, 32, 207–214.

Alexander, P.J. (2002), Peer-to-Peer File Sharing: The Case of the Music Recording Industry, *Review of Industrial Organization*, 20(2), 151–161.

Alexander, P.J. (2013), The Music Recording Industry, Ch. 7 in Brock, J. *The Structure of American Industry*, 12th edn, Waveland Press.

Allmendinger, J. and Hackman, J.R. (1995), The More, the Better? A Four-Nation Study of the Inclusion of Women in Symphony Orchestras, *Social Forces*, 74(2), 423–460.

Alpert, L. (1983), Estimating a Multi-Attribute Model for Different Music Styles, *Journal of Cultural Economics*, 7(1) 63–81.

Amegashie, J.A. (2009), *American Idol*: Should it be a Singing Contest or a Popularity Contest? *Journal of Cultural Economics*, 33(4) 265–278.

Andersen, B. and Frenz, M. (2010), Don't Blame the P2P File-Sharers: The Impact of Free Music Downloads on the Purchase of Music CDs in Canada, *Journal of Evolutionary Economics*, 20(5), 715–740.

Anderson, B., Hesbacker, P., Etzkorn, K.P. and Denisoff, R. (1980), Hit Record Trends 1940–1977, *Journal of Communications*, 30(2), 31–43.

Anderson, C. (2006), *The Long Tail*, Random House.

Appleton, J. and Govinda, M. (2009), UK Arts and Culture Cancelled, by Order of the Home Office, Manifesto Club.

Asai, S. (2011), Demand Analysis of Hit Music in Japan, *Journal of Cultural Economics*, 35(2) 101–117.

Attali, J. (1985), *Noise: Political Economy of Music*, University of Minnesota Press.

Axelrod, R. (1984), *The Evolution of Cooperation*, Basic Books.

Axelsson, A., Eliasson, A. and Israelsson, B. (1995), Hearing in Pop Rock Musicians: A Follow-Up Study, *Ear and Hearing*, 16(3), 245–253.

B

Bacache-Beauvallet, M., Bourreau, M. and Moreau, F. (2012), Piracy and Creation: The Case of the Music Industry, *European Journal of Law and Economics*, DOI: 10.1007/s10657-012-9360-1.

Bacache-Beauvallet, M., Bourreau, M. and Moreau, F. (2013), Information Asymmetry and Contracts in the Recorded Music Industry, Unpublished ms.

Baker, A.J. (1991), A Model of Competition and Monopoly in the Record Industry, *Journal of Cultural Economics*, 15(1), 29–54.

Bakker, G. (2006), The Making of a Music Multinational: PolyGram's International Businesses 1945–1998, *Business History Review*, 80, 81–123.

Banerjee, A. (1992), A Simple Model of Herd Behavior, *Quarterly Journal of Economics*, 107, 797–818.

Banerjee, D. and Chatterjee, I. (2010), The Impact of Piracy on Innovation in the Presence of Technological and Market Uncertainty, *Information Economics and Policy*, 22(4), 391–397.

Barker, G.R. (2012), Assessing the Economic Impact of Copyright Law: Evidence of the Effect of Free Music Downloads on the Purchase of Music CDs, ANU College of Law Working Paper No. 2, Australia.

Barlow, W. (1998), *Voice Over: Making of Black Radio*, Temple University Press.

Baumol, W.J. and Baumol, H. (1994), On the Economics of Musical Composition in Mozart's Vienna, *Journal of Cultural Economics*, 18(2), 171–198.

Bayaan, I. (2004), Technology and the Music Industry: Effects on Profits, Variety and Welfare, Working Paper, Emory University, GA.

Bayton, M. (1993), *Feminist Musical Practice: Problems and Contradictions, in Rock and Popular Music: Politics, Policies, Institutions*, Routledge.

Bayton, M. (1999), *Frock Rock*, Oxford University Press.

Becchetti, L. and Eleeuteri, S. (2006), Piracy Repression and "Proustian" Effects in Popular Music, Unpublished ms.

Becker, G.S. (1965), A Theory of the Allocation of Time, *Economic Journal*, 75, 493–517.

Becker, G.S. (1991), *A Treatise on the Family*, Harvard University Press.

Becker, G.S. and Murphy, K. (1988), A Theory of Rational Addiction, *Journal of Political Economy*, 96, 675–700.

Becker, G.S. and Stigler, G.J. (1977), De Gustibus Non Est Disputandum, *American Economic Review*, 67(1), 76–90.

Behar, A., Wong, W. and Kunov, H. (2006), Risk of Hearing Loss in Orchestra Musicians: Review of the Literature, *Medical Problems of the Performing Arts*, 21(4), 164–168.

Belinfante, A. and Davis, R.R. (1978/9), Estimating the Demand for Record Albums, *Review of Business and Economic Research*, 14(2), 47–53.

Belinfante, A. and Johnson, R.L. (1982), An Economic Analysis of the U.S. Recorded Music Industry, *Journal of Cultural Economics*, 6(2), 11–25.

Belk, R. (1995), Collecting as Luxury Consumption, *Journal of Economic Psychology*, 16(3), 477–490.

Belleflamme, P. and Peitz, M. (2010), Digital Piracy: Theory, CORE Discussion Papers 2010060, Universite Catholique de Louvain.

Bellis, M., Hennell, T., Lushey, C., Hughes, K., Tocque, K. and Ashton, J.R. (2007), Elvis to Eminem: Quantifying the Price of Fame through Early Mortality of European and North American Rock and Pop Stars, *Journal of Epidemiology and Community Health*, 61(10), 896–901.

Benjamin, T. (2009), The Economics of New Music, PhD thesis, Oxford University.

Bennett, A. and Peterson, R. (2004), *Music Scenes: Local, Translocal and Virtual*, Vanderbilt University Press.

Benson, D. (2006) *Music: A Mathematical Offering*, Cambridge University Press.

Bentley, R.A., Lipo, C.P., Herzog, H.A. and Hahn, M.W. (2007), Regular Rates of Popular Culture Change reflect Random Copying, *Evolution and Human Behaviour*, 28(3), 151–158.

Bentley, R.A. and Maschner, H.D.G. (1999), Subtle Criticality in Popular Album Charts, *Advances in Complex Systems*, 2(3), 197–209.

Bernheim, D. (1994), A Theory of Conformity, *Journal of Political Economy*, 102, 841–877.

Berry, S.T. and Waldfogel, J.L. (1999), Public Radio in the U.S.: Does it Correct Market Failure or Cannibalize Commercial Stations? *Journal of Public Economics*, LXXI, 189–211.

Beyers, W., Bonds, A., Wenzl, P. and Sommers, P. (2004), The Economic Impact of Seattle's Music Industry: A Report for the City of Seattle's Office of Economic Development, Seattle.

Bhattacharjee, S., Gopal, R.D., Lertwachara, K. and Marsden, J.R. (2006), Impact of Legal Threats on Online Music Sharing Activity: An Analysis of Music Industry Legal Actions, *Journal of Law and Economics*, 49(1), 91–114.

Bhattacharjee, S., Gopal, R.D., Lertwachara, K. and Marsden, J.R. (2007), Stochastic Dynamics of Music Album Lifecycle: An Analysis of the New Market Landscape, *International Journal of Human-Computer Studies*, 65, 85–93.

Bikhchandani, S., Hirshleifer, D. and Welch, I. (1992), A Theory of Fads, Fashion, Custom and Cultural Change in Informational Cascades, *Journal of Political Economy*, 100(5), 992–1026.

Bishop, J. (2004), Who are the Pirates? The Politics of Piracy, Poverty, and Greed in a Globalized Music Market, *Popular Music and Society*, 27(1), 101–106.

Bishop, J. (2005), Building International Empires of Sound: Concentration of Power and Property in the Global Music Market, *Popular Music and Society*, 28(4), 443–471.

Black, G.C., Fox, M.A. and Kochanowski, P. (2007), Concert Tour Success in North America: An Examination of the Top 100 Tours from 1997 to 2005, *Journal of Popular Music and Society*, 30(2), 149–172.

Black, M. and Greer, D. (1987), Concentration and Non-Price Competition in the Recording Industry, *Review of Industrial Organization*, 3, 13–37.

Blackburn, D. (2004), On-line Piracy and Recorded Music Sales, Working Paper, Harvard University.

Blackburne, S. Mr Justice, Decision (2006) Case between Matthew Fisher, Claimant, and Gary Brooker and Onward Music, Defendant, High Court of Justice, Chancery Division London, Neutral Citation Number [2006] EWHC3239 (CH) Case No. HC05101374.

Boldrin, M. and Levine, D.K. (2010), *Against Intellectual Monopoly*, Cambridge University Press.

Boone, C.L. (1995), All Male Programming: An Antitrust Violation? *International Alliance for Women in Music Journal*, 2–4 October.

Boorstin, E.S. (2004), Music Sales in the Age of File Sharing, Working Paper, Princeton University.

Borowiecki, K.J. and Kavetsos, G. (2011), Does Competition Kill? The Case of Classical Composers, Trinity Economic Papers, TEP Working Paper No. 1111, Dublin.

Botstein, L. (2008), The Unsung Success of Classical Music, *Wall Street Journal*, 3 October.

Bounie, D., Bourreau, M. and Waelbroeck, P. (2007), Pirates or Explorers? Analysis of Music Consumption in French Graduate Schools, *Brussels Economic Review*, 50(2), 167–192.

Bourdieu, P. (1979/1984) *Distinction: A Social Critique of the Judgement of Taste*, Routledge.

Bowmaker, S., Phillips, R.J. and Johnson, R.D. (2005), Economics of Rock'n'Roll, pp. 389–422 in Bowmaker, S. (ed.), *Economics Uncut: A Complete Guide to Life, Death, and Misadventure*, Edward Elgar.

Boyle, D. (2000), *The Tyranny of Numbers: Why Counting can't make us Happy*, Harper-Collins (2001 edition).

Bradley, L. (2013), *Sounds Like London: 100 Years of Black Music in the Capital*, Serpent's Tail.

Bradlow, E.T. and Fader, P.S. (2001), A Bayesian Lifetime Model for the Hot 100 Billboard Songs, *Journal of the American Statistical Association*, 96(454), 368–381.

Bradshaw, A. and Shankar, A. (eds) (2010), *Production and Consumption of Music*, Routledge.

Brandes, L., Franck, E.P. and Nüesch, S. (2011), Selling the Drama: Death-Related Publicity and its Impact on Music Sales, Working Paper, University of Zurich, 21 June.

Broughton, S., Ellingham, M. and Trillo, R. (1994), *World Music: The Rough Guide*, Rough Guides.

Brown, A., O'Connor, J. and Cohen, S. (2000), Local Music Policies within a Global Music Industry: Cultural Quarters in Manchester and Sheffield, *Geoforum*, 31, 437–451.

Brown, H. (2003), The Caribbean Music Industry: Building Competitiveness and Enhancing Export Capabilities in an Emerging Sector, Caribbean Export Development Agency.

Brown, La T. (2006), Estimating the Economic Impact of the Music Industry on Local City Governments, International Academy of Management and Business, Conference Paper Publication Proceedings.

Brown, W.G., Brown, K. and Alexander, P.J. (2002), Radio Market Structure and Music Diversity, Federal Media Ownership Working Group Paper 9, September.

Bryson, B. (1996), Anything but Heavy Metal: Symbolic Exclusion and Music Dislikes, *American Sociological Review*, 61(5), 884–899.

Bryson, B. (1997), What about the Univores? Music Dislikes and Group Based Identity Construction among Americans with Low Levels of Education, *Poetics*, 25(2), 141–156.

Buchanan, J.M. (1965), An Economic Theory of Clubs, *Economica*, 32(1), 1–14.

Bufwack, M.A. and Oermann, R.K. (1993), *Finding Her Voice: The Saga of Women in Country Music*, Crown Publishers.

Bull, M. (2000), *Sounding Out the City*, Berg.

Bull, M. (2002), The Seduction of Sound in Consumer Culture: Investigating Walkman Desires, *Journal of Consumer Culture*, 2(1), 81–101.

Bull, M. (2004), Automobility and the Power of Sound, *Theory, Culture and Society*, 21(4–5), 243–259.

Bull, M. (2005), No Dead Air! The iPod and the Culture of Mobile Listening, *Leisure Studies*, 24(4), 343–355.

Burke, A.E. (1994), The Demand for Vinyl L.P.s 1975–1988, *Journal of Cultural Economics*, 18(1), 41–64.

Burke, A.E. (1996), The Dynamics of Product Differentiation in the British Record Industry, *Journal of Cultural Economics*, 20(2), 145–164.

Burnett, R. (1993), The Popular Music Industry in Transition, *Popular Music and Society*, 17, 87–114.

Burnett, R. (1996), *The Global Jukebox: The International Music Industry*, Routledge.

Bustinza, O., Vendrell-Herrero, F., Parry, G. and Myrthianos, V. (2013), Music Business Models and Piracy, *Industrial Management and Data Systems*, 113(1), 4–22.

Buzzarte, M. and Bickly, T. (eds) (2012), *Anthology of Essays on Deep Listening*, Deep Listening.

Byrne, D. (1999), Crossing Music's Borders: "I Hate World Music", *New York Times*, 3 October.

C

Cage, J. (1994), *Silence: Lectures and Writings*, Marion Boyars.

Cain, G. (1976), The Challenge of Segmented Labor Market Theory to Orthodox Theory, *Journal of Economic Literature*, 14(4), 1215–1257.

Camerer, C.F. and Thaler, R.H. (1995), Anomalies: Ultimatums, Dictators and Manners, *Journal of Economic Perspectives*, 9(2), 209–219.

Cameron, S. (1995), On the Role of Critics in the Culture Industry, *Journal of Cultural Economics*, 19(4), 321–331.

Cameron, S. (2002), *The Economics of Sin: Rational Choice or No Choice at All?* Edward Elgar.

Cameron, S. (2003), The Political Economy of Gender Disparity in Musical Markets, *Cambridge Journal of Economics*, 27(6), 905–918.

Cameron, S. (2005), Pop and Judicial Efficiency: Economic Considerations in the Spandau Ballet Case, *Journal of Interdisciplinary Economics*, 17(3), 327–344.

Cameron, S. (2008), E-baying for Blood: Non-competitive Flexible Pricing in Entertainment Ticketing: Some Demand Side Evidence, *Applied Economics*, 40(10–12), 1315–1322.

Cameron, S. (2011), Criticism, pp. 139–141 in Towse. R. (ed.), *Handbook of Cultural Economics*, 2nd edn, Edward Elgar.

Cameron, S. and Collins, A. (1997), Transaction Costs and Partnerships: The Case of Rock Bands, *Journal of Economic Behavior and Organization*, 32(2), 171–183.

Cameron, S. and Ward, D.R. (2000), Abstinence, Excess, Success? Alcohol, Cigarettes, Wedlock and Earnings, *Economic Issues*, 5(2), 37–52.

Campbell, D. (1975), Black Musicians in Symphony Orchestras: A Bad Scene, *The Crisis*, January, 12–17.

Cantor, P. (2001), An Interview with Paul Cantor, *Austrian Economics Newsletter*, 21(1).

Carroll, M.W. (2003), Whose Music is it Anyway? How We Came to View Musical Expression as a Form of Property, Part 1, Villanova University School of Law Working Paper Series.

Carter, E.L. (2002), *Who and Where are They? Black Symphonic Musicians.*

Cassy, J. (2003), Old School Earners: Sanctuary Proves Safe in Global Music Downturns, *Guardian*, 21 January.

Ceulemans, C. (2009), Commercial Success of Rock Artists in the U.S.A.: The Role of Internal Competition, Working Paper ECARES, Université Libre de Bruxelles.

Ceulemanns, C. and Detry, L. (2008), Musical Characteristics and Success in Popular Music, Unpublished ms.

Ceulemans, C., Ginsburgh, V. and Legros, P. (2011), Rock and Roll Bands, (In)Complete Contracts and Creativity, *American Economic Review*, 101(3), 217–221.

Chace, Z. (2011), How Much Does it Cost to Make a Hit Song? www.npr.org/blogs/money/2011/07/05/137530847/how-much-does-it-cost-to-make-a-hit-song (accessed 8 September 2014).

Chace, Z. (2013), The Real Story of how Macklemore got "Thrift Shop" to No. 1, www.npr.org/blogs/money/2013/02/08/171476473/the-real-story-of-how-macklemore-got-thrift-shop-to-number-one4 (accessed 8 September 2014).

Chan, T.W. and Goldthorpe, J.H. (2007), Social Stratification and Cultural Consumption: Music in England, *European Sociological Review*, 23(1), 1–19.

Chang, J. (2007), *Can't Stop Won't Stop: A History of the Hip-Hop Generation*, Ebury Press.

Chapman, R. (1992), *Selling the Sixties: The Pirates and Pop Music Radio*, Routledge.

Chapman, R. (2010), *Syd Barrett: A Very Irregular Head*, Faber and Faber.

Chi, W. (2008), Does File Sharing Crowd out Copyrighted Goods? Evidence from the Music Recording Industry, Working Paper, Department of Economics, Johns Hopkins University.

Chiang, E.P. and Assane, D. (2002), Copyright Piracy on the University Campus: Trends and Lessons from the Software and Music Industries, *International Journal of Media Management*, 4(3), 145–149.

Chiang, E.P. and Assane, D. (2007), Determinants of Music Copyright Violation on the University Campus, *Journal of Cultural Economics*, 31(3), 187–204.

Choi, P., Sang, H.B. and Jun, J. (2010), Digital Piracy and Firms' Strategic Interactions: The Effects of Public Copy Protection and DRM Similarity, *Information Economics and Policy*, 22(4), 354–364.

Christgau, R. (1970), Look at that Stupid Girl, *Esquire*, June.

Clawson, M.A. (1999), When Women Play the Bass: Instrument Specialization and Gender Interpretation in Alternative Rock Music, *Gender and Society*, 13(2), 193–210.

Cloonan, M. and Brennan, M. (2013), Alien Invasions: The British Musicians Union and Foreign Musicians, *Popular Music*, 32(2), 277–295.

Coase, R.H. (1937), The Nature of the Firm, *Economica*, 4, 386–405.

Cohen, A.I. (1987), *International Encyclopedia of Women Composers*, Books and Music.

Cohen, R. (2005), *The Record Men: Chess Records and the Birth of Rock and Roll*, Profile Books.

Cohen, S. (2007), *Decline, Renewal and the City in Popular Music Culture: Beyond the Beatles*, Ashgate.

Coleman, J.S. (1987), Norms as Social Capital, pp. 133–155 in Radniitzky, G. and Bernholz, P. (eds), *Economic Imperialism: The Economic Approach Applied Outside the Field of Economics*, Paragon House.

Collin, M. (2001), *This is Serbia Calling: Rock'n'Roll Radio and Belgrade's Underground Resistance*, Serpent's Tail.

Collins, A., O'Doherty, R. and Snell, M. (2006), Rising Stars, Superstars and Dying Stars: Hedonic Explorations of Autograph Prices, University of the West of England, Discussion Papers 0603.

Collins, P. and Morton, B. (eds) (1992), *Contemporary Composers*, St. James Press.

Colonna, C.M., Kearns, P.M. and Anderson, J.E. (1993), Electronically Produced Music and its Effects on the Performing Musician and Music Industry, *Journal of Cultural Economics*, 17(1), 69–74.

Competition Commission (2009), Ticketmaster and Live Nation: A Report on the Anticipated Merger between Ticketmaster Entertainment, Inc. and Live Nation, Inc., London (pdf on website).

Condry, I. (2004), Cultures of Music Piracy: An Ethnographic Comparison of the U.S. and Japan, *International Journal of Cultural Studies*, 7(1), 343–363.

Connolly, M. and Krueger, A.B. (2006), Rockonomics: The Economics of Popular Music, pp. 667–719 in Ginsburgh, V. and Throsby, D. *Handbook of the Economics of Art and Culture*, Vol. 1, Elsevier.

Cook, K.L. (1989), Laws of Scattering Applied to Popular Music, *Journal of the American Society for Information Science*, 40(4), 277–288.

Cooper, L. (2010), Charting the Success of Male Recording Duos: Billboard Recognition of Country, Pop, and R and B/Rap Pairs, 1944–2004, *Journal of Popular Music and Society*, 33(2), 237–257.

Coopey, R. (2011), "You Say You Want a Revolution": Sport, Music and Entertainment from the Eighteenth to the Twentieth Century, pp. 155–169 in Eisenberg, C. and Gestricht, A. *The Cultural Industries in Britain and Germany: Historical and Comparative Perspectives*. Arbeitkries Deustsch England Forschung.

Coulangeon, P. and Yammick, L. (2007), Is "Distinction" Really Outdated? Questioning the Meaning of the Omnivorization of Musical Taste in Contemporary France, *Poetics*, 35(2–3), 93–111.

Coulthard, A. (2000), Copyright in Musical Arrangements: Spandau Ballet and Beyond, NIPC Newsletter, Spring, reproduced at: www.nipclaw.com/copy/ac01.htm (accessed 23 June 2004).

Courty, P. (2000), An Economic Guide to Ticket Pricing in the Entertainment Industry, *Recherches Économiques de Louvain – Louvain Economic Review*, 66(1), 167–192.

Courty, P. (2003), Some Economics of Ticket Resale, *Journal of Economic Perspectives*, 17(2), 85–97.

Cowen, T. (1996), Why Women Succeed and Fail, in the Arts, *Journal of Cultural Economics*, 20(2) 93–113.

Cowen, T. (1998), In Praise of Commercial Culture, Harvard University Press.

Cowen, T. and Tabbarok, A. (2000), An Economic Theory of Avant Garde and Popular Art, or High and Low Culture, *Southern Economic Journal*, 67(2), 232–253.

Cox, J., Collins, A. and Drinkwater, S. (2010), Seeders, Leechers and Social Norms: Evidence from the Market for Illicit Digital Downloading, *Information Economics and Policy*, 22(4), 299–305.

Cox, R.A.K., Felton, J.M. and Chung, K.H. (1995), The Concentration of Commercial Success in Popular Music: An Analysis of the Distribution of Gold Records, *Journal of Cultural Economics*, 19(4), 333–340.

Crain, M.W. and Tollison, R. (1997), Economics and the Architecture of Popular Music, *Journal of Economic Behaviour and Organization*, 32(2), 185–205.

Crain, M.W. and Tollison, R. (2002), Consumer Choice and the Popular Music Industry: A Test of the Superstar Theory, *Empirica*, 29(1), 1–9.

Craswell, R. (2001), Two Economic Theories of Enforcing Promises, Ch. 1 in Benson, P. (ed.) *Readings in the Theory of Contract Law*, Cambridge University Press.

Cummings, A.S. (2013), *Democracy of Sound: Music Piracy and the Remaking of American Copyright in the Twentieth Century*, Oxford University Press.

Curien, N. and Moreau, F. (2005), The Music Industry in the Digital Era: Towards New Business Frontiers, Unpublished working paper.

D

Dahl, L. (1984), *Stormy Weather*, Quartet Books.

Danaher, B., Smith, M.D., Telang, R. and Chen, S. (2012), The Effect of Graduated Response Anti-Piracy Laws on Music Sales: Evidence from an Event Study in France, Discussion Paper.

Danay, R. (2006), Copyright vs. Free Expression: The Case of Peer-to-Peer File-Sharing of Music in the United Kingdom, *Yale Journal of Law and Technology*, 8, Fall, 32–62.

Dane, C. (1998), *The UK Record Industry Annual Survey 1998*, Media Research Publishing.

Dannen, F. (1991), Hit Men: Power Brokers and Fast Money Inside the Music Business, Vintage.

Davis, B.G. (2006–2007), Identity Theft: Tribute Bands, Grand Rights, and Dramatico-Musical Performances, *Cardozo Arts and Entertainment Law Journal*, 24, 845–882.

Day, E. (2008), Why Are Our Orchestras So White? *Observer*, 14 September.

Day, T. (2000), *A Century of Recorded Music. Listening to Musical History*, Yale University Press.

DCMS (2000), Consumers Call the Tune: Music Industry Forum, New Technology Group, London.

De Alessi, L. and Staaf, R.J. (1994), What Does Reputation Really Assure? The Relationship of Trademarks to Expectations and Legal Remedies, *Economic Inquiry*, 32(3), 1–9.

De Waard, A. (2008), It's Up to You … No Really it's Up to You: Radiohead, Big Music and the Future of the Record Industry, Ch. 9 in Sickels, R.C. (ed.), *The Business of Entertainment: Popular Music* vol. 2, Praeger Publishers.

DeBoer, L. (1985), Is Rock'n'Roll a Symptom of Baumol's Disease? *Journal of Cultural Economics*, 9, 48–59.

Dejean, S. (2008), What Can We Learn from Empirical Studies about Piracy? Faculté des Sciences Economiques, University of Rennes.

Dejean, S., Nguyen, G.D. and Moreau, F. (2014), On the Complementarity Between Online and Offline Music Consumption: The Case of Free Streaming, *Journal of Cultural Economics*, 38(4), 315–330.

DeKoenig, M. and Cane-Honeysett, K. (2003), *Young, Gifted and Black: The Story of Trojan Records*, Sanctuary Publishing.

Dempster, D. (2000), Whither the Audience for Classical Music? *Harmony*, 11, 43–55.

Denisoff, R.S. (1996), *Tarnished Gold: The Record Industry Revisited*, Transaction Books.

Department for Education/DCMS (2011), The Importance of Music: A National Plan for Music Education, UK, Government Publications.

Derogatis, J. (1996), *Kaleidoscope Eyes*, Fourth Estate.

Dertouzos, J. (2008), Radio Airplay and the Record Industry: An Economic Analysis, for the National Association of Broadcasters.

Dewenter, R., Haucap, J. and Wenzel, T. (2011), On File Sharing with Indirect Network Effects between Concert Ticket Sales and Music Recordings, *Journal of Media Economics*, 25(3), 168–178.

Di Federico, E. and Le Sourd, M. (2012), On The Move: Artists' Mobility and Visas: A Step Forward, Final report of On the Move's workshop on artists' mobility and Schengen visas, http://on-the-move-org (accessed 4 January 2015).

Diamond, P.A. and Maskin, E. (1979), An Equilibrium Analysis of Search and Breach of Contract I: Steady States, *Bell Journal of Economics*, 10(1), 282–316.

Diamond, P.A. and Maskin, E. (1981), An Equilibrium Analysis of Search and Breach of Contract II: A Non-Steady State Example, *Journal of Economic Theory*, 25(2), 165–195.

Dibben, N. and Williamson, N.J. (2007), An Exploratory Survey of In-Vehicle Music Listening, *Psychology of Music*, 35(4), 571–589.

Disdier, A.C., Tai, S.H.T., Fontagne, L. and Mayer, T. (2010), Bilateral Trade of Cultural Goods, *Review of World Economics*, 145(4), 575–595.

Dixon, R.D. (1983), LP Chart Careers: Indices and Predictors of Ascent and Descent in Popularity, *Popular Music and Society*, 8(3/4), 19–42.

Dobusch, L. and Quack, S. (2012), Framing Standards, Mobilizing Users: Copyright Versus Fair Use in Transnational Regulation, *Review of International Political Economy iFirst*, 20(1), 52–88.

Dolfsma, W. (1999), The Consumption of Music and the Expression of Values: A Social Economic Explanation for the Advent of Pop Music, *American Journal of Economics and Sociology*, 58(4), 1019–1046.

Dolgins, A. (1993), *Rock Names: How Rock Groups got their Names*, Pan Macmillan.

Doucleff, M. (2012), Anatomy of a Tear-Jerker Why does Adele's "Someone Like You" Make Everyone Cry? Science has Found the Formula, *Wall Street Journal*, 11 February, http://online.wsj.com/news/articles/SB10001424052970203646004577213010291701 378 (accessed 21 May 2014).

Douglas, M. and Isherwood, B. (1979), *The World of Goods: Towards an anthropology of Consumption*, Allen Lane/Penguin.

Dowd, T.J. (2003), Structural Power and the Construction of Markets: The Case of Rhythm and Blues, pp. 147–201 in Engelstad, F. (ed.) *Comparative Studies of Culture and Power (Comparative Social Research, Volume 21)*, Emerald Group Publishing Limited.

Dowd, T.J. (2004), Concentration and Diversity Revisited: Production Logics and U.S. Mainstream Recording Market, 1940–1990, *Social Forces*, 82(4), 1411–1455.

Dowd, T.J., Liddle, K. and Blyler, M. (2005), Charting Gender: The Success of Female Acts in the U.S. Mainstream Recording Market, 1940–1990, pp. 81–124 in Jones, C. and Thornton, P.H. (eds) *Transformation in Cultural Industries: Research in the Sociology of Organizations*, Vol. 23, Elsevier.

Drummond, B. (2008), *The 17*, Beautiful Books.

Drummond, B., Cauty, J. and Savage, J. (1999), Introduction, in *The Manual: How To Have a Number One Hit the Easy Way*, 2nd edn, Ellipsis.

Dubina, H. (2013), Decomposing the Precarious Future of American Orchestras in the Face of Golan v. Holder, *UCLA Law Review*, 60(4), 950–1005.

Dubini, P. and Provera, B. (2008), Chart Success and Innovation in the Music Industry: Does Organizational Form Matter? *Journal of Media Business Studies*, 5(1), 41–65.

Duchêne, A. and Waelbroeck, P. (2006), The Legal and Technological Battle in the Music Industry: Information-push versus Information-pull Technologies, *International Review of Law and Economics*, 26(4), 565–580.

Dumbreck, A., Hermnanns, K.S. and McBain, K. (2003), Sounding Out the Future: Key Skills, Training and Education in the Music Industry, Commissioned by the National Music Council, Paisley.

E

Earl, P.E. (2001), Simon's Travel Theorem and the Demand for Live Music, *Journal of Economic Psychology*, 22(3), 335–358.

Ederington, J. and Minier, J. (2006), Why Tariffs, Not Subsidies? A Search for Stylized Facts, *Contributions to Economic Analysis and Policy*, 5(1) Article 31.

Edgar, A.M. (2013), Blackvoice and Adele's Racialized Musical Performance: Blackness, Whiteness, and Discursive Authenticity, *Critical Studies in Media Communication*, 31(3), 1–15.

Edmiston, K. and Thomas, M. (2003), The Commercial Music Industry in Atlanta and the State of Georgia: An Economic Impact Study, Fiscal Research Program Georgia State University (report FRC-85), August.

Ehrlich, C. (1976), *The Piano: A History*, Clarendon.

Ehrlich, C. (1989), *Harmonious Alliance: History of the Performing Rights Society*, Oxford University Press.

Eijk, Van N. (2001), Social Differentiation in Musical Taste Patterns, *Social Forces*, 79(3), 1163–1185.

Eijk, Van N., Poort, J. and Rutten, P. (2010), Legal, Economic and Cultural Aspects of File Sharing, *Communications and Strategies*, 77, 1st quarter 35–54.

Einhorn, M.A. (2006), Transaction Cost and Administered Markets: License Contracts for Music Performance Rights, *Review of Economic Research on Copyright*, 3(1), 61–74.

Ekelund, R.B. and Ritenour, S. (1999), An Exploration of the Beckerian Theory of Time Costs: Symphony Orchestra Demand, *American Journal of Economics and Sociology*, 58(4), 887–899.

Elberse, A. (2009), Bye Bye Bundles: The Unbundling of Music in Digital Channels, Harvard Business School Working Paper.

Elliott, C. and Simmons, R. (2011), Factors Determining UK Album Success, *Applied Economics*, 43(30), 4699–4706.

Elliott, M. (1993), *Rockonomics: The Money Behind the Music*, Citadel Press.

Ericsson, S. (2011), The Recorded Music Industry and the Emergence of Online Music Distribution: Innovation in the Absence of Copyright (Reform), Max Planck Institute for Intellectual Property and Competition Law Research Paper No. 11-09.

Etzioni, A. (1987), Toward a Kantian Socio-Economics, *Review of Social Economy*, 45(1), 37–47.

Evans, L. (ed.) (1994), *Women, Sex and Rock n' Roll: In their Own Words*, Pandora.

Evans, R.D. Jr., Hart, P.M., Cicala, J.E. and Sherrell, D.L. (2009), Elvis: Dead and Loving It: The Influence of Attraction, Nostalgia, and Risk in Dead Celebrity Attitude Formation, *Journal of Management and Marketing Research*, 3(1), 1–13.

Ewoudou, J. (2008), Understanding Culture Consumption in Canada 2005, Culture, Tourism and the Centre for Education Statistics, Research Paper.

F

Falk, M. and Falk, R. (2011), An Ordered Probit Model of Live Performance Attendance for 24 EU Countries, Austrian Institute of Economic Research.

Farrell, G. (1998), The Early Days of the Gramophone Industry in India: Historical, Social and Musical Perspectives, pp. 57–82 in Leyshon, A., Matless, D. and Revill, G. (eds) *The Place of Music*. Guilford Press.

Favaro, D. and Frateschi, C. (2007), A Discrete Choice Model of Consumption of Cultural Goods: The Case of Music, *Journal of Cultural Economics*, 31(3), 205–234.

Feist, A., Manton, K. and Dane, C. (1999), A Sound Performance: The Economic Value of Music to the United Kingdom, National Music Council, London.

Ferreira, F. and Waldfogel, J. (2010), Pop Internationalism: Has a Half Century of World Music Trade Displaced Local Culture? NBER Working Paper 15964, Cambridge, MA.

Filer, R.K. (1986), The "Starving Artist-Myth or Reality" Earnings of Artists in the United States, *Journal of Political Economy*, 94(1), 56–75.

Filer, R.K. (1990), Art and Academe: The Effect of Education on Earnings of Artists, *Journal of Cultural Economics*, 14(1), 15–38.

Fisher, C.G. and S.B. Preece (2003), Evolution, Extinction, or Status Quo? Canadian Performing Arts Audiences in the 1990s, *Poetics*, 31(2), 69–86.

Flanagan, R.J. (2008), The Economic Environment of American Symphony Orchestras, Report to Andrew W. Mellon Foundation, March.

Foster, P. (2010), Pirates Cost UK Music Industry £219m a Year, *The Times*, 17 December.

Fox, M.A. (2002), E-Commerce Business Models for the Music Industry, *Popular Music and Society, Special Issue: Digital Music Delivery: Its Past, Present, and Future*, 27(2), 201–220.

Fox, M.A. (2005), Market Power in Music Retailing: The Case of Wal-Mart, *Popular Music and Society*, 28(4), 501–519.

Fox, M. and Kochanowski, P. (2007), Multi-Stage Markets in the Recording Industry, *Journal of Popular Music and Society*, 30(2), 173–195.

Frederick, R. (2013), Study the Hits: Songs by Adele, http://robinfrederick.com/tag/how-to-write-songs-like-adele/ (accessed 4 June 2014).

Frey, B.S. (1994), The Economics of Music Festivals, *Journal of Cultural Economics*, 18(1), 29–39.

Friedman, M. (1953), The Methodology of Positive Economics, pp. 3–16, 30–43 in *Essays in Positive Economics*, Aldine.

Frith, S. (2004), Does British Music Still Matter? A Reflection on the Changing Status of British Music in the Global Music Market, *European Journal of Cultural Studies*, 7(1), 43–58.

Frith, S. (2006), *Performing Rites: On the Value of Popular Music*, Oxford University Press.

Frith, S. (2007), Live Music Matters, *Scottish Music Review*, 1(1), 1–17.

Frontier Economics (2007), The Feasibility of a Live Music Impact Study, DCMS.

Fuller, S. (1994), *The Pandora Guide to Women Composers: Britain and the United States 1629–Present*, Pandora.

G

Gaar, G.G. (1992), She's a Rebel: The History of Women in Rock 'n' Roll, Seal Press, Seattle.

Galloway, T. and Kinnear, D. (2001), Unchained Melody: A Price Discrimination-Based Policy Proposal for Addressing the MP3 Revolution, *Journal of Economic Issues*, 35(2), 279–287.

Gander, J. and Rieple, A. (2002), Creative Relationships in the Worldwide Recorded Music Industry, *Creativity and Innovation Management*, 11(4), 248–254.

Gander, J. and Rieple, A. (2004), How Relevant is Transaction Cost Economics to Inter-Firm Relationships in the Music Industry? *Journal of Cultural Economics*, 28(1), 57–79.

García-Álvarez, E., Katz-Gerro, T. and López-Sintas, J. (2007), Deconstructing Cultural Omnivorousness 1982–2002: Heterology in Americans' Musical Preferences, *Social Forces*, 86(2), 417–443.

Gayer, A. and Shy, O. (2003), Internet and Peer-to-Peer Distribution in Markets for Digital Products, *Economics Letters*, 81(2), 197–203.

Gayer, A. and Shy, O. (2006), Publishers, Artists, and Copyright Enforcement, *Information Economics and Policy*, 18(4), 374–384.

Gaze, R.C. and Schwer, R.K. (1997), The Economic Impact of the Grateful Dead on a Local Economy, *Journal of Cultural Economics*, 21(1), 41–55.

Geary, K. (2004-2005), Tribute Bands: Flattering Imitators or Flagrant Infringers, *Southern Illinois University Law Journal*, 29, 481.

George, N. (2008), *The Death of Rhythm and Blues*, Penguin.

Georges, P. and Seçkin, A. (2013), Black Notes and White Noise: A Hedonic Approach to Auction Prices of Classical Music Manuscripts, *Journal of Cultural Economics*, 37(1), 33–60.

Ghafele, R. and Gilbert, B. (2011), Counting the Costs of Collective Rights: Management of Music Copyright in Europe, MPRA Paper 3646, Munich.

Gibbons, F. (2002), Cor Baby that's Really Mean, Otway tells Shops, *Guardian*, 11 October.

Gibson, C. and Connell, J. (2003), Bongo Fury: Tourism, Music and Cultural Economy at Byron Bay, Australia, *Tijdschrift voor economiche en sociale geografie*, 94(2), 164–187.

Gibson, C. and Connell, J. (2005), Music and Tourism: On the Road Again, *Channel View Press*.

Gifford, A. Jr (1999), Being and Time: On the Nature and the Evolution of Institutions, *Journal of Bioeconomics*, 1(1), 127–149.

Giles, D.C., Pietrzykowski, S. and Clark, K.E. (2007), The Psychological Impact of Personal Record Collections and the Impact of Changing Technological Forms, *Journal of Economic Psychology*, 28(4), 429–443.

Giles, D.E. (2006), Superstardom in the U.S. Popular Music Industry, *Economics Letters*, 92(1), 68–74.

Giles, D.E. (2007a), Increasing Returns to Information in the U.S. Popular Music Industry, *Applied Economics Letters*, 14(5–6), 327–331.

Giles, D.E. (2007b), Survival of the Hippest: Life at the Top of the Hot 100, *Applied Economics*, 39(15), 1877–1887.

Ginsburgh, V. and van Ours, J. (2003), Expert Opinion and Compensation: Evidence from a Musical Competition, *American Economic Review*, 93(1), 289–296.

Gisser, M., McClure, J., Ökten, G. and Santon, G. (2009), Some Anomalies Arising from Bandwagons that Impart Upward Sloping Segments to Market Demand, *Econ Journal Watch*, 6(1), 21–34.

Gladwell, M. (2009), *Outliers: The Story of Success*, Penguin.

Glejser, H. and Heyndels, B. (2001), Efficiency and Inefficiency in the Ranking in Competitions: The Case of the Queen Elisabeth Music Contest, *Journal of Cultural Economics*, 25(2), 109–129.

Gloor, S. (2011), Just How Long Is Your "Fifteen Minutes"? An Empirical Analysis of Artists' Time on the Popular Charts, *Music and Entertainment Industry Educators Association Journal*, 11(1): 61–82.

Godbolt, J. (2010), *A History of Jazz in Britain, 1919–1940*, Northway Productions.

Goldin, C. and Rouse, C. (2000), Orchestrating Impartiality: The Impact of "Blind" Auditions on Female Musicians, *American Economic Review*, 90(4), 715–741.

Gopal, R.D., Bhattacharjee, S. and Sanders, G.L. (2006), Do Artists Benefit from Online Music Sharing? *Journal of Business*, 79(3), 1503–1533.

Gould, J.E. (2012), Mozart vs. the Gangstas: How Classical Music is Changing Young People's Lives, *Time US*, 8 January.

Gourvish, T. (2009), The British Popular Music Industry, 1950–1975: Archival Challenges and Solutions, *Business History*, 51, 25–40.

Gourvish, T. and Tennent, K. (2010), Peterson and Berger Revisited: Changing Market Dominance in the British Popular Music Industry, *c*.1950–1980, *Business History*, 52(2), 187–206.

Gowers, A. (2006), *Gowers Review of Intellectual Property*, HMSO.

Gracie, C. and Sinha, R. (2012), Gracie Management Music Consumption Model™ Report, 4 September, www.graciemgt.com (accessed 3 January 2015).

Graddy, K. and Margolis, P.E. (2011), Fiddling with Value: Violins as an Investment, *Economic Inquiry*, 49(4), 1083–1097.

Graham, G., Burnes, B., Lewis, B.J. and Langer, J. (2004), The Transformation of the Music Industry Supply Chain, *International Journal of Operations and Production Management*, 24(11), 1087–1103.

Granovetter, M. (1979), Threshold Models of Collective Behavior, *American Journal of Sociology*, 83, 1420–1443.

Grassmuck, V. (2010), Academic Studies on the Effect of File-Sharing on the Recorded Music Industry: A Literature Review, *Grupo de Pesquisa em Política Pública para o Acesso à Informação (GPOPAI)*, 14 May, http://ssrn.com/abstract=1749579 (accessed 4 January 2015).

Grazian, D. (2004), The Production of Popular Music as a Confidence Game: The Case of the Chicago Blues, *Qualitative Sociology*, 27(2), 137–158.

Greene, R. (2005), Black Classical Music Composers: Compact Disc Listing, Ardmore, PA.

Gregory, G. (2012), *Send in the Clones: A Cultural Study of the Tribute Band, Studies in Popular Music*, Equinox Publishing.

Greig, C. (1989), *Will You Still Love Me Tomorrow? Girl Groups from the 50s On*, Virago Press.

Grolleau, G., El Harbi, S. and Bekir, I. (2014), Substituting Piracy with a Pay-What-You-Want Option: Does it Make Sense? *European Journal of Law and Economics*, 37(2), 277–297.

Gronow, P. and Saunio, N. (1998), *An International History of the Recording Industry*, Trans. C. Murray, Cassell.

Guerzoni, M. (2013), Music Consumption at the Dawn of the Music Industry: The Rise of a Cultural Fad, *Journal of Cultural Economics*, 38, 145–171.

Guinness (1997), *British Hit Singles*, 11th Edn, Introduced by Mark Lamarr.

Gundel, S., Hecker, A. and Muthmann, E. (2006), Incentive, Control and Firm Boundaries in the Music Industry: Explaining the Recent Downturn, Working Paper, Albert-Ludwigs-Universität Freiburg.

H

Halcousis, D. and Matthews, T. (2007), eBay Auctions for *Third Eye Blind* Concert Tickets, *Journal of Cultural Economics*, 31(1), 65–78.

Hamlen, W.A. Jr (1991), Superstardom in Popular Music: Empirical Evidence, *Review of Economics and Statistics*, 73(4), 729–733.

Hamlen, W.A. Jr (1994), Variety and Superstardom in Popular Music, *Economic Inquiry*, 32(3), 395–406.

Hammond, R.G. (2012), Profit Leak? Pre-Release File Sharing and the Music Industry, Working Paper, North Carolina State University.

Hand, C. (2009), Modelling Patterns of Attendance at Performing Arts Events: The Case of Music in the United Kingdom, *Creative Industries Journal*, 2(3), 259–271.

Hanser, S.B. and Thomson, I.W. (1994), Effects of Music Therapy Strategy on Depressed Older Adults, *Journal of Gerontology*, 49(6), 265–269.

Hansman, H., Mulder, C. and Verhoeff, R. (1999), The Adoption of the Compact Disk Player: An Event History Analysis for the Netherlands, *Journal of Cultural Economics*, 23(3), 221–232.

Hanson, T., Hayward, B. and Phelps, A. (2007), *A Survey of Live Music in England and Wales*, DCMS.

Harchaoui, T.M. and Hamdad, M. (2000), Prices of Recorded Classical Music, *International Journal of Industrial Organisation*, 18(3), 497–514.

Hardy, P. (2012), *Download! How the Internet Transformed the Record Business*, Omnibus Press.

Harker, D. (1997), The Wonderful World of IFPI: Music Industry Rhetoric, the Critics and the Classical Marxist Critique, *Popular Music*, 16(1), 45–79.

Harper, G., Cotton, C. and Benefield, Z. (2013), Nashville Music Industry: Impact, Contribution and Cluster Analysis, Nashville Area Chamber of Commerce Research Center.

Harries, S. and Harries, M. (1989), A Pilgrim Soul: The Life and Work of Elisabeth Lutyens, Faber & Faber.

Harris, J. (2005), The Sins of Sir Freddie, *Guardian*, www.theguardian.com/music/2005/jan/14/2 (accessed 8 September 2014).

Harrison, A. (2011), *The Music Business: The Essential Guide to the Law and the Deals*, Virgin Books.

Harrison, T. (2007), "Empire": Chart Performance of Hard Rock and Heavy Metal Groups, 1990–1992, *Journal of Popular Music and Society*, 30(2), 197–225.

Hayward, P. (ed.) (1998), *Sound Alliances: Indigenous Peoples, Cultural Policy and Popular Music in the Pacific*, Cassell.

Heikkinen, M. and Karhunen, P. (1996), Does Public Support Make a Difference and for Whom? *Journal of Cultural Economics*, 20(4), 341–358.

Heiner, R.A. (1983), The Origins of Predictable Behavior, *American Economic Review*, 73, 560–595.

Hendricks, K. and Sorensen, A. (2009), Information and the Skewness of Music Sales, *Journal of Political Economy*, 117(2), 324–369.

Hennion, A. (1989), An Intermediary between Production and Consumption: The Production of Popular Music, *Science, Technology and Human Values*, 14(4), 400–424.

Henry, R., Daniell, A. and Trotman, S. (2001), The Music Industry in Trinidad and Tobago Report prepared for UNCTAD/WIPO.

Hervas-Drane, A. and Noam, E.M. (2011), Online Sharing and Cultural Globalization, Universitat Pompeu Fabra Working Paper.

Hesmondhaugh, D. (1998), The British Dance Music Industry: A Case Study of Independent Cultural Production, *British Journal of Sociology*, 49(2), 234–251.

Hesmondhaugh, D. (1999), Indie: The Institutional Politics and Aesthetics of a Popular Music Genre, *Cultural Studies*, 13(1) 34–61.

Hesmondhaugh, D. (2013), *Why Music Matters*, Wiley Blackwell.

Hewett, I. (2006), *Why They are Hooked on Classical? Daily Telegraph*, 20 May.

Heylin, C. (2012), *All the Madmen: Barrett, Bowie, Drake, the Floyd, The Kinks, The Who and the Journey to the Dark Side of English Rock*, Constable.

Hiller, S. (2011), Exclusive Dealing and its Effects: The Impact of Large Music Festivals on Local Music Venues, University of Colorado Working Paper.

Hirschman, A.O. (1970), *Exit, Voice and Loyalty: Response to Decline in Firms, Organisations and States*, Harvard University Press.

Hirshleifer, D. (1995), The Blind Leading the Blind: Social Influence, Fads, and Informational Cascades, Ch. 12 in Tommasi, M. and Ierulli, K. (eds) *The New Economics of Human Behavior*, Cambridge University Press.

Hiscock, J. and Hojman, D.E. (2004), Interpreting Suboptimal Business Outcomes in the Light of the Coase Theorem: Lessons from Sidmouth International Festival, *Tourism Management*, 31(2), 240–249.

Hitters, E. and van de Kamp, M. (2010), Tune In, Fade Out: Music Companies and the Classification of Domestic Music Products in the Netherlands, *Poetics*, 38(5), 461–480.

Hoeven, van der A. (2012), The Popular Music Heritage of the Dutch Pirates: Illegal Radio and Cultural Identity, *Media, Culture and Society*, 34(8), 927–943.

Holbrook, M. (2013), Consumption Criteria in Arts Marketing, Ch. 19 in O'Reilly, D., Rentschler, R. and Kirchner, T. (eds) *The Routledge Companion to Arts Marketing*, Routledge.

Holbrook, M.B. and Schindler, R.M. (1989), Some Exploratory Findings on the Development of Musical Tastes, *Journal of Consumer Research*, 16(1), 119–124.

Holmstrom, B. and Milgrom, P. (1991), Multi-task Principal-Agent Analyses: Incentive Contracts, Asset Ownership and Job-Design, *Journal of Law, Economics and Organization*, 7, 24–52.

Holt, F. (2010), The Economy of Live Music in the Digital Age, *European Journal of Cultural Studies*, 13(2), 243–261.

Homan, S. (ed.) (2006), *Access All Eras: Tribute Bands and Global Pop Culture*, Open University Press.

Hong, B. (2010), A Comment on Survival of the Hippest: Life at the Top of the Top 100, *Applied Economics Letters*, 19(10–12), 1101–1115.

Hong, S-H. (2007), The Recent Growth of the Internet and Changes in Household-Level Demand for Entertainment, *Information Economics and Policy*, 19(3–4), 304–318.

Hong, S-H. (2011), Measuring the Effect of Napster on Recorded Music Sales, *Journal of Applied Econometrics*, 28(2), 297–324.

Hosokawa, S. (1984), The Walkman Effect, *Popular Music*, 4: Performers and Audiences, 165–180.

Hudson, H.D. (2011), Disruptive Disruption in the Music Business, Part 1: An Historical Perspective, *Four Peaks Review*, 1(1), 37–48.

Hudson, R. (1995), Making Music Work? Alternative Regeneration Strategies in a Deindustrialised Locality: The Case of Derwentside, *Transactions of the Institute of British Geographers*, 20(4), 460–473.

Hughes, T. (2004), *Analog Man's Guide To Vintage Effects*, For Musicians' Only Publishing.

Hui, K-L. and Png, I. (2003), Piracy and the Legitimate Demand for Recorded Music, *Contributions to Economic Analysis and Policy*, 2(1), 1–22.

Hull, G.P. (2000), The Structure of the Recorded Music Industry, Ch. 4 in Greco, A.N. (ed.) *The Media and Entertainment Industries*, Allyn and Bacon.

Hull, G.P. (2004), *The Recording Industry*, Routledge.

I

IFPI (2012), Digital Music Report 2011, available at: www.ifpi.org/content/library/DMR2011.pdf (accessed 28 December 2014).

IFPI (2013), Digital Music Report 2013, available at: www.ifpi.org/digital-music-report-2013.php (accessed 12 July 2014).

Illes, A. and Mattin, (2009), *Noise and Capitalism*, Areteleku Audiolab.

International Centre for Tourism and Hospitality Research, University of Bournemouth (2009), *The Contribution of Music Festivals and Major Concerts to Tourism in the UK*, Destination Music.

J

Jahn, B. and Weber, T. (1998), *Reggae Island: Jamaican Music in the Digital Age*, Da Capo Press.

James, V. (2001), The Caribbean Music Industry Database 2000, Report prepared for UNCTAD/WIPO.

Janssens, J., Van Daele, S. and Vander Beken, T. (2009), The Music Industry on (the) Line? Surviving Music Piracy in a Digital Era, *European Journal of Crime, Criminal Law and Criminal Justice*, 17(1), 77–96.

Jeppesen, L.B. and Frederiksen, L. (2006), Why Do Users Contribute to Firm-Hosted Communities? The Case of Computer-Controlled Musical Instruments, *Organization Science*, 17(1), 45–63.

Jezic, D.P. (1989), *Women Composers: The Lost Tradition Found*, Feminist Press, CUNY.

Johansson, D. and Larsson, M. (2009), The Swedish Music Industry in Graphs, Economic Development Report 2000–2008, Trend Maze of the Royal Institute of Technology, http://60eparallele.owni.fr/files/2011/05/swedish_music_industry_2000-2008.pdf (accessed 4 January 2015).

Johnstone, J. and Katz, E. (1957), Youth and Popular Music: A Study in the Sociology of Taste, *American Journal of Sociology*, 62, 563–568.

Jones, S.R.G. (1984), *The Economics of Conformism*, Basil Blackwell.

Jong, S.J. (2004), Criminalizations of Netizens for their Access to On-Line Music, *Journal of Korean Law*, 4(1), 51–72.

Joo, T.W. (2011) Remix without Romance, *Connecticut Law Review*, 44(2), 415–479.

Jung, S. (2011), K-pop, Indonesian Fandom, and Social Media, *Transformative Works and Cultures*, http://journal.transformativeworks.org/index.php/twc/article/view/289/219 (accessed 25 July 2014).

K

Kam, J. (2004), Success in Failure: The National Centre for Popular Music, *Prometheus*, 22(2), 169–187.

Kandori, M. (1992), Social Norms and Community Enforcement, *Review of Economic Studies*, 59(1), 63–80.

Kassabian, A. (2004), Would You like Some World Music with Your Latte? Starbucks, Putumayo and Distributed Tourism, *Twentieth Century Music*, 1(2), 209–223.

Kassabian, A. (2013), *Ubiquitous Listening: Affect, Attention, and Distributed Subjectivities*, University of California Press.

Katz-Gerro, T. and Lopez-Sintas, J. (2013), The Breadth of Europeans' Musical Tastes: Disentangling Individual and Country Effects, *Advances in Sociology Research*, 14, 97–122.

Kenlock, N. (2013), After the Demise of Choice FM, is it Back to Pirate Radio for Black Britons? *Guardian*, 14 November.

Kennedy, M. (1980), *The Concise Oxford Dictionary of Music*, Oxford University Press.

Keyes, J.M. (2004), Musical Musings: The Case for Rethinking Music Copyright Protection, *Michigan Telecommunications and Technology Law Review*, 10, 407–444.

Kim, E.M. and Ryoo, J. (2007), South Korean Culture Goes Global: K-Pop and the Korean Wave, *Korean Social Science Journal*, 34(1), 117–152.

Kim, J.G. and Ahn, J.Y. (2012), An Empirical Study on Effects of Korea's Cultural Exports, *Journal of Korea Trade*, 16(2), 25–48.

King, S. (2004), Blues Tourism in the Mississippi Delta: The Functions of Blues Festivals, *Popular Music and Society*, 27, 4.

Klaes, M. (1997), Sociotechnical Constituencies, Game Theory and the Diffusion of Compact Discs: An Interdisciplinary Investigation into the Market for Recorded Music, *Research Policy*, 25, 1221–1234.

Kloosterman, R.C. and Qispel, C. (1990), Not Just the Same Old Show on my Radio: An Analysis in the Diffusion in Black Music among Whites in South of the United States of America, *Popular Music*, 9(2), 151–164.

Knopper, S. (2009), *Appetite for Self-Destruction: The Spectacular Crash of the Record Industry in the Digital Age*, Free Press.

Kolb, B. (2000), *Marketing Cultural Organisations: New Strategies for Attracting Audiences to Classical Music, Dance, Museums, Theatre and Opera*, Oak Tree Press.

Kozinets, R.V. (2002), Can Consumers Escape the Market? Emancipatory Illuminations from Burning Man, *Journal of Consumer Research*, 29(1), 20–38.

Kozinn, A. (2006), Check the Numbers: Rumours of Classical Music's Demise are Dead Wrong, *New York Times*, 28 May.

Kozul-Wright, Z. and Stanbury, L. (1998), Becoming a Globally Competitive Player: The Case of the Music Industry in Jamaica, UNCTAD No. 138, Geneva.

Kretschmer, M., George, M. and Wallis, R. (1999), The Changing Location of Intellectual Property Rights in Music: A Study of Music Publishers, *Collecting Societies and Media Conglomerates Prometheus*, 17(2), 163–186.

Kretschmer, M., George, M. and Wallis, R. (2001), Music in Electronic Markets: An Empirical Study, *New Media and Society*, 3(4), 417–441.

Krueger, A.B. (2005), The Economics of Real Superstars: The Market for Rock Concerts in the Material World, *Journal of Labor Economics*, 23(1), 1–30.

Kruse, H. (2010), Local Identity and Independent Music Scenes, Online and Off, *Journal of Popular Music and Society*, 33(5), 625–639.

Kuhlman, K. (2004), The Impact of Gender on Students' Instrument Timbre Preferences and Instrument Choices, *Visions of Research in Music Education*, 5, www-usr.rider.edu/~vrme/ (accessed 1 August 2014).

Kumari, K. (2014), I Find the Men Here Uncivilised, says Biddu, *Times of India*, 8 February.

Kurabayashi, Y. and Ito, T. (1992), Socio-Economic Characteristics of Audiences for Western Classical Music in Japan, pp. 275–288 in Towse, R. and Khakee, A. (eds) *Cultural Economics*, Springer-Verlag.

Kureshi, H. and Savage, J. (eds) (1995), *The Faber Book of Pop*, Faber & Faber.

Kusek, D. (2011), Music Business 101: The Future of Global Music, Berklee College of Music, www.futureofmusicbook.com/ (accessed 25 July 2014).

Kusek, D. and Leonhard, G. (2005), The Future of Music: Manifesto for the Digital Music Revolution, Berklee Press and Hal Leonard Publishing.

L

Lacher, K.T. and Mizerski, R. (1994). An Exploratory Study of the Response and Relationships Involved in the Evaluation of and in the Intention to Purchase New Rock Music, *Journal of Consumer Research*, 21(2), 366–380.

LaFrance, M. (2011), From Whether to How: The Challenge of Implementing a Full Public Performance Right in Sound Recordings, *Harvard Journal of Sports and Entertainment Law*, 2(2), 221–264.

Lange, M.D. and Luksetich, W.A. (1993), The Cost of Producing Symphony Orchestra Services, *Journal of Cultural Economics*, 17(2), 1–15.

Lange, M.D. and Luksetich, W.A. (1995), A Simultaneous Model of Nonprofit Symphony Orchestra Behavior, *Journal of Cultural Economics*, 19(1), 49–68.

Larkin, C. (ed.) (1995), *The Guinness Who's Who of Jazz*, 2nd edn, Guinness Publishing.

Larsen, G. and Hussels, S. (2011), The Significance of Commercial Music Festivals, Ch. 13 in Cameron, S. (ed.) *Handbook of the Economics of Leisure*, Edward Elgar.

Larsen, G., Lawson, R. and Todd, S. (2010), The Symbolic Consumption of Music, *Journal of Marketing Management*, 26(7/8), 671–685.

Leary, C. (2012), Composing in the Internet Age of Post-Auratic Art, PhD thesis submitted, Newcastle University.

Lebrecht, N. (1992), *The Companion to 20th Century Music*, Simon & Schuster.

Lebrecht, N. (1999), Going Cheaply, *Telegraph*, 17 November, www.telegraph.co.uk/culture/4719009/Going-cheaply.html (accessed 31 December 2014).

Lebrecht, N. (2008), *Who Killed Classical Music? Maestros, Managers and Classical Music?* Penguin Books.

Lee, J.A (2003a), A Bayesian Model for Prelaunch Sales Forecasting of Recorded Music, *Management Science*, 49(2), 179–196.

Lee, J.A. (2003b), A Requiem for Classical Music, *Regional Review*, Q2, 14–23.

Lee, S. (2006), The Effect of File Sharing on Consumer's Purchasing Pattern: A Survey Approach, Working Paper, University of Florida.

Leibenstein, H. (1950), Bandwagon, Snob and Veblen Effects in the Theory of Consumer Demand, *Quarterly Journal of Economics*, 64(2), 183–207.

Leibenstein, H. (1966), Allocative Efficiency vs. "X-Efficiency", *American Economic Review*, 57, 392–415.

Leibenstein, H. (1978), X-Inefficiency Exists: A Reply to an Xorcist, *American Economic Review*, 69(1), 203–211.

Létourneau, A.É. (2010), Pirate Radio and Manoeuvre: Radical Artistic Practices in Quebec, pp. 145–160 in Langlois, A., Sakolsky, P. and Van der Zorn, M. (eds) *Pirate Radio in Canada*, trans. C. Gabriel, New Star Books.

Leung, T.C. (2009), Should the Music Industry sue its own Customers? Impacts of Music Piracy and Policy Suggestions, Working Paper, Chinese University of Hong Kong.

Levitin, D.J. (2007), *This is Your Brain on Music: The Science of a Human Obsession*, Plume/Penguin.

Lewis, G.H. (1983), The Meanings in the Music and the Music's in Me: Popular Music as Symbolic Communication, *Theory, Culture and Society*, 1(3), 133–141.

Leyshon, A. (2001), Time-Space (and Digital) Compression: Software Formats, Musical Networks, and the Reorganization of the Music Industry, *Environment and Planning A*, 33, 49–77.

Liebesman, Y.J. (2012), Downstream Copyright Infringers, Saint Louis University Legal Studies Research Paper No. 2011-10.

Liebowitz, S.J. (2004), The Elusive Symbiosis: The Impact of Radio on the Record Industry, *Review of Economic Research on Copyright Issues*, 1(1), 93–118.

Liebowitz, S.J. (2006), File Sharing: Creative Destruction or Just Plain Destruction? *Journal of Law and Economics*, 49(1), 1–28.

Liebowitz, S.J. (2008), Testing File Sharing's Impact on Music Album Sales in Cities, *Management Science*, 54(4), 852–859.

Liebowitz, S.J. (2016), The Metric is the Message: How Much of the Decline in Sound Recording Sales is due to File-Sharing? *Journal of Cultural Economics*, forthcoming.

Liebowitz, S.J. and Watt, R. (2006), How Best to Ensure Remuneration for Creators in the Market for Music? *Journal of Economic Surveys*, 20(4), 513–545.

Lipsey, R.G. and Rosebluth, G. (1971), A Contribution to the New Theory of Demand: A Rehabilitation of the Giffen Good, *Canadian Journal of Economics*, 4(2), 131–163.

Liu, J. (2010), The Tough Reality of Copyright Piracy: A Case Study of the Music Industry in China, *Cardozo Arts and Entertainment Law Journal*, 27, 621–551.

Llewellyn, E.A. (2010), Boundaries, Hybridity and the Problem of Opposing Cultures, PhD thesis, University of Southampton.

Lopes, P.D. (1992), Innovation and Diversity in the Popular Music Industry, 1969 to 1990, *American Sociological Review*, 57(1), 56–71.

Lorenzen, M. and Frederiksen, L. (2005), On the Economics of Innovation Projects Product Experimentation in the Music Industry, DRUID Working Papers 05-23, DRUID, Copenhagen Business School.

Lovering, J. (1998), The Global Music Industry: Contradictions in the Commodification of the Sublime, pp. 31–56 in Leyshon, A., Matles, D. and Revill, E. (eds) *The Place of Music*, Guilford Press.

M

Macaulay, S. (1963), Noncontractual relations in business, *American Sociological Review*, 28, 55–66.

McCain, R. (1990), Humanistic Economics Again, *Forum for Social Economics*, 19(2), 78–87.

McDonnell, E. and Powers, A. (eds) (1995), *Rock She Wrote*, Delta.

McKenzie, J. (2009), Illegal Music Downloading and its Impact on Legitimate Sales: Australian Empirical Evidence, *Australian Economic Papers*, 48(4), 296–307.

McLeod, K. (2005) MP3s are Killing Home Taping: The Rise of Internet Distribution and its Challenge to the Major Label Music Monopoly, *Popular Music and Society*, 28(4), 521–531.

McLeod, K. and DiCola, P. (2011), *Creative License: The Law and Culture of Digital Sampling*, Duke University Press.

Maffioletti, A. and Ramello, G.B. (2004), Should We put Them in Jail? Copyright Infringement, Penalties and Consumer Behavior: Insights from Experimental Data, *Review of Economic Research on Copyright Issues*, 35(1), 19–48.

Manitoba Audio Recording Industry Association (2005), Economic Impact Analysis of Manitoba's Music Industry, Full Report Final Revision 3 by kisquared.

Manitoba Music (2011), Annual Report 2010–2011, manitobamusic.com (accessed 25 June 2014).

Mansfield, J. (2014), *Beat Box: A Drum Machine Obsession*, Gingko Press.

Manski, C.F. (2000), Economic Analysis of Social Interactions, *Journal of Economic Perspectives*, 14(3), 115–136.

March, I., Greenfield, E. and Layton, R. (1992), The Penguin Guide to Compact Discs and Cassettes, Penguin Books.

Marcone, S. (2013), The Poverty of Artist Royalties, *Music Business Journal* (Berklee College of Music) May.

Marcus, S. (2010), *Girls to the Front: The True Story of the Riot Grrrl Revolution*, Harper Perennial.

Martorella, R. (1975), The Structure of the Market and Musical Style: The Economics of Opera Production and Repertoire: An Exploration, *International Review of the Aesthetics and Sociology of Music*, 6, 241–254.

Maslow, A.H. (1971), *The Farther Reaches of Human Nature*, Penguin Harmondsworth (1977 reprint of original book).

Mason, K. (2013), Adele Hits New Dance Club Songs Peak with "Skyfall", Billboard, January, www.billboard.com/articles/news/1489091/adele-hits-new-dance-club-songs-peak-with-skyfall (accessed 3 June 2014).

Maymin, P. (2011). Music and the Market: Song and Stock Volatility, Unpublished paper NYU Poly, Department of Finance and Risk Engineering, http://papers.ssrn.com/sol3/papers.cfm?abstract_id=1295584 (accessed 18 June 2014).

Meier, L.M. (2011), Promotional Ubiquitous Musics: Recording Artists, Brands, and "Rendering Authenticity", *Journal of Popular Music and Society*, 34(4), 399–415.

Meiseberg, B. (2014), Trust the Artist Versus Trust the Tale: Performance Implications of Talent and Self-Marketing in Folk Music, *Journal of Cultural Economics*, 38(1), 9–42.

Melly, G. (2008), *Revolt Into Style*, Faber.

Merseyside Music Development Agency (1999), The Hidden Economy: An Economic Assessment of the Music Sector on Merseyside, Liverpool, MDMA.

Messerlin, P. and Shin, W. (2013), The K-Pop Wave: An Economic Analysis, Unpublished ms (JCE sub).

Michel, N.J. (2006), The Impact of Digital File-sharing on the Music Industry: An Empirical Analysis, *Topics in Economic Analysis and Policy*, 6(1), 1–24.

Mill, J.S. (1909), *Autobiography*, Watts and Co.

Milner, G. (2009), *Perfecting Sound Forever: The Story of Recorded Music*, Granta Books.

Minniti, A. and Vergari, C. (2010), Turning Piracy into Profits: A Theoretical Investigation, *Information Economics and Policy*, 22(4), 379–390.

Minor, M., Wagner, T., Brewerton, F. and Hausman, A. (2004), Rock On! An Elementary Model of Consumer Satisfaction with Musical Performances, *Journal of Services Marketing*, 18(1), 7–18.

Mintel (2008), Music Festivals and Concerts – UK – August 2008, Mintel International Group Limited, London.

Mitchell, T. (1996), *Popular Music and Local Identity: Rock, Pop and Rap in Europe and Oceania*, Leicester University Press.

Mittelstaedt, R.A. and Zorn, T.S. (1984), Econometric Replication: Lessons from the Experimental Sciences, *Quarterly Journal of Business and Economics*, 23, 9–15.

Mixon, F.G. and Ressler, R.W. (2000), A Note on Elasticity and Price Dispersions in the Music Recording Industry, *Review of Industrial Organization*, 17(4), 465–470.

MMC (1994), The Supply of Recorded Music, HMSO Cm 2599.

MMC (1996), Performing Rights, HMSO 3147.

Moe, A.G. and Earl, P.E. (2009), *Bandwagon and Reputation Effects in the Popular Music Charts*, University of Queensland.

Moist, K. (2008), To Renew the Old World: Record Collecting as Cultural Production, *Studies in Popular Culture*, 31(1), 99–122.

Moller, A.R. (2006), *Hearing: Anatomy, Physiology, and Disorders of the Auditory System*, 2nd edn, Academic Press.

Molteni, L. and Ordanini, A. (2003), Consumption Patterns, Digital Technology and Music Downloading, *Long Range Planning*, 36(4), 389–406.

Montgomery, A.L. and Moe, W.W. (2002). Should Music Labels Pay for Radio Airplay? Investigating the Relationship between Album Sales and Radio Airplay, Unpublished ms.

Montoro-Pons, J. and Cuadrado-Garcia, M. (2008), Legal Origin and Intellectual Property Rights: An Empirical Study in the Prerecorded Music Sector, *European Journal of Law and Economics*, 26(2), 153–173.

Montoro-Pons, J. and Cuadrado-Garcia, M. (2011), Live and Prerecorded Popular Music Consumption, *Journal of Cultural Economics*, 35(1), 19–45.

Montoro-Pons, J., Cuadrado-Garcia, M. and Casasus-Estelles, T. (2013), Analysing the Popular Music Audience: Determinants of Participation and Frequency of Attendance, *International Journal of Music Business Research*, 2(1), 35–62.

Moreau, F. (2013), The Disruptive Nature of Digitization: The Case of the Recorded Music Industry, *International Journal of Arts Management*, 15(2), 18–31.

Mortensen, D.T. (1982), Property Rights and Efficiency in Mating and Racing Games, *American Economic Review*, 72(5), 968–979.

Mortimer, J., Nosko, C. and Sorenson, A. (2012), Supply Responses to Digital Distribution: Recorded Music and Live Performances, *Information Economics and Policy*, 24, 3–14.

Mundy, S. (2001), *Music and Globalisation: A Guide to the Issues*, International Music Council.

Music Canada (2012), *Economic Impact Analysis of the Sound Recording Industry in Canada*, PriceWaterhouseCooper.

Music Week (2011), Label's Release Strategy Key to Adele's US Break, 7 March 2011, www.musicweek.com/news/read/labels-release-strategy-key-to-adeles-us-break/045059 (accessed 22 May 2014).

Musicians Union (2000), Nice Work if You Can Get It! Employment Trends for British Musicians, 1978–1998, London.

Myer, L. and Kleck, C. (2007), From Independent to Corporate: A Political Economic Analysis of Rap Billboard Toppers, *Journal of Popular Music and Society*, 30(2), 137–148.

Mysliwski, M. (2011), A Microeconometric Analysis of Album Sales Success in the Polish Market, Department of Applied Econometrics, Working Paper 54, Warsaw School of Economics.

N

Navas, E. (2012), *Remix Theory: The Aesthetics of Sampling*, Springer.

Negus, K. (1995), When the Mystical Meets the Market: Creativity and Consumption in the Production of Popular Music, *Sociological Review*, 43, 316–341.

Negus, K. (1998), Cultural Production and the Corporation: Musical Genres and the Strategic Management of Creativity in the US Recording Industry, *Media Culture and Society*, 20(3), 359–379.

Newman, M.S. (2012), Imitation is the Sincerest Form of Flattery, But is it Infringement? The Law of Tribute Bands, *Touro Law Review*, 28(2), 391–419.

Nicholson, S. (2005), *Is Jazz Dead? Or has it Moved to a New Address?* Routledge.

NME (2014), Kasabian's Serge Pizorno says Rock 'n' Roll is Dying Out, www.nme.com/news/kasabian/77558 (accessed 3 June 2014).

North, A. and Oishi, A. (2006), Music CD Purchase Decisions, *Journal of Applied Social Psychology*, 36(12), 3043–3084.

North, A.C. and Hargreaves, D.J. (2007), Lifestyle Correlates of Musical Preferences: 3. Travel, Money, Education, Employment and Health, *Psychology of Music*, 35(3), 473–497.

Nurse, K. (2003), The Caribbean Music Industry: Building Competitiveness and Enhancing Export Capabilities in an Emerging Sector, Caribbean Export Development Agency.

Nurse, K. (2007), The Cultural Industries in Caricom: Trade and Development Challenges, Report Prepared for the Caribbean Regional Negotiating Machinery (with Demas, A., Tull, J., Paddington, B., O'Young, W., Gray, M., Hoagland, H., Reis, M. (revised version) Chapter 3, Music Industry.

O

O'Brien, K. (1996), *Hymn to Her: Women Musicians Talk*, Virago.

O'Brien, L. (2002), *She Bop II: The Definitive History of Women in Rock, Pop, and Soul*, Continuum.

O'Reilly, D. (2011). Leisure Tribe-nomics, pp. 239–249 in Cameron, S. (ed.) *Handbook on the Economics of Leisure*, Edward Elgar.

O'Reilly, D., Larsen, G. and Kubacki, K. (2013), *Music, Markets and Consumption*, Goodfellow Publishers.

Oberholzer-Gee, F. and Strumpf, G. (2007), The Effect of File Sharing on Record Sales: An Empirical Analysis, *Journal of Political Economy*, 115(1), 1–42.

Oberholzer-Gee, F. and Strumpf, G. (2009), File-Sharing and Copyright, Working Paper 09-132, Harvard Business School.

Oestreich, J.R. (2010), Japanese Musicians Still Turn to the West, *New York Times*, 14 September, p. C1.

Ogg, A. (2002), *The Men Behind Def Jam*, Omnibus Books.

Oliver, P. (1990), *Black Music in Britain: Essays on the Afro-Asian Contribution to Popular Music*, Open University Press.

Ophem, H., Stam, P. and van Praag, B. (1999), Multichoice Logit: Modeling Incomplete Preference Rankings of Classical Concerts, *Journal of Business and Statistics*, 17(1), 117–128.

Ordanini, A. (2006), Selection Models in the Music Industry: How a Prior Independent Experience may affect Chart Success, *Journal of Cultural Economics*, 30(3), 183–200.

Osborne, B. (1999), *The A–Z of Club Culture*, Sceptre Books.

Oxoby, R. (2007), On the Efficiency of AC/DC: Bon Scott versus Brian Johnson, University of Calgary MPRA Paper No. 3196.

P

Palin, S.L. (1994), Does Classical Music Damage the Hearing of Musicians? A Review of the Literature, *Occupational Medicine*, 44(3), 130–136.

Palmieri, R. (1996), *Encyclopedia of the Piano: Garland Reference Library of the Humanities*, Garland Publishing, *New York and London*.

Park, Y.S. (2014), Trade in Cultural Goods: A Case of the Korean Wave in Asia, *Journal of East Asian Economic Integration*, 18(1), 83–107.

Parry, G., Bustinza, O.F. and Vendrell-Herrero, F. (2012), Servitisation and Value Coproduction in the UK Music Industry: An Empirical Study of Consumer Attitudes, *International Journal of Production Economics*, 135(1), 320–332.

Parsons, L. (2002), Thompson's Rubbish Theory: Exploring the Practices of Value Creation, *European Advances in Consumer Research*, 8, 390–393.

Partridge, C. (2006), The Spiritual and the Revolutionary: Alternative Spirituality, British Free Festivals, and the Emergence of Rave Culture, *Culture and Religion*, 7(1), 41–60.

Patmore, D. (2013), The Marketing of Orchestras and Symphony Concerts, Ch. 35 in O'Reilly, D., Rentschler, R. and Kirchner, T. (eds) *The Routledge Companion to Arts Marketing*, Routledge.

Pavlov, O.V. (2005), Dynamic Analysis of an Institutional Conflict: Copyright Owners Against Online File Sharing, *Journal of Economic Issues*, 39(3), 633–663.

Peitz, M. and Waelbroeck, P. (2003), Piracy and Digital Products: A Critical Review of the Economics Literature, CESifo Working Paper 1071.

Peitz, M. and Waelbroeck, P. (2004a), The Effect of Internet Piracy on Music Sales: Cross-Section Evidence, *Review of Economic Research on Copyright Issues*, 1(2), 71–79.

Peitz, M. and Waelbroeck, P. (2004b), An Economist's Guide to Digital Music, GESY Discussion Paper No. 32.

Peitz, M. and Waelbroeck, P. (2004c), File-Sharing, Sampling and Music Distribution, Working Paper 26/2004, International University in Germany.

Peitz, M. and Waelbroeck, P. (2006), Why the Music Industry May Gain From Free Downloading: The Role of Sampling, *International Journal of Industrial Organization*, 24(5), 907–913.

Percival, M.J. (2011), Music Radio and the Record Industry: Songs, Sounds, and Power, *Journal of Popular Music and Society*, 34(4), 455–473.

Pesendofer, W. (1995), Design Innovation and Fashion Cycles, *American Economic Review*, 85(4), 771–792.

Peterson, R.A. and Berger, D.G. (1996), Measuring Industry Concentration, Diversity and Innovation in Popular Music, *American Sociological Review*, 61(1), 175–178.

Peterson, R.A. and DiMaggio, P. (1975), From Region to Class, the Changing Locus of Country Music: A Test of the Massification Hypothesis, *Social Forces*, 53(3), 497–506.

Peterson, R.A. and Kern, R.M. (1996), Changing Highbrow Taste: From Snob to Omnivore, *American Sociological Review*, 61(5), 900–907.

Peterson, R.A. and Simkus, A. (1992), How Musical Tastes Mark Occupational Status Groups, Ch. 7 in Lamont, M. and Fournier, M. (eds) *Cultivating Differences: Symbolic Boundaries and the Making of Inequality*, University of Chicago Press.

Pettijohn, T.F. II and Sacco, D.F. (2009a), Tough Times, Meaningful Music, Mature Performers: Billboard Songs and Performer Preferences across Social and Economic Conditions in the USA, *Psychology of Music*, 37(2), 155–179.

Pettijohn, T.F. II and Sacco, D.F. Jr (2009b), The Language of Lyrics: An Analysis of Popular Billboard Songs across Conditions of Social and Economic Threat, *Journal of Language and Social Psychology*, 28(3), 297–311.

Pettijohn, T.F. II, Jason, T.E. and Richard, K.G. (2012), And the Beat Goes On: Popular *Billboard* Songs Beat per Minute and Key Signatures Vary with Social and Economic Conditions, *Current Psychology*, 31, 313–317.

Phillips (Record Label) (1998), Great Pianists of the 20th Century: Selections from the Definitive Collection, two-CD sampler.

Phillips, J.R. (2016), Breaking Up is Hard to Do: The Resilience of the Rock Group as an Organizational Form for Creating Music, *Journal of Cultural Economics*, forthcoming.

Phillips, M.B. (2013), African American "Classical" Musicians: Exceeding Hegemony and Debunking the Myths, Paper presented at the Graduate Center, New York, 1 November.

Piekut, B. (2010), New Thing? Gender and Sexuality in the Jazz Composers Guild, *American Quarterly*, 62(1) 25–47.

Pinch, T.J. and Bijsterveld, K. (2003), Should One Applaud? Breaches and Boundaries in the Reception of New Technology in Music, *Technology and Culture*, 44(3), 536–559.

Pitt, I. (2010), Superstar Effects on Royalty Income in a Performing Rights Organization, *Journal of Cultural Economics*, 34(3), 219–236.

Pompe, J., Tamburi, L. and Munn, J. (2011), Factors that Influence Programming Decisions of US Symphony Orchestras, *Journal of Cultural Economics*, 35(3), 167–184.

Poort, J., Rutten, P. and Van Eijk, N. (2010), Legal, Economic and Cultural Aspects of File Sharing, *Communications and Strategies*, 77(1), 35–54.

Porter, S.Y. and Abeles, H.F. (1978), The Sex Stereotyping of Instruments, *Journal of Research in Music Education*, 26(2), 65–75.

Porter, S.Y. and Abeles, H.F. (1979), So Your Daughter Wants to be a Drummer, *Music Educators Journal*, 65(5), 47–49.

Powers, D. (2011), Bruce Springsteen, Rock Criticism, and the Music Business: Towards a Theory and History of Hype, *Journal of Popular Music and Society*, 34(2), 203–219.

Pratt, A.C. (2004), The Music Industry in Senegal: The Potential for Economic Development, UNCTAD-Report 11.

Prieto-Rodríguez, J. and Fernández-Blanco, V. (2000), Are Popular and Classical Music Listeners the Same People? *Journal of Cultural Economics*, 24(2), 147–164.

PRS for Music (2009), British Festivals to Generate £450m in 2009, 11 June, www.prsformusic.com (accessed 3 August 2014).

Pulley, B. (2011), Record Sales Rise as Lady Gaga, Adele Find a Future with Spotify, Radio Bloomberg News, 14 November, www.bloomberg.com/news/2011-11-14/record-sales-rise-as-lady-gaga-adele-find-a-future-with-spotify.ht (accessed 28 June 2014).

R

Ragot, S. (2008), Pirates versus Majors: A Game Theory Modelling, Conference Paper, 15th International Conference on Cultural Economics (Association of Cultural Economics International), Northeastern University, Boston, MA.

Raines, P. and Brown, La T. (2007), Evaluating the Economic Impact of the Music Industry of the Nashville, Tennessee Metropolitan Statistical Area, *Music and Entertainment Industry Educators Association Journal*, 7(1), 13–37.

Regev, M. (1994), Producing Artistic Value: The Case of Rock Music, *Sociological Quarterly*, 35(1), 85–102.

Regner, T. and Barria, J.A. (2009), Do Consumers Pay Voluntarily for Online Music? *Journal of Economic Behavior and Organization*, 71(2), 395–406.

Reid, G. (2006), The Politics of City Imaging: A Case Study of the MTV Europe Music Awards Edinburgh 03, *Events Management*, 10(1), 35–46.

Reid, G. (2010), Formanta Polivoks Synthesizer: The Story Of The Polivoks, *Sound on Sound*, July.

Rentfrow, P.J. and Gosling, S.D. (2003), The Do Re Mi's of Everyday Life: The Structure and Personality Correlates of Music Preferences, *Journal of Personality and Social Psychology*, 84(6), 1236–1256.

Reynolds, S. (2004), Lost in Music: Obsessive Record Collecting, pp. 289–307 in Weisbard, E (ed.) *This Is Pop: In Search of the Elusive at Experience Music Project*, Harvard University Press.

Reynolds, S. and Press, J. (1995), *The Sex Revolts: Gender, Rebellion, and Rock 'n' Roll*, Harvard University Press.

Riall, B.W. (2011), Economic and Fiscal Impact Analysis of the Music Industry in Georgia, Study commissioned by Georgia Music Partners, Atlanta, GA.

Ribowsky, M. (2009), *Supremes: A Story of Motown, Success and Betrayal*, Da Capo Press.

Riesman, D. (1950), Listening to Popular Music, *American Quarterly*, 2, 359–371.

Rob, R. and Waldfogel, J. (2006), Piracy on the High C's: Music Downloading, Sales Displacement, and Social Welfare in a Sample of College Students, *Journal of Law and Economics*, 49(1), 29–62.

Rochelandet, F. and Le Guel, F. (2005), P2P Music Sharing Networks: Why the Legal Fight Against Copiers may be Inefficient, *Review of Economic Research on Copyright Issues*, 2(2), 69–82.

Rochelandet, F. and Nandi, T.K. (2008), The Incentives for Contributing Digital Contents over P2P Networks: An Empirical Investigation, *Review of Economic Research on Copyright Issues*, 5(2), 19–35.

Rodman, G.B. and Vanderdonckt, C. (2006), Music for Nothing or, I Want My MP3, *Cultural Studies*, 20 (2/3), 245–261.

Rogers, J. (2013), *The Death and Life of the Music Industry in the Digital Age*, Bloomsbury Academic.

Rohr, D. (2001), *The Careers of British Musicians, 1750–1850: A Profession of Musicians*, Cambridge University Press.

Ross, P.G. (1996), An Organizational Analysis of the Emergence, Development, and Mainstreaming of British Punk Rock Music, *Popular Music and Society*, 20(1), 155–173.

Ross, P.G. (2005), Cycles in Symbol Production Research: Foundations, Applications, and Future Directions, *Popular Music and Society*, 28(4), 473–487.

Rosselli, J. (1989), From Princely Service to the Open Market: Singers of Italian Opera and their Patrons, 1600–1850, *Cambridge Opera Journal*, 1(1), 1–32.

Rothenbuhler, E.W. and Dimmick, J.W. (1982), Popular Music: Concentration and Diversity in the Industry, 1974–1980, *Journal of Communication*, 32(1), 143–149.

Rothfield, L., Coursey, D., Lee, S., Silver, D. and Norris, W., with Hotze, T., Felkner, J. Savage, J., Wang, F. and Morre, A. (2006), Chicago Music City: A Report on the Music Industry in Chicago, Prepared for the Chicago Music Commission by the Cultural Policy Center at the University of Chicago.

Rushton, M. and Thomas, M. (2005), The Economics of the Commercial Music Industry in Atlanta and the State of Georgia: Industrial Organization and New Estimates of Economic Impacts, Fiscal Research Program Georgia State University, February.

Rutten, P. (1991), Local Popular Music on the National and International Markets, *Cultural Studies*, 5, 294–305.

S

Sadler, D. (1993), Consumer Electronics Companies, Technological Change and the Music Industry, Paper presented at "The Place of Music: Culture and Economy", Conference held at University College, London, 13–14 September.

Sadler, D. (1997), The Global Music Business as an Information Industry: Reinterpreting Economies of Culture, *Environment and Planning A*, 29, 1919–1936.

Saha, A. (2011), Negotiating the Third Space: British Asian Independent Record Labels and the Cultural Politics of Difference, *Journal of Popular Music and Society*, 34(4), 437–454.

Salganik, M.J., Dodds, P.S. and Watts, D.J. (2006), Experimental Study of Inequality and Unpredictability in an Artificial Cultural Market, *Science*, 311, 854–856.

Sanjek, R. (1998), *American Popular Music and its Business: The First Four Hundred Years*, Oxford University Press.

Sanner, S. (1991), The Legendary Pink Dots, *Alternative Press*, 6(42), November, http://brainwashed.com/common/htdocs/publications/lpd-1991-ap.php?site=lpd08 (accessed 6 August 2014).

Saskmusic (2008), Economic Impact Asssessment of the Music Seskatchewan Music Industry, Final Report by kisquared.

Schelling, T. (1984), Self Command in Practice, in Policy, and in a Theory of Rational Choice, *American Economic Review*,74(2), 1–11.

Schink, T., Kreutz, G., Busch, V., Pigeot, I. and Ahrens, W. (2014), Incidence and Relative Risk of Hearing Disorders in Professional Musicians, *Occupational and Environmental Medicine*, 71, 472–476.

Schoenberg, H.C. (1962), The Distaff Side: Many Women are Fine Artists but Find it Hard to get Public Acceptance, *New York Times*, 25 March.

Schulze, G.G. and Anselm, R. (1999), Public Orchestra Funding in Germany: An Empirical Investigation, *Journal of Cultural Economics*, 22(4), 227–247.

Schwartz, P. (1972), *The New Political Economy of J.S. Mill*, LSE/Weidenfeld and Nicholson, English translation of 1968 book.

Schwartz, S. (1991a), Inter-Firm Employment Differences by Gender: A Case Study of Major Orchestras, *Eastern Economic Journal*, 17(3), 331–336.

Schwartz, S. (1991b), Economic Behavior of Symphony Orchestras in the Decade of the 1970s: A U.S.–Canada Comparison, *Journal of Cultural Economics*, 15(2), 95–101.

Scott, A. (1999), The Global Music Business as an Information Industry: Reinterpreting Economies of Culture, *Environment and Planning A*, 31, 1965–1984.

Scott, D.M. and Halligan, B. (2010), *Marketing Lessons from the Grateful Dead*, John Wiley & Sons.

Shank, B. (1994), Dissident Identities: The Rock'n'Roll Scene in Austin Texas, *Wesleyan University Press*.

Shapiro, H. (2003), *Waiting for the Man: The Story of Drugs and Popular Music*, 2nd revd edn, Helter Skelter Publishing.

Shefrin, H.M. and Thaler, R. (1988), The Behavioral Life-Cycle Hypothesis, *Economic Inquiry*, 26(4), 609–643.

Shevey, S. (1972), *The Ladies of Pop-Rock*, Scholastic Book Services.

Shiller, B. and Waldfogel, J. (2008), Music for a Song: An Empirical Look at Uniform Song Pricing and its Alternatives, the Wharton School Working Paper Series, 17 June.

Shiller, B. and Waldfogel, J. (2009), The Challenge of Revenue Sharing with Bundled Pricing: An Application to Digital Music, the Wharton School Working Paper Series, University of Pennsylvania, Philadelphia, PA.

Shin, I. and Illtae, A. (2010), Growth of Online Music Industry and DRM-Free Digital Music Sales, *International Telecommunications Policy Review*, 17(2), 27–54.

Sibelius Academy (1998), Entrepreneurship in the Music Industry: Developing Competitiveness in the Finnish Music Industry, Research and Information Unit of the Arts Council of Finland, Sibelius Academy, Helsinki.

Sintas, J.L., Zerva, K. and Garcia-Alvarez, E. (2012), Accessing Recorded Music: Interpreting a Contemporary Social Exchange System, *Acta Sociologica*, 55(2), 179–184.

Siwek, S.E. (2007), The True Cost of Sound Recording Piracy to the U.S. Economy, Institute for Policy Innovation, Policy Report 188, Lewisville, TX.

Skoff, J. (2014), Does the Market Reward Musical Talent? Vulfpeck, Spotify, and the Changing Face of the Music Industry, WUPR Political Review, St. Louis, MO.

Smith, A. (2009). Contemporary Dancers and Orchestral Musicians in Line for Visa Concession, *Stage*, 5 May, www.thestage.co.uk/news/2009/05/contemporary-dancers-and-orchestral-musicians-in-line-forvisa-concessions/ (accessed 23 June 2014).

Smith, M.D. and Telang, R. (2012), Assessing the Academic Literature Regarding the Impact of Media Piracy on Sales, mimeo, Carnegie Mellon University, Pittsburgh, PA.

Soloveichik, R. (2010), Music as a Capital Asset, Working Paper, Bureau of Economic Analysis, Washington DC.

Soloveichik, R. (2011), Artistic Originals as Capital Assets, *Survey of Current Business*, June, 43–51.

Solow, J. (1998), An Economic Analysis of Droit de Suite, *Journal of Cultural Economics*, 22(4), 209–226.

Speaks, C., Nelson, D. and Wars, W.D. (1970), Hearing Loss in Rock-and-Roll Musicians, *Journal of Occupational Medicine*, 12(6), 216–219.

Spencer, L. (1999), *Lilith Fair: VH1 Behind the Music*, Pocket Books.

Stamm, K.B. (2000), *Music Industry Economics: A Global Demand Model for Pre-Recorded Music*, Mellen Studies in Economics 5, Edwin Mellen Press.

Stevans, L. and Sessions, D. (2005), An Empirical Investigation into the Effect of Music Downloading on the Consumer Expenditure of Recorded Music: A Time-Series Approach, *Journal of Consumer Policy*, 28(3), 311–324.

Stewart, S. (2005), What was Mill's Problem Really? *Radical Psychology*, www.radicalpsychology.org/vol.4-2/Stewart2a.html (accessed 27 May 2014).

Stewart, S. and Garrett, S. (1984), Signed, Sealed and Delivered: The True Life Stories of Women in Pop, *Pluto Press*.

Straw, W. (1991), Systems of Articulation, Logics of Change: Communications and Scenes in Popular Music, *Cultural Studies*, 6, 368–388.

Straw, W. (1997), Sizing up Record Collections: Gender and Connoiseurship in Rock Music Culture, pp. 3–16 in Whiteley, S. (ed.) *Sexing the Groove: Popular Music and Gender*, Routledge.

Straw, W. (2000), Exhausted Commodities: The Material Culture of Music, *Canadian Journal of Communication*, 25(1), 175–185.

Straw, W. (2009), In Memoriam: The Music CD and its Ends, *Design and Culture*, 1(1), 79–91.

Strobl, E. and Tucker, C. (2000), The Dynamics of Chart Success in the U.K.: Pre-Recorded Popular Music Industry, *Journal of Cultural Economics*, 24(2), 113–134.

Sublette, N. (2004), The Missing Cuban Musicians, Cuba Research and Analysis Group, Albuquerque, NM.

Sullivan, O. and Katz-Gerro, T. (2007), The Omnivore Thesis Revisited: Voracious Cultural Consumers, *European Sociological Review*, 23(2), 123–137.

Sutcliffe, P. (1998), Small Town Girls, *Mojo*, 57, 16–18 August.

Suzor, N. and Fitzgerald, B. (2011), The Legitimacy of Graduated Response Schemes in Copyright Law, *University of New South Wales Law Journal*, 34(1), 1–40.

Sweeting, A. (2000), *Cover Versions: Singing Other People's Songs*, Pimlico.

Sweeting, A. (2006), Too Much Rock'n'Roll? Station Ownership, Programming and Listenership in the Music Radio Industry, Northwestern University, Unpublished ms.

Sweeting, A. (2011), Dynamic Product Positioning in Differentiated Product Markets: The Effect of Fees for Musical Performance Rights on the Commercial Radio Industry, NBER Working Paper.

T

Tanaka, T. (2004), Does File Sharing Reduce Music CD Sales? A Case of Japan, IIR Working Paper WP#05-08, Institute of Innovation Research, Hitotsubashi University, Tokyo.

Tang, P. (2005), Digital Copyright and the "New" Controversy: Is the Law Moulding Technology and Innovation? *Research Policy*, 34(6), 852–871.

Tarlach, G. (2002), Highway to History: Tribute Bands Rock Out: Salutes to the Likes of AC/DC, *Milwauke Journal Sentinel*, 29 August.

Tennent, K. (2013), A Distribution Revolution: Changes in Music Distribution in the UK 1950–1976, *Business History*, 55(2), 327–347.

Thaler, R. and Shefrin, H.M. (1981), An Economic Theory of Self Control, *Journal of Political Economy*, 89, 392–406.

The Leading Question/music:)ally (2009), Digital Music Attitudes and Behaviour, UK Music, London.

Thomes, T.P. (2011), An Economic Analysis of Online Streaming: How the Music Industry can Generate Revenues from Cloud Computing, Discussion Paper No. 11-039, ZEW, Centre for European Economic Research.

Thompson, B. (2001), *Ways of Hearing: A User's Guide to the Pop Psyche from Elvis to Eminem*, Phoenix.

Thompson, M. (1979), *Rubbish Theory*, Oxford University Press.

Thomson, K. (2010), Taking the Pulse: Survey on Health Insurance and Musicians, *Future Music Coalition*, 27 May.

Thorne, S. (2011), An Exploratory Investigation of the Theorized Levels of Consumer Fanaticism, *Qualitative Market Research: An International Journal*, 14(2), 160–173.

Thornton, S. (1996), *Club Cultures: Music, Media and Subcultural Capital*, Wesleyan University Press.

Throsby, D. (1992), Artists as Workers, Ch. 19 in Towse, R. and Khakee, A. (eds) *Cultural Economics*, Springer-Verlag.

Throsby, D. (2002), The Music Industry in the New Millennium: Global and Local Perspectives, Paper prepared for the Global Alliance for Cultural Diversity Division of Arts and Cultural Enterprise UNESCO, Paris.

Throsby, D. and Thompson, B. (1994), But What do You do for a Living? A New Economic Study of Australian Artists, Australia Council, Redfern, Australia.

Tindall, B. (2006), *Mozart in the Jungle: Sex, Drugs and Classical Music*, Grove/Atlantic.

Tohmo, T. (2005), Economic Impacts of Cultural Events on Local Economies: An Input–Output Analysis of the Kaustinen Folk Music Festival, *Tourism Economics*, 11(3), 431–451.

Tollison, R. and Crain, M.W. (1997), Economics and the Architecture of Popular Music, *Journal of Economic Behavior and Organization*, 32(2), 185–205.

Tomlinson, D. (2002), Federal Versus State Jurisdiction and Limitations Versus Laches in Songwriter Disputes: The Split among the Federal Circuits in Let the Good Times Roll, Why Do Fools Fall in Love? and Joy to the World, *Loyola of Los Angeles Entertainment Law Review*, 23, 55–79.

Toop, D. (1999), *Rap Attack 3: African Rap to Global Hip Hop*, 3rd revd edn, Serpent's Tail.

Toop, D. (2010), *Sinister Resonance: The Mediumship of the Listener*, Continuum Publishing.

Towse, R. (1997), The Monopolies and Mergers Commission's Investigation of U.K. Music Market, *Journal of Cultural Economics*, 21(2), 147–151.

Towse, R. (2001), *Singers in the Marketplace*, Clarendon Place.

Towse, R. (2010), *Textbook of Cultural Economics*, Cambridge University Press.

Troilo, M. (1999), Collecting, pp. 88–92 in Earl, P.E. and Kemp, S. (eds) *The Elgar Companion to Consumer Research and Economic Psychology*, Edward Elgar.

Trondman, M. (1990), Rock Taste: On Rock as Symbolic Capital, pp. 71–85 in Carlsson, U. and Roe, K. (eds) *Popular Music Research*, Nordicom.

Tschmuck, P. (2001a), From Court Composers to Self-made Men: An Analysis of the Changing Socio-Economic Status of Composers in Austria from the Seventeenth to the Nineteenth Century, pp. 157–172 in Janssen, S., Halbertsma, M., Ijdens, T. and Ernst, K. (eds) *Trends and Strategies in the Arts and Cultural Industries*, Erasmus University, Rotterdam.

Tschmuck P. (2001b), The Court's System of Incentives and the Socio-Economic Status of Court Musicians in the Late 16th Century, *Journal of Cultural Economics*, 25(1), 47–62.

Tschmuck, P. (2002), Creativity without a Copyright: Music Production in Vienna in the Late Eighteenth Century, pp. 210–220 in Towse, R. (ed.) *Copyright in the Cultural Industries*, Edward Elgar.

Tschmuck, P. (2003), How Creative are the Creative Industries? A Case of the Music Industry, *Journal of Arts Management, Law and Society*, 33(2), 127–141.

Tschmuck, P. (2009), Copyright, Contracts and Music Production, *Information, Communication and Society*, 12(2), 87–102.

Tschmuck, P. (2010), The Cycles of Creativity in the Music Industry, pp. 179–188 in Anheier, H. and Isar, Y.R. (eds) *Cultural Expression, Creativity and Innovation*, Sage.

Tu, Y. and Lu, M. (2006), An Experimental and Analytical Study of On-Line Digital Music Sampling Strategies, *International Journal of Electronic Commerce*, 10(3), 39–70.

Tussey, D.S. (2005), Music at the Edge of Chaos: A Complex Systems Perspective on File Sharing, *Loyola University Chicago Law Journal*, 37, 101–167.

U

UK Music (2012), Destination Music: The Contribution of Music Festivals and Major Concerts to Tourism in the UK. Foreword by Feargal Sharkey, preface by Michael Eavis.

UNESCO (2000), International Flows of Selected Cultural Goods 1980–98, UNESCO Institute for Statistics.

UNESCO (2005), International Flows of Selected Cultural Goods and Services, 1994–2003, UNESCO Institute for Statistics.

Upright, C.B. (2004), Social Capital and Cultural Participation: Spousal Influence on Attendance at Arts Events, Princeton University Center for Arts and Cultural Policy Studies, Unpublished ms.

V

Valentine, G. (1993), The Space that Music Makes, Paper presented at "The Place of Music: Culture and Economy", Conference held at University College, London, 13–14 September.

Vernik, D.A., Purohit, D. and Desai, P.S. (2011), Music Downloads and the Flip Side of Digital Rights Management, *Marketing Science*, 30(6), 1011–1027.

Voegelin, S. (2010), *Listening to Noise and Silence: Toward a Philosophy of Sound Art*, Continuum Publishing.

Vogel, H. (1998), *Entertainment Industry Economics*, 4th edn, Cambridge University Press.

Volz, I.P. (2006), The Impact of Online Music Services on the Demand for Stars in the Music Industry, Working Paper, Johann Wolfgang Goethe University, Frankfurt.

W

Waldfogel, J. (1998), The Family Gap for Young Women in the United States and Britain: Can Maternity Leave make a Difference? *Journal of Labor Economics*, 16(3), 505–545.

Waldfogel, J. (2010), Music File Sharing and Sales Displacement in the iTunes Era, *Information Economics and Policy*, 22(4), 306–314.

Waldfogel, J. (2011a), Bye, Bye, Miss American Pie? Supply of New Recorded Music since Napster, NBER Working Paper 16882, Cambridge, MA.

Waldfogel, J. (2011b), Copyright Protection, Technological Change, and the Quality of New Products: Evidence from Recorded Music since Napster, NBER Working Paper 17503, Cambridge, MA.

Wall, D.S. (2003), Policing Elvis: Legal Action and the Shaping of Post-Mortem Celebrity Culture as Contested Space, *Entertainment Law*, 2(3), 35–69.

Wallis, M., Kretschmer, G., Baden-Fuller, C. and Klimis, M. (1999), Contested Collective

Administration of Intellectual Property Rights in Music: The Challenge to the Principles of Reciprocity and Solidarity, *European Journal of Communication*, 14(1), 5–35.

Wallis, M., Kretschmer, G. and Klimis, M. (1999), Globalisation, Technology and Creativity: Current Trends in the Music Industry, Final report to the ESRC Programme, Media Economics and Media Culture, Bournemouth University.

Wallis, R. and Malm, K. (1984), *Big Sounds from Small Peoples: The Music Industry in Small Countries*, Pendragon Press.

Warren, R.L. (1972), The Nazi Use of Music as an Instrument of Social Control, pp. 72–78 in Denisoff, R.S. and Peterson, R.A. (eds) *The Sounds of Social Change*, Rand McNally & Company.

Wassall, G. and Alper, N. (1998), Earnings of American Artists: 1940–1990, Paper given at the 10th International Conference on Cultural Economics, Barcelona.

Weisser, J. (2012), Not All Musicians are Entrepreneurs: Successful and Professional Ones Are, www.hypebot.com/hypebot/2012/05/ (accessed 4 January 2015).

White, C.G. (2001), The Effects of Class, Age, Gender and Race on Musical Preferences: An Examination of the Omnivore/Univore Framework, Thesis submitted to the Faculty of the Virginia Polytechnic and State University in partial fulfillment of the requirements for the degree of Master of Science in Sociology, Blacksburg, VA.

White, P. (2010), Music: A Human Right, *Sound on Sound*, April, available at: http://www.soundonsound.com/apr10/articles/leader_0410.htm (accessed 19 December 2014).

Wikström, P. and Burnett, R. (2009), Same Songs, Different Wrapping: The Rise of the Compilation Album, *Journal of Popular Music and Society*, 32(4), 507–522.

Williamson, J. and Cloonan, M. (2006), Rethinking "the Music Industry", Working Paper, University of Paisley, Glasgow.

Wills, G. and Cooper, C.L. (1988), *Pressure Sensitive: Popular Musicians Under Stress*, Sage.

Wilson, N. and Stokes, D. (2002), Cultural Entrepreneurs and Creating Exchange, *Journal of Research in Marketing and Entrepreneurship*, 4(2), 37–52.

Wire (1995), Interview with Karlheinz Stockhausen, Transcripts from Broadcast on BBC Radio 3, November.

Withers, G. (1980), Unbalanced Growth and the Demand for the Performing Arts: An Econometric Analysis, *Southern Economic Journal*, 46, 735–742.

Witter, M. (2002), Music and the Jamaican Economy, Report prepared for UNCTAD/WIPO.

Wood, N., Duffy, M. and Smith, S.J. (2007), The Art of Doing (Geographies of) Music, *Environment and Planning D: Society and Space*, 25(5), 867–888.

Y

Yazicioglu, E.T. and Fuat Firat, A. (2007) Glocal Rock Festivals as Mirrors into the Future of Culture(s), pp. 101–117 in Belk, R. (ed.) *Consumer Culture Theory: Research in Consumer Behaviour*, 11, Elsevier.

Yoon, K. (2007), On the Impact of Digital Music Distribution, Working Paper, Hitotsubashi University, South Korea.

Young, P. (1992), The Economics of Convention, *Journal of Economic Perspectives*, 10(1), 105–122.

Young, S. and Collins, S. (2010), A View from the Trenches of Music 2.0, *Journal of Popular Music and Society*, 33(3), 339–355.

Yu, P.K. (2011), Digital Copyright and Confuzzling Rhetoric, Research Paper Series No. 11-23, Drake University Legal Studies.

Z

Zablocka, A. (2008), Antitrust and Copyright Collectives: An Economic Analysis, *Yearbook of Antitrust and Regulatory Studies*, CSAIR, University of Warsaw, 1(1), 151–165.

Zendel, B.R. and Alain, C. 2011. Musicians Experience Less Age-related Decline in Central Auditory Processing, *Psychology and Aging*, 27(2), 410–417.

Zentner, A. (2005), File Sharing and International Sales of Copyrighted Music: An Empirical Analysis with a Panel of Countries, *Topics in Economic Analysis and Policy*, 5, article 21, 1–17.

Zentner, A. (2006), Measuring the Effect of File Sharing on Music Purchases, *Journal of Law and Economics*, 49(1), 63–90.

Zentner, A. (2007), Online Sales, Internet Use, File Sharing, and the Decline of Retail Music Specialty Stores, Working Pape, University of Texas at Dallas.

Zullow, H.M. (1991), Pessimistic Rumination in Popular Songs and News Magazines predict Economic Recession via Decreased Consumer Optimism and Spending, *Journal of Economic Psychology*, 12(3), 501–526.

Zwaan, K., Tom, F.M. ter Bogt (2010), From Zero to Hero? An Exploratory Study of the Predictors of Success in the Dutch Idols Competition, *Journal of Popular Music and Society*, 33(3), 319–337.

INDEX OF MUSICAL PERSONS AND ENTITIES

Page numbers in *italics* denote tables.

INDEX

Page numbers in *italics* denote tables, those in **bold** denote figures.